D1523871

MORAL ORDER/WORLD ORDER

Also by Hugh C. Dyer

THE STUDY OF INTERNATIONAL RELATIONS: THE STATE OF THE ART (*co-editor*)

Moral Order/World Order

The Role of Normative Theory in the Study of International Relations

Hugh C. Dyer
Lecturer in International Studies
University of Leeds

First published in Great Britain 1997 by
MACMILLAN PRESS LTD
Houndmills, Basingstoke, Hampshire RG21 6XS and London
Companies and representatives throughout the world

A catalogue record for this book is available from the British Library.

ISBN 0–333–68906–2

 First published in the United States of America 1997 by
ST. MARTIN'S PRESS, INC.,
Scholarly and Reference Division,
175 Fifth Avenue, New York, N.Y. 10010

ISBN 0–312–17317–2

Library of Congress Cataloging-in-Publication Data
Dyer, Hugh C., 1957–
Moral order/world order : the role of normative theory in the
study of international relations / Hugh C. Dyer.
    p.   cm.
Includes bibliographical references and index.
ISBN 0–312–17317–2 (cloth)
1. International relations—Philosophy.   2. International
relations—Moral and ethical aspects.   I. Title.
JX1395.D94 1997
327.1'01—dc21   96–49388
                                                                        CIP

This book is printed on paper suitable for recycling and made from fully managed and
sustained forest sources.
10   9   8   7   6   5   4   3   2   1
06   05   04   03   02   01   00   99   98   97

Printed in Great Britain by
The Ipswich Book Company Ltd
Ipswich, Suffolk

Contents

vi   *Contents*

Contents

Preface

The origins of this book lie in a discomfort with the policies of states, which in pursuing some vaguely defined national purpose abroad, seem to contradict the values held to underpin their own societies. This contradiction could be accounted for by limiting moral concern to members of a given society, but this is hardly plausible in a world where national societies are interdependent. Contradiction and hypocrisy are not themselves surprising, since contradictions are everywhere and hypocrisy is a common vice, but they lend confusion to the understanding of national purposes and international relations. Whatever values justify a particular form of social life, they cannot easily be sustained in a limited social sphere without finding purchase in the unlimited global sphere. Similarly, the values reflected in the conditioned anarchy of international relations must have some relation to the lives and aspirations of the world's peoples. The lives of individuals and societies everywhere must be diminished when the fragile artifices of social organisation are undermined by incoherence in their fundamental points of reference. Consequently, the normative dimensions of international relations seem worthy of attention. However, traditional theories of international relations are limited in this respect, being largely preoccupied with concrete material circumstances which impinge upon these relations, and little concerned with the normative parameters which endow purpose and meaning. What is commonly referred to as normative theory is often a marginalised adjunct of theories about power and wealth, to which awkward ethical issues are relegated. Though it does not purport to construct a specific theory, both human concern and theoretical challenge direct this book to an investigation of the role of normative theory, or rather normative styles of theorising, in the study of international relations.

Academic colleagues and students encountered along the way have all influenced this book, although their aggregate effect could hardly be disassembled. Discussions with Michael Banks, Chris Brown, Robin Brown, Michael Donelan, Mervyn Frost, Owen Hartley, Mark Hoffman, Robert Jackson, Hayo Krombach, Cornelia Navari, Rob Walker, Daniel Warner and Philip Windsor have left their mark. Robin Brown, Mervyn Frost, Owen Hartley, Mark Hoffman, Friedrich Kratochwil, Terry Nardin, and John Vincent were kind enough to give me written comments on my work. I am grateful to them for challenging me to make the most of my argument. Along with many others, I benefited from the late John Vincent's remarkable wit and insight. The Department of International Relations at the London School of Economics, the Department of Politics at Queen Mary College, the Department of Politics at the University of Natal, and the Institute for International Studies at the University of Leeds have contributed to the intellectual and social environment in which this book was written. I was fortunate to have the support and toleration of many friends (they know who they are) who shared in my life and work during the preparation of this book, and they are more important to me than I can easily say. My family has always nurtured and endured me, and I am ever grateful for that unconditional support which I now know to be something of a rarity. In acknowledging the assistance of these people I also absolve them of responsibility for this book, which is my own folly.

Hugh C. Dyer

Introduction

THE PRESENT ARGUMENT

This book critically assesses the role of normative theory in the study of international relations, and as an initial premise, it characterises this role as a central one: the attendance to essential questions of values. How and why it plays a central role, and what this role amounts to, are the questions this book seeks to answer. Values are considered in juxtaposition to interests or facts, although their intimate relationship is an important issue, and the importance is twofold: distinguishing values brings this latter variable into focus, but has also permitted its marginalisation in the study of international relations. The argument develops amidst conflicting attitudes to norms, since what is largely a philosophical sociology of international relations, exposing underlying theoretical assumptions and claims, is at some points an applied sociology of international relations indicating agreed norms in practice (such as inform the idea of 'international society') which inevitably imposes some limitations on the philosophical sociology because of the relation between theory and practice. Therefore, the use of the term 'normative' here does *not* mean simply 'prescriptive', but is used more generally to mean 'of or having to do with norms'. Thus it is not the purpose of this book to describe, prescribe or sanction a particular 'Normative' theory with a capital 'N' (such as, for example, Frost's 'constitutive theory of individuality'[1]), but rather to indicate the significance of theorising about norms. Neither should use of the term 'normative theory' be taken to suggest either that there is 'non-normative theory' or that international relations can be separated from norms – it is precisely the argument of this book that neither is possible and that theories of international relations must be self-conciously aware of that condition. Consequently, in critically assessing the role of normative theory in the study of international relations, this book is itself an exercise in normative theory.

Because of the broad implications and the various facets of a normative approach, various modes of analysis are employed as seem appropriate to the issue at hand, without straying from commitment to a normative perspective.[2] In identifying the role of normative theory, this work is also a critical assessment of traditional views of that role, and those dominant

1

theoretical approaches which have limited the role. This critique reflects a concern with the apparent divergence, during the course of this century, of two complementary elements in political theory, with the consequence that political theory generally (though here we are concerned with international theory in particular) has in some sense lost touch with its traditional concerns, and perhaps with its own political character as well as that of its subject:

> ... it is necessary to appreciate that there are two aspects to political theory, traditionally conceived. It involves the analysis of what is politically feasible on the one hand, and of what is desirable on the other.[3]

The divergence of these two aspects is exacerbated in the study of international relations by the assumption that politics occurs within the context of the state and national society, prompting Martin Wight to ask 'Why is there no international theory?'[4]

In theories of international relations, the dominant ones having considerable influence on the conduct of world affairs, this has had the unfortunate effect of rather marginalising the exploration of the desirable ends of the state or of the international system as a whole (in any fundamental way, at any rate), and marginalising the problems of difference and identity in respect to the values which inform desired ends – 'given the widespread presumption that science deals with facts only, philosophers were loath to present themselves as defenders of any particular values'.[5] Similarly, a distinction can be made between descriptive empirical accounts of the norms of international relations which give rise to claims or actions, and prescriptive abstract critiques of the values which underlie these norms, understood as signposts of meaning. However, such distinctions are challenged when seen in the context of a dialogue between the two aspects. The division of labour in political theorising may now be nearing its end, although the debate about method is not closed, of course, and attempts at closure or assumptions about the unique validity of a given method are futile. The present normative approach makes room for both informal modes of phenomenological and ordinary language analysis, while tending toward pragmatism,[6] or instrumentalism,[7] in as much as these latter result in 'a forward-looking attitude in which analytic emphasis falls on the promise that an idea carries'.[8]

Normative theory is critical in another sense, shared with critical theory and post-modernist thought: it implies the necessity of continuous critique and questioning of foundations, such that whatever philosophical or theoretical foundations underwrite the study of international relations they must be viewed as ultimately contextual or contingent, and not in any full sense absolute. It is argued that this is nevertheless a sound enough basis for both ethics and epistemology as applied in this field, and as 'practically' useful as any empirically based system of knowledge, while sharing none of the constraining features of pure empiricism, or scientific positivism. It thus retains some of the emancipatory or utopian aspirations of philosophical and theoretical tradition. Benhabib makes the relation between normative and critical theory more cogent by placing the latter between practical philosophy and social science:

> What distinguishes critical social theory from positivistic sociology then is its emphatic *normative* dimension...[which] preserves the intentions of practical philosophy to rationally articulate a more adequate form of human existence and to enlighten them in its attainment.[9]

Benhabib employs Habermas's theory of communicative action to argue that social action is not to be regarded in terms of subject–object relations:

> Communicative for social action is the subject–subject relation, which we can understand as a form of linguistically mediated communication.[10]

This is also the perspective of normative theory as characterised here, in which the meaning of the object is determined by inter-subjectively agreed norms, and for which the role of language – as the medium of agreement – is clearly central. Thus Horkheimer's view of the social constitution of nature is preferred over the 'modern, mechanistic conception of nature which Durkheim takes for granted'.[11]

This is also a position which permits a universal rationalism, although this is not a necessary condition of normative theorising. Linklater suggests that in Hedley Bull's later writings, rationalism came nearer to 'considering the rights and duties which might underpin a different form of universal political organisation' and that as a consequence, rationalism 'may be regarded as a bridge between realism and the critical theory of international relations', in as much as states are committed (in practice) to consensus and order, which requires that 'certain norms are regarded as universally binding'.[12] This last is an empirical sociological observation about the international system, typical of the English School theorists of international society, and will be criticised here for reifying (that is, positing the static reality of) the norms of the states-system. While normative theory accounts for existing norms, it also enables a critique of given norms and their sources.

The emphasis on values allows for two themes within the overall argument, related to the two aspects of political theory noted above –

feasibility and desirability – and reflected in the recurrent opposing pairs of fact/value, is/ought, description/prescription.

The first theme concerns the epistemological framework provided by a normative account of knowledge, where values such as the security and stability of knowledge and the orderly apprehension of the world can be explained and comprehended (without giving way to conservativism, and allowing ample opportunity for critique). It is necessary to distinguish this epistemological dimension because while the moral dimension of normative structures is commonly acknowledged, the epistemological aspect is not so readily incorporated into political thinking. While maintaining a heightened consciousness of the uncertain and contingent nature of epistemological foundations, a normative approach to epistemological values can nevertheless provide a systematic account of knowledge which is sensitive to changing or competing values (for example, paradigms), as well as the distinction between sensory experience and the assignment of meaning.[13]

The second theme concerns the political conditions of knowledge, which determine the role of different theories. This political dimension indicates the need for an adaptation of the traditional role of normative scholarship as moral commentary, which arises from the critique of traditional approaches which limit the role of normative theory. Normative theory, as defined here, denies the separation of ethics from politics arising from the natural rights tradition and realist conceptions of the state which have led to a separate and easily marginalised study of morals.[14]

The argument presented here is that values are central phenomena in international relations; that international relations, and knowledge of them, are essentially normative in form; that consideration of value questions cannot not be limited to moralising or otherwise peripheral qualifications of traditional explanations of international relations; and that normative theory places values at the heart of international theory.

The two thematic trends (noted above) often meet one another in the overall argument, and are elaborated separately below to provide the reader with some guidance as to their relationship and distinctiveness.

Values in Knowledge

A normative account of knowledge, as discussed here, denies the traditional separation of is–ought, fact–value, description–prescription, and argues that they are inseparable characteristics of the world as it is apprehended by humans. Because knowledge is acquired, validated and shared through the collective process of assigning meaning, to what only then may be considered objects of knowledge, all such contributions to knowledge are subject to collective human valuations which inevitably employ norms as their point of reference in the medium of communication.

Taking into account the limits to human comprehension of human affairs (beyond which any greater certainty would require a Kierkegaardian leap of faith) a normative approach provides the closest proximity to 'absolute' knowledge or truth as is necessary, desirable, or possible, leaving the matter of faith to transcendent beliefs or confidence in human nature. Thus it can, in a sense, approximate the goals of secular/rational scientism, but without resort to absolutist foundations.

In providing a framework of political understanding that remains flexible in its foundations, while recognising the need for structured knowledge (viewed as a normative structure in this case), a normative approach offers a potential universal background theory for the study of international relations.[15] On this account, partial knowledge and particular investigations can be linked meaningfully to a greater whole without the necessity of 'complete' knowledge (in the absolute sense), since the framework is one of form or relationship rather than content, and hence adaptable.

Values in International Relations

The difficulty of identifying values has given rise to value non-cognitivist theories which dismiss the subject matter out of hand. While traditional theories of international relations often refer to moral concerns, it is generally to dismiss the matter of values more gently, but with equal effect. One reason for this dismissive attitude is the assumption that values are strictly prescriptive (in an uninteresting way), have no descriptive function, no substance, and hence no significance in the analysis of politics.

Here, it is argued that prescription and description ('ought' and 'is') are intimately related, and that values are implicit in both functions (as discussed above in reference to systematic knowledge). Thus, the political significance of values – as distinct from desired objects, or objective interests – is their role as mediators in both prescriptive and descriptive accounts of politics. Values are necessary points of reference both in prescribing what would be good to do or what ought to be done, and in describing what already is, in terms of those existing political values which determine interests or objects of desire. On this account, values are the substance of political systems and structures, and the appropriate objects of study.

Benhabib says (noting Hegel's argument, as against legalistic Kantian ethics) that the institutions and practices of collective life – ethical life –

are 'to be viewed as part of a functionally interdependent totality of social relations and practices'.[16] Similarly, and despite the absence of a 'global state', any comprehension of interests or tangible assets in international relations depends on a comprehension of the values at play, for it is these latter which give political meaning to the pursuit of interests and the formulation of purposes. As opposed to the traditional moral standpoint, playing into the discrepancy between is and ought and projecting universalised subjective values into an unfriendly world of facts, the properly collective ethical standpoint contains the individual moral standpoint but also allows that

> within an intersubjectively shared context of institutional action, one's action and purposes become recognisable by others in accordance with socially shared rules and meaning patterns.[17]

Structure of the Argument

The argument begins in the context of an ongoing debate about the status of international relations as an academic discipline, or field of study (and a similar debate concerning the status of normative theorising). Ensuing problems of defining the subject matter, and paradigmatic differences, mean that the appropriate method of understanding is not settled (as well as it is in the natural sciences, for example). That the study and practice of international relations continues nevertheless thus implies a significant body of contested concepts and problematic assumptions. Normative theory is therefore employed as a means of revealing and addressing epistemological questions in this field. Chapter 1 examines methodological issues arising from this application of values, and the relationship of values to facts through the medium of theoretical accounts of reality. In particular the consequences of adopting a hermeneutic rather than positivist approach are considered, and also the 'is–ought' problem, 'understood to be the manifold of general and fundamental problems about the nature of practical thinking in general, whether it is moral or not'.[18]

The first task is to discern the means by which an agreed understanding of the subject matter has been obtained, in the midst of epistemological uncertainty. It is shown that this has been achieved primarily by the dominance of one paradigm: realism. This provides, therefore, the starting point for a critical assessment of the discipline and the role of normative theory in it. It is argued that realism, as a dominant paradigm, ignores values and leaves open the issue of political purposes, relying instead on the categories of 'national interest' and 'power' of states, but without providing any foundation for their existence let alone their interests. Chapter 2 provides an analysis of the literature and the dominant place of realism there, while Chapter 3 introduces the role of normative theory in contrast. Normative theory is presented as a means of revealing value structures that underlie and inform interests, and a means of accounting for political purposes in terms of social values rather than in terms of such sterile categories as states and their interests.

Having already made the connection between values and facts, the next task is to consider how these value-laden facts are related to political ideas through conciousness and the need for action. Hence the normative characteristics of ideas and ideologies are examined. Ideas are presented as a fundamental influence on political events; on the historical progression of international politics. Ideologies are seen as the means of conveying ideas about political purposes, and ideology in general is characterised as the form of political engagement. These, then, are fitted to the pattern of normative structures which link values (and ideas about them) to the facts of political practice. Chapter 4 examines the place of ideas from a range of philosophical perspectives, and the connection between ideas and ideology in political life.

Because ideas and ideology give meaning to political purposes, the values that underlie these political purposes are connected to knowledge of both purposes and the political environment in which they are defined and pursued. Thus it is important to locate the relationship between systems of values and systems of knowledge: between ethics and epistemology. Chapter 5 undertakes an investigation of this relationship, suggesting that political ideas give rise to normative concepts through the use of moral language in descriptions of international politics, thus revealing the relative similarity of form between ethics and epistemology.

The argument continues by examining the key relationship between values and interests. The above mentioned normative concepts, reflecting values, provide the foundation of beliefs and expectations in political practice, which are then held to be interests. In order to determine the role of normative theory in the study and practice of international relations, it is necessary to identify the processes by which values inform and influence the practical pursuit of interests through foreign policy. It is argued in Chapter 6 that the array of values and consequent interests displayed by a state (or other potential actor) are encapsulated in a world view which guides and limits the formation of foreign policy. Furthermore, it is argued that such a settled world view is necessary to the stable apprehension of reality, and provides the only basis for political choice and action. The consequent dilemma for international politics is the resolution of differing world views which may be the source of either cognitive dissonance or outright conflict, or both.

In order to examine the effects of a world view on political choice and on the outcome of policy decisions, the argument then focuses on the substantive policy area of nuclear strategy, on foreign policy formation and analysis, and on the implications of environmental change in Chapter 7. Because of the central importance of nuclear policy in world affairs, it provides a suitable case for the general argument: the possibility of collective self-destruction suggests at least one universal political value and focuses attention on the potential of human agency. More specifically, this historically significant area of policy provides a clear example of the normative content and structure of political choice, and indicates the predominant importance of normative judgements even in a policy-formation process which is so burdened with empirical and technical considerations. The normative character of policy choice is emphasised by an examination of the particular debate about the ethics of deterrence, but this examination reveals problems with the rationale and justification of nuclear policies which would be of general concern even were the ethical implications thought to be uninteresting. Value-informed beliefs underlie 'interests' for which a strategy of defence, or its realisation, is devised. This chapter inevitably returns to the question of political purpose and its foundations, in as much as a proper understanding of strategic issues requires an appreciation of the political goals to which strategies are directed.

Drawing on insights from the specific case of nuclear deterrence, the argument turns to an assessment of normative influences in policy formation and analysis generally. Here the problems of identifying political goals and the appropriate means to achieve them are shown to have profound normative implications, which cannot be escaped in even the most mundane policy-processes. Bringing the central themes of the argument to bear on the practical and (given the predominance of state actors) essential activity of foreign policy decision-making shows the extent to which norms and values pervade political structures. It also indicates that the traditional emphasis on state-centric realist forms of political behaviour and on the manipulation of empirical data (both in policy-making and policy analysis) does not permit normative questions to be dismissed, but only ignored. The trend in the literature towards a greater interest in normative approaches is discussed, as are the implications for policy formation which follow from a growing awareness of normative issues as a significant and substantial aspect of political life.

Finally, the implications of global environmental change are examined, in order to illustrate how normative considerations are of increasing importance in relation to the challenges of the post Cold War period. This period is characterised by both broad consensus and clear schisms in the international community: in relation to environment change there is general agreement on the key aspects of the problem and the urgency of finding solutions, yet there are sharp divisions concerning responsibility, sharing of costs, and the mechanisms of collective decision-making. In one sense, there are signs of emerging global values which might favour liberal democratic aspirations and the gradual decline of state-centric policy-making in favour of global institution-building, yet at the same time violent nationalisms and strictly delimited interpretations of national interest lead to war, economic protectionism, and aggravated environmental degradation. The prospects for transforming a traditional preoccupation of International Relations are examined through a treatment of 'environmental security', which stands as a benchmark for the significance of environmental change both in terms of human living conditions and in terms of shifting global value structures which inform the theory and practice of international relations.

The argument is drawn to a close with a concluding discussion of actual and possible roles for normative theory which have already been introduced in the course of uncovering the extent of normative structures and influences. The notion of a normative background theory, as a basis for particular investigations or theoretical constructs, is examined once again in the light of discussions above. Similarly, the central question of whether values or interests should be the principal focus of political inquiry is addressed once more. The argument that normative theory cannot address practical or 'real' political problems, and that these can only be understood in terms of objective material interests and empirically observed facts, is dismissed with the conclusion that normative theory can, should, and does play a fundamental role in the study of international relations.

The following section is a further introductory exploration of the nature of normative theory.

NORMATIVE THEORY

While the term 'normative' is frequently used in the literature, and generally understood to suggest either a moral element or some other prescriptive character, it is usually left undefined. Equally, 'normative theory' is a phrase often used but seldom defined. Because of such omissions, and because these terms will be widely employed in the following arguments, it is approriate to set out their various meanings here. A fuller exploration of definitions is presented in the following chapter.

Because of the nature of his project, Mervyn Frost provides a useful definition in his book, *Towards a Normative Theory of International Relations*.[19] In setting out the critical question on the second page – 'What ought to be done in international relations?' – he already identifies the traditional distinguishing feature of normative statements: the use of 'ought' as distinct from 'is'. Subsequently, he refers to

...the set of ideas and rules constituting the civil and political relationships between them [states]...

and observes that

...the evaluation of these rules – which activity I have called normative theory – is clearly of cardinal importance.[20]

Frost also points to the convergence of international relations theory with critical social science (cf. Brian Fay)[21] as surpassing interpretation and descriptivism in questioning practices and developing new ones.[22] This suggests that normative theory, being tied up in this convergence, is a particularly adaptable theoretical approach which is sensitive to political change, and thus suitable for addressing it.

Another useful definition appears in Chris Brown's *International Relations Theory: New Normative Approaches*:

By normative international relations theory is meant that body of work which addresses the moral dimension of international relations and the wider questions of meaning and interpretation generated by the discipline.[23]

Brown argues that while it is possible to have theory which is not involved with norms, 'a very great deal of what is traded in international relations as non-normative theory is steeped in normative assumptions', and says that it is possible (if controversial) to defend the view that *all* theory is normative.[24]

What has perhaps most commonly characterised normative theory, while at the same time constraining it in some respects, is a close association with morality and ethics. This sort of view is taken by Charles Beitz, though the focus on moral and ethical issues clearly does not diminish the breadth of implications:

In international politics as in other areas of social inquiry, normative ideas have their most powerful effects when they operate, so to speak, in the background: they motivate empirical investigation, shape research agendas, and affect the choice of methods in a variety of subtle ways.[25]

What arises from such uses of the term 'normative' indicates that there is something called a 'norm' from which the adjective is derived. For the moment we may define a norm as a standard (a fuller definition of norms is provided in Chapter 1), and among the most common standards in social and political life are moral norms. The relation between morality and ethics is, indeed, defined in terms of norms: Morality is otherwise known as *normative ethics*, indicating that ethical judgements are made in reference to a particular norm (or set of norms), which might be altered subsequently or might only apply to particular persons or circumstances.

Thus there is an ambiguity in the term 'normative': it may be descriptive either of that which makes reference to a given norm, or of norms themselves in general. Some theorists demand a distinction between the normative (by which is meant 'the prescriptive') and the descriptive; between a deontic modality and the actual circumstance of that modality. Here, the normative is viewed as inclusive of both the prescriptive and the descriptive, on the grounds that these roles of a normative international theory are coexistent and complementary, notwithstanding the difference between the two roles. This double meaning gives normative theory a broad range, in that it may be employed in addressing particular practices which refer to a norm, or in addressing the way in which norms exist, evolve, are promulgated, and perhaps eventually superceded.

What is essential to the present undertaking, however, is the necessity of revealing the values at play both in international relations (the 'object' of study) and in the epistemological foundations of our understanding of it. Normative theory is presented here as being uniquely concerned with values as a significant aspect of both the practice and study of international relations, and consequently a fruitful theoretical approach.

NOTES

1. Mervyn Frost, *Ethics in International Relations: A Constitutive Theory* (Cambridge: Cambridge University Press, 1996), especially Chapter 5.
2. '...an inquiry may move at need from mode to mode, with no sense of changing imposing school commitments in so doing.' Abraham Edel,

Analyzing Concepts in Social Science: Science, Ideology, and Value, Vol. 1 (New Brunswick, NJ: Transaction Books, 1979), p. 138.

3. Chandran Kukathas and Philip Pettit, *Rawls: A Theory of Justice and its Critics* (Cambridge: Polity Press, 1990), pp. 1–2.

4. This being the title of Wight's essay in Herbert Butterfield and Martin Wight (Eds), *Diplomatic Investigations: Essays in the Theory of International Politics* (London: George Allen and Unwin Ltd., 1966), first published in *International Relations* (Vol. 2, No. 1, April 1960).

5. Kukathas and Pettit, *op. cit.*, p. 4.

6. See subsequent references to Peirce, James, and Rorty.

7. See subsequent references to Dewey.

8. Edel, *op. cit.*, p. 14. For a useful discussion of conceptual analysis, see his philosophical overview of modes of analysis, pp. 1–41.

9. Seyla Benhabib, *Critique, Norm, and Utopia: A Study of the Foundations of Critical Theory* (New York: Columbia University Press, 1986), p. 5.

10. *Ibid.*, p. xi.

11. *Ibid.*, p. 3.

12. Andrew Linklater, *Beyond Realism and Marxism: Critical Theory and International Relations* (London: Macmillan, 1990), p. 20–1.

13. See, Jerzy Wróblewski, 'Cognition of Norms and Cognition Through Norms', in di Bernardo (ed), *Normative Structures of the Social World* (Amsterdam: Editions Rodopi, 1988), especially p. 244.

14. See the argument in Benhabib, *Critique, Norm, and Utopia*, p. 6.

15. Note again Beitz's remark that normative ideas are most powerful when operating 'in the background'. Charles R. Beitz, 'Recent International Thought', *International Journal* (Vol. 43, No. 2, Spring 1988), p. 203.

16. Seyla Benhabib, *Critique, Norm, and Utopia*, *op. cit.*, p. 309. It is worth noting here that the later Hegel maintained a distinction between the state, as an expression of the Spirit, and civil society. See the discussions in Torbjörn L. Knutsen, *A History of International Relations Theory* (Manchester: Manchester University Press, 1992) and Philip Windsor, 'The State and War' in Cornelia Navari (ed), *The Condition of States* (Milton Keynes: Open University Press, 1991).

17. *Ibid.*, p. 79.

18. Hector-Neri Castañeda, 'Ought, Reasons, Motivation, and the Unity of the Social Sciences: The Meta-theory of the Ought–Is Problem', in Giuliano di Bernardo (ed) *op. cit.*, p. 7.

19. Mervyn Frost, *Towards a Normative Theory of International Relations* (Cambridge: Cambridge University Press, 1986), p. 2.

20. *Ibid.*, p. 64.

21. See Brian Fay, *Social Theory and Political Practice* (London: Allen and Unwin, 1975), pp. 90–1, concerning the characterisation of interpretive and critical social science, as being essentially conservative and potentially innovative respectively. Following Fay's distinction, one might consider the two aspects of normative theory as having similar characteristics: as descriptive theory it may be necessarily conservative in describing the status quo order (though nevertheless sufficiently insightful to allow for immanent change), while as prescriptive theory it may allow for alternative interpretations of the reality it addresses, since choices must be made.

22. *Ibid.*, pp. 26–7. See also Andrew Linklater, *Beyond Realism and Marxism*, *op. cit.* The relation between normative theory and critical theory will be addressed further below.

23. Chris Brown, *International Relations Theory: New Normative Approaches* (London: Harvester Wheatsheaf, 1992), p. 3.

24. *Ibid.*, and note 4.

25. Charles R. Beitz, 'Recent International Thought', *op. cit.*, p. 203.

1 Methodology: Values, Theory, Facts

This chapter on methodology investigates the role of norms in international relations theory in the context of epistemological traditions, and characterises the special relationship between values and facts that arises from the interpretive function of theory.

In this respect normative approaches to the study of international relations reflect concern with issues larger than the description and prediction of events in the analysis of substantive issue and policy areas. This is not to belittle the conventional or traditional activities of international relations scholars, but rather to assess critically the assumptions and philosophical foundations of these undertakings. The rationale for such a critical assessment is simply that the soundness and character of these assumptions bears directly on the efficacy and propriety of the practical activities which they support.

To date the methodological significance of normative international theory has been little discussed, in spite of a considerable body of work which can be described as being of a normative character. While some of the literature is specifically indicated as normative theory, the history of normative thought in the study of international relations (such as there is of it) is somewhat chequered, and comprised of eclectic and competing ideas which seldom receive systematic attention.[1] Before examining the literature, however, we must attend to a prior task: the definition and explication of norms, and those normative concepts which will be applied in various ways throughout the work.

DEFINITION OF TERMS

Norms are, ordinarily speaking, standards or measures (from the Latin *norma*, a carpenter's square or rule). More generally, a norm is 'a standard or pattern or type considered representative of a group'.[2] In the social or political context norms are (descriptively) standards of behaviour – of social and political action – and (prescriptively) reasons which dictate such action.

It is central to this book that the common practice in philosophy is to make a distinction between the prescriptive and the descriptive, thus tempting an assumption that the normative belongs only to the prescriptive. Avrum Stroll, for one, argues that this is a mistake – norms are primarily descriptive. Only when it is determined (descriptively) what is normal in a given context, may deviation or conformity be viewed as either a perjorative or commendatory basis for prescription.

> Norms are, in their basic use, descriptions or reports of the average or median outcome of certain activities or achievements by a person or group of persons. The adjective 'normal' and the adverb 'normally' bear the logical weight in this connection. They are used to characterise typical or customary behaviour...[3]

Thus the traditional distinction between the normative and the descriptive that is so widely assumed in international relations and social science generally arises from the mutually exclusive distinction between prescription and description – thus generating the faulty premise that norms are prescriptions (only). The present argument denies this definition of 'normative', and employs the term as one encompassing both description and prescription, thus endowing it with considerably greater significance than is generally allowed in the theory of international relations.

As Stroll notes, in the tradition the term 'normative' is a creation, 'designed to capture the extended prescriptive use... and plays only that restricted role',[4] and therefore we should not look to this definition for an indication of its function. The prescriptive–descriptive distinction is reflected in closely related distinctions of ought–is and value–fact which also pervade traditional approaches and theories, indicating the extensive implications of the normative approach as described here.

Hume's well-known observation, held to make out the case for the is–ought distinction, is that discussion of 'ought' tends to become discussion of 'is' without acknowledgement of the change in mode; however, this could equally be taken as evidence of the intimate relation between the two and of the dual character of norms.

Having insisted on the dual character of norms, it does not follow that the descriptive–prescriptive distinction is meaningless:

> ...the conventional way of summarizing Hume's insight as the gap between 'is' and 'ought' is misleading; ...the reason behind this confusing manner of expression probably lies in a too simplistic equation of the occurrence of a verb in the is-form with descriptivity. If that is the

case we need a better convention for differentiating descriptions from prescriptions, rather than giving up the whole distinction altogether.[5]

Similarly, Stroll writes that the distinction may stand for present purposes, since it is accepted that prescriptions don't describe anything (are only based on description), but the 'further ascription of norms to the prescriptive side of that distinction' is contested.[6] Thus we must not make the error of assuming that 'normative' means only or evenly chiefly 'prescriptive'. The point is made by Kuno Lorenz in summarising the main thesis of Nelson Goodman's *Ways of Worldmaking* as stating that

> the division between the given and the constructed, between that which is found and that which is made, between the fact and the artefact, is outdated and has, actually, been challenged since the times of the pre-Socratics though it was seldom understood in that way.[7]

The epistemological significance of norms in science is complemented by a similar significance in the particular social context of ethics, where norms are moral standards. Morals are sometimes called substantive or *normative* ethics (in contrast to theoretical ethics) – 'moral' being derived from the Latin *mos*, meaning custom. The normative reference indicates that *a priori* concepts are in play, establishing a standard from which measurements may be taken; by which judgements may be made. (Note, however that the concepts may be *a priori* only in the restricted sense of being relative to a given context, rather than absolute.) In application to international relations, normative analysis can be used to evaluate the ethical implications of possible norms of behaviour, and also to evaluate the efficacy and status of substantive customary behaviour.

Therefore, taking the ethical content and connotation into account, normative theory may be (and has been) characterised as employing *a priori* concepts and propositions to formulate an essentially (but, it is argued here, not exclusively) prescriptive theoretical framework. However, we may still view normative theory as being primarily descriptive, with its prescriptive import being derivative. If the norms in question are proven or assumed, the theory may address their consequences, and the prescriptive function will be incidental to this purpose. Thus Lauener writes:

> Pragmatic considerations induce us to establish, in given situations, what I call *contexts* by adopting particular rules. We thus produce a pragmatically relativized a priori providing us with a clearcut distinction between the analytic and the synthetic, between language and theory, etc.[8]

Normative international theory is consequently concerned with prescribing the parameters of political organisation and action or with describing those parameters (political norms) which are already established and acted upon – not ignoring the inference from the descriptive to the prescriptive. Frost describes normative theory as the *evaluation* (which implies both description and prescription) of ideas and rules which constitute civil and political relationships.[9]

The predominant difficulty in this sort of theorising is establishing that political norms exist, this being an assumption of normative explanations. The general point that a structure of some kind is fundamental to communication, coordination, cooperation, and even comprehension is not difficult to make. Neither is it unreasonable to posit that social and political structures are comprised largely of rules, which may be arbitrary in comparison to physical laws, but are of similar definitional significance. Unger makes a distinction between prescriptive rules (imperatives) and constitutive rules (as in games) and value ('the social face of desire' dependent on individual will).[10] It is thus rather difficult to describe all norms as rules, and not least because 'norm' is a complex and evasive concept. For example, Stroll argues that 'norm', 'standard', 'convention', 'rule' and 'criterion' are all different, but closely related – he states that norms are linguistic locutions, standards are prescriptive measures, while criteria are types of test. He also mentions patterns and models as being descriptive and prescriptive concepts respectively, and implies a virtually unlimited range of concepts all being distant cousins while retaining some specific meaning in each case: no doubt this situation is the result of norms being contextually defined.

In the process of examining the concept of norms, we will see that its complexity is indicative of its pervasiveness in the social and political realm, and that the ubiquity of norms (difficult as they may be to identify with empirical precision) is in itself justification for considering their methodological and theoretical implications.

In the conceptual field of the term 'norm' (see Appendix to Chapter 1) the most notable characteristic is best described by the notions of continuity or regularity (a characteristic of all systems). From this characteristic of the related concepts, we may define a norm as being some form of constant. A further characteristic is the reference to social activity which is shared by many of the concepts. From this we may be inclined to describe norms as a social concept, yet there are also references which are not exclusively social and could equally well apply to the physical realm.

Consider the type of norm called a directive, or 'technical norm', which indicates the means to an end – conforming to the norm is a logical necessity for the achievement of the end in question (for example, operating instructions). If we further consider the characteristic brought out in the definition of rules, that is, the dual role of definition and regulation (description and prescription), we can view the concept of a norm as one which concerns the ascription of meaning. This understanding of norms accounts for the notion of a constant, and allows for applications which are not necessarily social – although meaning itself arises in a social context.

Other characteristics, such as the notions of guidance, judgement, and common practice, are indicative of fluctuation and change, from which we may conclude that norms are of greater significance in the social or political realm where the vagaries of human behaviour present a substantial difficulty in ascribing meaning. The subject matter of the natural sciences being rather more predictable, the demand for reference to a norm may be reduced, or infrequent. It is nevertheless significant that norms serve the function of regulating the value of facts. The regulation of the value of facts, in conjunction with the closely related function of ascribing meaning, indicates that norms are central to our apprehension of reality. If we add that a norm is a linguistic locution, after Stroll (as above), this view is further supported by the consideration that such ascriptions and apprehensions must be expressed in language.

Taking these various characteristics, we may define norms as *constants which define and regulate the value of phenomena in the apprehension of reality such that meaning can be ascribed.* For our purposes, this is a useful definition of norms, being general enough for us to investigate their methodological and theoretical significance. As social structures are contingent, a given structure being sufficient but not necessary to communal life, it is clear that norms are vital to their maintenance. This is true whether norms are the dependent or independent variable – that is, the product or producer of a social structure (as products, norms are 'constants' in relation to a given context, and contexts change) – and perhaps especially true when the social structure is relatively weak (as in international society).[11]

Norms can be seen as the means by which an organised apprehension of a social structure is secured. That norms determine the value of social phenomena is shown by the reference to norms in judging such phenomena as desirable or undesirable in the context of the broader social structure. In the physical realm, a similar demand for organised apprehension can be met by norms, even though we may wish to ascribe some objectivity to physical phenomena which is independent of the accepted norms which define them. Thus there is an epistemological function for norms, whether distinctly ontological or simply methodological: ontological where there is consensus on what exists, and methodological where there is consensus on how to determine what exists or how to organise knowledge of what exists.

In addressing the problem of the existence of social and political norms, as distinct from the abstract concept of norms, it will be useful to consider their origin, and some demonstrable examples of identifiable norms. Earlier it was seen that norms exist, as von Wright says, when they are in force. Subsequently, he says:

> The existence of a norm is a fact. The truth-grounds of normative statements and of norm-propositions are thus certain facts. In the facts which make such statements and propositions true lies the reality of norms.[12]

Hence the 'ontological problem of norms' is to determine the nature of these facts, and what it means to say that a norm exists. Having already concluded that norms exist when they are in force – when they are facts – we now want to know the source of these facts (norms). This source must be the beneficiary of the norms, and perhaps also the instrument of their enforcement, which thereby constitutes norms as facts: this source is therefore the political and social system (whether state or society) for which the norms operate. Thus one important aspect of the existence and reality of norms is their validity in respect to the social system as a whole. Validity may be understood either in legal terms or in terms of efficacy (as in the phrases 'law which is in force' or 'law which is in existence' or 'law which is valid', these being synonymous), but in both cases the validity of the norm lies in the ability of the social system to uphold it – whether it is brought into existence by means of efficacious force or by a legal act. The same applies for norms which are less rigorously defined and enforced (e.g. customs). Validity is, in this sense, determined by a political, legal, or moral authority for which, importantly, legitimacy is generally a prerequisite. Thus the validity of a norm stands in relation to the higher order norms of socio-political organisation which are the bases of all human institutions. The origins of norms are therefore similar to those of political organisation.

The origin of political norms may be seen, from a contractarian point of view, as roughly parallel to the evolution of social conventions. David Hume describes the need for social conventions in reference first to the stability of external goods,[13] and subsequently to the origin of justice.[14] A social convention is not strictly contractual ('This convention is not of the nature of a promise'[15]), but is the implicit agreement arrived at when rational agents of limited generosity fully recognise their mutual interests, and regulate their conduct such that their interests are best served.[16] Where conduct is regulated in a coordinated fashion according to generally agreed principles, we can say that a norm exists. The established norm assumes an identity independent of its origins, in the manner that states become distinct entities, even though both are, as Hume would say, artifices. Similar contractarian views are found in the work of Hobbes, Locke and Rousseau, and in the neo-contractarian work of John Rawls and Robert Nozick. While these are theorists of political organisation, the first step in establishing a political system is to establish the 'rules of the game', and in doing so one establishes fundamental norms.

This explanation of the origin of norms is both abstract and historical, but nevertheless adequate to account for the existence of norms in present societies. 'A norm is the resultant of complex patterns of a large number of people over a protracted period of time',[17] yet once properly established is independent of individual people, particular circumstances, and its own origins. The norm becomes an objective phenomenon, and questions about the origins of norms then exclude the purely historical and focus on the reasons for given norms existing for given societies – that is, on the meaning of norms in the social context. Here, the inquiry into norms is not so much intended to enhance knowledge of norms themselves (with respect to their origin), but of the society for which the norms operate.

We must also take into account theories which deny that existing norms are the product of a genuinely collective experience or of shared ideas, but rather are the consequence of socio-economic (and socio-historical) structures generally favourable to a dominant class. A similar argument can be made on the basis of gendered social structures. Equally, some societies have excluded groups on the basis of race or religion. Here there is room for debate about the relation between ideas, societies, and socio-historical conditions, although debates about causal direction tend to exhibit a 'chicken–egg' circularity. One pertinent example is Mannheim's

> 'sociology of knowledge' which would demonstrate the partisan, contextual and existentially determined nature of all cognition, thought and theories

and his

> attempts to produce a social theory that transcended the limitations of particular world views[18]

which Horkheimer criticised as idealism, and the result of an inadequate theory of society which relates ideas to social groups but is insensitive to the particular socio-historical conditions in which a society is grounded.

Critiques drawing on specific aspects of social inequality or discrimination are entirely valid, but are not immediately troublesome to the present line of argument, since the necessity and habit of reference to a normative system may still be explained by an evolutionary approach, whether or not a particular system results, in whole or in part, from foreign or indigenous domination or particular historical conditions – it simply becomes a descriptive exercise in applied sociology. Similarly, the abstract origin of Hobbes' Leviathan has a normative aspect, although this solution to the state of nature problem does not readily acknowledge the normative agreement implied by voluntary subjegation to authority (largely because the tangible origins were not likely voluntary).

It should also be said that an evolutionary approach does not necessitate Darwinism or historical determinism, or a teleological requirement of progress or 'improvement' at every evolutionary stage, rather than simple difference. An evolutionary account of norms merely indicates the social context of their origin, rather than some transcendent truth towards which our thoughts and actions are directed. Thus it is important to recognise that while norms, once established, are objective elements of the social milieu (objective in their social influence) they are not objective in their origins; society itself is indeed an 'artifice', and its contingent foundations may well result, for example, in the perpetuation of apparently arbitrary discrimination in the distribution of social benefits. There is ample room, on this account, for fundamental critiques of society and its political institutions, and for critical philosophy addressing itself to the influence of dominant norms in thought and discourse. It remains the case that such critical activity depends on having identified norms which perpetuate assumptions.

One response to the ubiquity of norms, and the extent of their influence once established, may be seen in the 'postmodern turn' in philosophy with its somewhat nihilistic, relativistic, contextual approach (as yet ill-defined in the literature[19]). This body of work comprises critiques of modern philosophy (by Derrida, and Rorty, for example),[20] and has been called 'an outgrowth of a society in which image, culture, consumption and spectacle become organizing principles of life'.[21] Modernists (such as Habermas) have, in turn, broadly criticised postmodernism – that with roots in Nietzsche and Heidegger – as irrationalist and perhaps even tending to fascism. The Critical Theory school concentrates its critique on Lyotard's *The Postmodern Condition: A Report on Knowledge*, and mounts 'defenses of universality and normativity against the postmodern attack'.[22] This debate may be viewed as one about the demise of the modern epoch – of Western Enlightenment – and of its conventional form of reason. The two commonly known categories of reasoning, inductivist and deductivist, were complemented by Charles S. Pierce's introduction of *abductive* reasoning: where induction finds a whole from parts (but perhaps having 'a whole' in mind), and deduction finds parts from their whole (favoured 'because it appears to be so conclusive'),[23] abduction relates wholes to wholes – it is necessarily a creative form of conjecture since the contents of these wholes 'are indeterminately different' when the option of deconstructing the parts for examination is denied by a direct relation of whole-to-whole. It is this element of conjecture, and inevitably paradox, that underlies the debate about knowledge and politics. Certainly, it is a debate about the influence of certain norms, and their role in establishing meaning. It is a particularly significant debate in the context of current international relations, since the critique of Western values coincides with their apparent success in the early years of the post Cold War world.

We are left with the further problem of identifying norms. This may be essentially a statistical problem, for example, which requires identifying the number (percentage) of members of a society who recognise and conform to a norm. Of course, although norms have a superorganic quality, there are likely to be dissenters in any society and indeed active critique. See, in spite of its shortcomings, the arguments within any 'open society'.[24] This does not disprove the existence of a norm, but any arbitrary statistical standard leaves the question of a statistical rationale open. This in turn leads us back to the fundamental conceptual and methodological problems discussed above. Without pursuing an account of what is sufficient to establish the status of a norm (beyond the analysis already undertaken), we may point to some examples of accepted and active norms.

In the interpersonal realm norms are familiar and apparent. For example, there is a norm about responding to a greeting. At the level of national societies there are norms pertaining to social and political activities, usually in the form of law – which in the case of common law is, interestingly, based in part on precedent. At the international level, norms are less immediately apparent to individuals, but function nevertheless. The most obvious examples are norms concerning the sovereignty of states over their people and territory, and the practice of diplomatic exchange. Less obvious but equally significant are norms concerning the proper use of force, the duty to aid foreign states and their citizens, and the maintenance of orderly international trade and finance, to name a few. That these norms are less familiar to individuals, for whom most normative activities are virtually instinctive (the use of language and facial expressions, driving on one or the other side of the road, respect for property, etc.), does not diminish their normative status. On the contrary it places them more clearly in the category of norms precisely because they have not been absorbed into the habitual behaviour of individuals, and remain more or less abstract and artificial constants (evidenced only by conformity) which are conciously used to define and regulate international behaviour.

At this point in the discussion a clarification of the ethical content of norms is required, since it is often scepticism about the cognitive status of morality that provides grounds for dismissing normative approaches.[25] On this view morality (being synonymous with a normative system), is indeterminate due to the absence of any objective moral truth. Even where some moral agreement is acknowledged for national societies, the constraints of this morality are not recognised in international society. So far morality has been only incidental to the present discussion, and our definition of norms does not make a specific or detailed reference to the subject. However, it should be noted that among the related concepts used in the derivation of the definition is the concept of customs – located in our scheme between rules and prescriptions. Customs that are regarded as exceedingly important, obligatory, and even indispensable to social welfare, are sometimes called mores (moral customs).[26] Morality and other normative systems share the evolutionary, contractarian origins described above. While there is room for debate about moral relativism,[27] the apprehension of social reality dictated by a moral system cannot be escaped, intact, unless morality is viewed (incorrectly) as referring only to *ad hoc* revelations of moral truth.

In short, morality evolves in a social context, and has the normative function of defining morally significant aspects of that social context. One may escape a given morality by entering a different social context, but must then adopt the corresponding morality in order to achieve a coherent perception of social reality. This is not to say that morality is the exclusive grounds for socio-political choice – though it obviously is for moral choice – or that there are not other normative systems at work, but it is nevertheless clear that morality is a necessary if not sufficient condition of social life. To adopt nihilism, or some undefined objective truth (such as a transcendent belief) which does not require a normative foundation in social structures, is to abandon all referents and enter an intellectual and political vacuum in which thought and action are meaningless; an invitation to existential and social crisis. To view a morality critically, in the context of coexisting moralities, is a rather different undertaking perhaps best captured by the term 'anti-foundationalism'. This latter position, in effect approximating moral relativism, emphasises rather than dismisses the need for a better understanding of the normative aspects of social and political life, if we are to avoid nihilism while coming to terms with relativism (whether moral, cultural or epistemological). The problem of relativism, and the anti-foundationalist perspective, will be addressed at greater length subsequently.

VALUES

The question of value-free social science is not new, and seems to have been settled in favour of there being no such thing. It is nevertheless possible to practice social science coherently by declaring value-laden assumptions at the outset, such that an internally consistent argument can lead to sound conclusions and, it is hoped, new insights. It should be recognised, however, that such practices do not address values directly, as an object of study, but merely acknowledge the influence of values while attempting to avoid their broader implications.[28]

The relationship between values and norms has been suggested earlier, in the analysis of related concepts. Norms provide the standards and criteria for the measurement and apprehension of values. Norms establish the value of other phenomena; of social facts. For a given society, some norms are synonymous with social values: those aspects of social life which are regarded as most important. In such cases the term 'value' indicates the high point on a scale of possible social values (an ideal, such as 'democracy' for example), this point on the scale also being the standard used to measure relative values on the scale. From the perspective of interpretive social science, any understanding of social phenomena depends on the recognition of the social values at play; that is, of the normative system. Other perspectives, however, will discount the significance of social values, on grounds that there are other objectively understandable means of explaining social phenomena, (such as interests, power, modes of production, institutional history, and so on) and that values belong to the private, not the public realm.[29] This view rests on the problematic is–ought distinction discussed earlier. For example, Marti-Huang debates John Searle's

> propensity to regard the truths of descriptive sentences as being objectively decidable, whereas value statements are matters of personal preferences...

on the grounds that:

> If evaluative conclusions are really a matter of personal preference, why should we bother to try to deduce them from factual premises?[30]

Whether or not values are exclusively significant in social explanations, when they underpin social norms they must be central to understanding, from any perspective. Through their relation to norms, values are determinant of meaning in a given society. If there are explanations from beyond the context of that society, they will not account for the particular motivations of actors within that context. This can only be accomplished by an appreciation of the normative parameters which define and regulate the scope of the actors' thought and action, and govern their apprehension of reality. It may be possible to comprehend the relative status and direction of a society as a whole, in some larger context of which that society is constituent, but it is not possible to penetrate a society coherently without an implicit analysis of its value system. It is a consequence of adopting a pluralistic world view that

> Once the matter concerning the choice of a linguistic system and an ontology is settled the question of truth...can only be raised internally while theories as a whole are compared on purely pragmatic grounds.[31]

Any theory of international relations must stand up to pragmatic comparison in terms of its ability to cope with various settled value choices, or contingent social norms, which must be taken as given features of the self-understanding of individual societies. Of course, any theory of international relations will itself have a standpoint in relations to possible value choices, whether or not it is a theory of values. Explanations which do not specifically refer to values are thus nevertheless conditioned by values and norms as a consequence of their epistemological priority.

Of course, employing normative analysis does not guarantee agreement about the significance of observed phenomena, for to further complicate matters every analyst brings to the task a set of personal value assumptions, which are themselves idiosyncratic reflections of the analyst's society or culture or part thereof. At best these personal values are acknowledged and experimentally controlled. At worst they are hidden assumptions which invade the analysis, making a rather poor joke of the term 'science'.

If it can be successfully argued that values are, for all practical purposes, constant across all social divisions, then most of our problems are solved. It seems unlikely, however, that this is the case. On the evolutionary, contractarian, pluralist view, there is little evidence to suggest a consistent pattern of socio-economic or political development across the globe (or even particular societies) which would provide a uniform context for the establishment of a universal value system. If, as structuralism has it, norms are largely determined by socio-economic structures, then the same inconsistency of development mentioned above denies universal values, although vertical, as well as horizontal differences are emphasised. From the perspective of realism, where interests and power are emphasised, the same inconsistencies in material and political circumstances clearly dictate disparate interests, and even if interests could be isolated from values, neither would be uniform.

This conclusion about the heterogeneity of values does not prejudice the possibility of a value system which is shared by societies, arising in the context of their mutual interactions, rather than their particular internal circumstances. Neither is it impossible that certain values or value systems transcend social boundaries, even where other values and value systems remain intact and distinct. Indeed it may be wise to seek out and foster those values which appear to be, for example, transnational in character. The question of an intersocietal or international value system, which refers to thought and action in those areas, is neither novel nor difficult. There are many instances of activity which is defined and regulated by an agreed code of behaviour, whether an institutionalised body of law, or treaties, or regulations, or simply a shared understanding of normative parameters.[32]

Of course it may, as Kratochwil suggests,

> seem necessary to separate the question of the strength or effectiveness of rules and norms from the issue of their existence and function.[33]

Obviously, at the extremes of isolation or violent interaction, internationally shared value systems are either irrelevant or abrogated, as are treaties and laws in such circumstances. This limit to the influence of norms is also evident in intrasocietal situations, yet only confirms by exception the existence and centrality of values in any functional social or political system.

METHODOLOGICAL IMPLICATIONS OF VALUES

The central methodological problem of a normative approach is the location of values. As suggested above, this is on the surface a simple empirical problem which could be solved by statistical analysis of adherence to recognised norms. As we will see in Chapter 2, ideology may be understood as the 'language of adherence', so an example of such an empirical analysis might be a survey of ideological identification among members of a society. Yet the prior requirement is an ability to identify a norm or value as such; as distinct from some other kind of social habit, or an 'empirical' condition of social existence. To begin with, the term 'norm' remains broad enough to present problems of identification. One author suggests that there are three basic types or characterisations of norms: norms as linguistic expressions, as complex situations, and as regularities of some phenomena.[34] The first type is relative to a given language, requiring consideration of grammatic structures, while the second adds to the linguistic expression a complex practical context of use, and requires consideration of other normative structures (such as politics, culture, society, etc.). The third is less troublesome for the present argument, and could be said to reflect the common meaning of regularity. It is the first two types of norm that raise problems of cognition, since they are only to be identified within a context that is itself normative in character. It is this latter consideration that points to the role of norms themselves as determinant of meaning ('cognition through norms'),[35] even as they are being socially determined.

It is the notion of facts standing separate from values that is the initial stumbling-block; but as the discussion above suggests, values are 'in' facts already and cannot be separated from them. This is particularly clear in the case of institutional facts, which are simply reflections of the institutional structure and the relationships which constitute it. Where the institution amounts to an entire society, these relationships are obviously complex and are in general taken for granted as a given social reality. Yet it is precisely in those hidden networks of social relations, and the institutional facts they generate, that values are located.

A norm becomes a fact when enforced by an acknowledged authority (see the argument above concerning the ontological problem of norms). In the pursuit of systematic knowledge (science), the acknowledged authority is the dominant theory (or paradigm) of the pertinent discipline: it is the value-structure of this theory which determines the validity of facts or theoretical propositions.

Thus, it is not methodologically fruitful to set out on a normative analysis or explanation by searching for values in isolation, and shunning investigation of social 'realities' or 'facts' which are held to be somehow unrelated to or independent of values. The appropriate method of a normative approach is to examine precisely those aspects of social and political life which seem to be determined entirely by factual circumstances rather than social norms, or exclusively by a calculus of interest rather than by political values, and through this examination to reveal their normative character and value content.

Conversely, as the present argument emphasises, it is fruitless to engage in purely empirical analyses of political life, and to attempt an isolation of facts from values – especially in international relations, where institutional facts are not as clearly settled and hence more obviously reliant on a normative frame of reference. The consequence of this epistemological condition – in science generally, in the social sciences certainly, and particularly in the field of international relations – is that any methodology must be sensitive to the normative character of both subject and method (implicating theory), such that the traditional distinction between 'is' and 'ought' gives way to an understanding of their intimate relationship.

Some, like Kegley and Raymond, respond to this issue by advocating a combination of methods or 'multiple paths':[36]

> Epistemologically, we feel that our understanding of world politics can best be advanced by an approach that combines the positivist's reliance on empirical evidence with the postmodernist's emphasis on the meanings that statesmen attach to the concepts that organise their vision of global reality and the legal narratives that shape their thinking.[37]

Alternatively, the problem of locating the foundations of empirical evidence, further complicated by the state-centric assumptions of realism, suggests that a more direct approach to the epistemological problem is required to uncover the full significance of such terms as 'meaning', 'vision', and 'narrative', since these may entirely undo any empirical foundations.

Friedrich Kratochwil, in his book *Rules, Norms, and Decisions,* suggests that human action is

> understandable against the background of norms embodied in conventions and rules which give meaning to an action. Thus, not only must an actor refer to rules and norms when he/she wants to make a choice, but the observer, as well, must understand the normative structure underlying the action in order to interpret and appraise choices.[38]

This view underlies the discussion which follows, emphasising the need to question prevailing assumptions, including those about the reliability of empirical evidence and the more general conception of world politics embodied in realism. The innovative critical character of normative theory is presented as an appropriate means of addressing both epistemological issues and the underlying substance of international relations. It is also an approach which goes some way to asserting the autonomy of the human sciences, as Greimas says,[39] by constituting world politics as a realm of human activity rather than a remote, alien and alienating phenomenon.

As a final example of the methodological implications of adopting a normative approach, Quentin Skinner's discussion of the role of ritual and ceremony in politics raises a 'question of deep concern to political theorists' which he notes has been addressed in different ways by such diverse authors as Nikos Poulantzas (e.g., in *Political Power and Social Classes*), Charles Taylor (writing on democracy) and John Dunn (e.g., in *Western Political Theory in The Face of the Future*):

> The question is whether our inherited traditions of political analysis may now be serving to inhibit rather than clarify our understanding not merely of alien cultures but also of ourselves.[40]

The following chapters examine the theoretical literature in international relations, revealing the inherent values and assumptions of traditional theory, and assessing those value-centred approaches which comprise the extant body of normative theory and hold the seeds of new approaches to international relations.

NOTES

1. Exceptions to the rule being Chris Brown, *International Relations Theory: New Normative Approaches* (London: Harvester Wheatsheaf, 1992) and Mervyn Frost, *Towards a Normative Theory of International Relations* (Cambridge: Cambridge University Press, 1986).
2. *Oxford English Dictionary.*
3. Avrum Stroll, 'Norms', *Dialectica* (Vol. 41, 1987; Proceedings of the VIIIth International Colloquium in Bienna/Biel May 1–4, 1986), from the summary, p. 7. See also Kuno Lorenz, 'Is and Ought Revisited' *Dialectica* (Vol. 41, 1987), p. 134.
4. Avrum Stroll, *op. cit.*, p. 17.
5. Duen Marti-Huang, 'The "Is" and "Ought" Convention', *Dialectica* (Vol. 41, 1987), p. 152.
6. Avrum Stroll, *op. cit.*, p. 22.
7. Kuno Lorenz, *op. cit.* See Nelson Goodman, *Ways of Worldmaking* (Indianapolis: Hackett Publishing, 1978), for a constructive nominalist view.
8. Henri Lauener, 'Philosophie als normative Tätigkeit (offener Transzendentalismus versus Naturalismus)', *Dialectica* (Vol. 41, 1987), from the summary in English, p. 23.
9. Mervyn Frost, *Towards a Normative Theory of International Relations* (Cambridge: Cambridge University Press, 1986). Note Frost's 'Theory of Constitutive Individuality'.
10. Roberto Mangabeira Unger, *Knowledge and Politics* (New York: The Free Press, 1975), p. 67ff.

11. See for example David Easton, *A Systems Analysis of Political Life* (New York: John Wiley, 1965), which describes a feedback loop of outputs from and inputs to a network of relationships (the system) through the medium of the system's external environment. While this refers to a system with a specific means of authoritative regulation, and an external environment, it may be applied to the international system if this is understood to provide its own environment and some degree of self-regulation. Equally, this may describe a normative system which generates its own 'transcendent' universe of values and means of self-regulation – as in, for example, an international society. Note Easton's definition of politics: the authoritative allocation of values.

12. Georg Henrik von Wright, *Norm and Action* (London: Routledge & Kegan Paul, 1977), p. 106.

13. David Hume, *A Treatise of Human Nature*, Book III, Part II, Section II, p. 489.

14. *Ibid.*, p. 491.

15. *Ibid.*, p. 490.

16. Hugh C. Dyer, *Justice in World Order: A conceptual Analysis* (unpublished MA thesis, Dalhousie University, 1984), pp. 182ff.

17. Edna Ullmann-Margalit, *The Emergence of Norms* (Oxford: Oxford University Press, 1977), p. 8.

18. Douglas Kellner, *Critical Theory, Marxism and Modernity* (Oxford: Polity Press, 1989), p. 24.

19. But see the characterisation of this approach in Chris Brown, *International Relations Theory: New Normative Approaches* (London: Harvester Wheatsheaf, 1992).

20. See Jacques Derrida, *On Grammatology* (Baltimore: Johns Hopkins University Press, 1976) and Richard Rorty, *Philosophy and the Mirror of Nature* (Princeton: Princeton University Press, 1979).

21. Kellner, *op. cit.*, p. 166.

22. *Ibid.*, p. 171. See also Jean-Francois Lyotard, *The Postmodern Condition: A Report on Knowledge* (Minneapolis: University of Minnesota Press, 1984).

23. Nicholas G. Onuf, *World of Our Making: Rules and Rule in Social Theory and International Relations* (Columbia, SC: University of South Carolina Press, 1989), pp. 98–100. See also, J. Buchler (ed), *Philosophical Writings of Pierce* (New York: Dover Publications, 1955), p. 150–156.

24. Karl Popper, *The Open Society and Its Enemies* (London: Routledge and Kegan Paul, 1945; 2nd Ed., revised, 1952).

25. See Mervyn Frost, *Towards a Normative Theory of International Relations*, *op. cit.*, p. 46.

26. Robert M. Williams, 'The concept of Norms' (*International Encyclopedia of Social Science*).

27. See Terry Nardin, 'The Problem of Relativism in International Ethics' (*Millennium: Journal of International Studies*, Vol. 18, No. 2, Summer 1989), pp. 149–161.

28. For a useful discussion of the role of social and cultural norms in both empirical science and (more particularly) social science, see Talcott Parsons, 'An Approach to the Sociology of Knowedge', *Transaction of the Fourth World Congress of Sociology* (Vol. 4, September 1959), reprinted as

Chapter 5 in his collection of essays, *Sociological Theory and Modern Society* (New York: The Free Press and London: Collier-Macmillan, 1967).

29. For an extensive discussion of the term 'value' (and its uses) which is sympathetic to the present argument, barring somewhat different distinctions made here between the terms 'value' and 'interest' because of their use in international relations scholarship, see Ralph Barton Perry, *Realms of Value: A Critique of Human Civilization* (Cambridge, MA: Harvard University Press, 1954).

30. Duen Marti-Huang, *op. cit.*, p. 152. See Searle's position in John R. Searle, 'How to Derive "Ought" from "Is"', *Philosophical Review* (Vol. 73, 1964).

31. Henri Lauener, *op. cit.*

32. See, for example, Charles W. Kegley, Jr. and Gregory A. Raymond, *When Trust Breaks Down: Alliance Norms and World Politics* (Columbia, SC: University of South Carolina Press, 1990), and Dorothy V. Jones, *Code of Peace: Ethics and Security in the World of Warlord States* (Chicago: University of Chicago Press, 1991).

33. Friedrich Kratochwil, 'Norms and Values: Rethinking the Domestic Analogy', *Ethics and International Affairs* (Vol. 1, 1987), p. 136.

34. Jerzy Wróblewski, 'Cognition of Norms and Cognition Through Norms', in Giuliano di Bernardo (ed), *Normative Structures of the Social World* (Amsterdam: Editions Rodopi, 1988), p. 223. See also in this useful edition Hector-Neri Castañeda, 'Ought, Reasons, Motivation, and the Unity of the Social Sciences: The Meta-theory of the Ought–Is Problem'.

35. Wróblewski, *op. cit.*, p. 241.

36. Kegley and Raymond, *op. cit.*, p. 99.

37. *Ibid.*, p. 4.

38. Friedrich V. Kratochwil, *Rules, Norms, and Decisions: On the conditions of practical and legal reasoning in international relations and domestic affairs* (Cambridge: Cambridge University Press, 1989), p. 11.

39. 'In the same way that the natural sciences have done, the human sciences can also assert their autonomy, which comes not from the "nature" of the objects of investigation – words or things, nature or culture – but from the method of approach that constitutes them all into human objects, into signifying objects'. Algirdas Julien Greimas, *On Meaning: Selected Writings in Semiology* (London: Francis Pinter, 1987), p. 19.

40. See Quentin Skinner's review of Clifford Geertz, *The World as a Stage. Negara: The Theatre State in Nineteenth-Century Bali* (Princeton, NJ: Princeton University Press, 1981), in *The New York Review*, 16 April 1981, pp. 35–7.

Appendix to Chapter 1: Conceptual Analysis of 'Norm'

The following conceptual analysis uses a representative group of terms or related concepts (definitions) from which significant characteristics are extracted and reorganised, or reconstructed. The outcome is a formulation of the concept of a norm (as given in the main text of Chapter 1). The formulation is necessarily general, although more specific definitions may apply for certain norms.

Figure 1   Types and Partial Synonyms of Norms

Guides

Patterns

RULES

Ideals   Customs

DIRECTIVES   Principles   PRESCRIPTIONS

Criteria   Regulations

Standards   Laws

The arrangement of the various concepts in Figure 1 is suggested by von Wright's classification of norms into three main types (Rules, Prescriptions, Directives) with related concepts, and three 'lesser' categories (Customs, Principles, Ideals) which exhibit shared characteristics (and are shown between the relevant groups).[1]

The preceding scheme is not rigid, but merely elucidates the main features of the central thematic concept of a 'norm'. The various interrelated concepts in Figure 1 belong to the same field of meaning, and are discussed briefly below.

RULES are established guides for action, usually applicable to specific circumstances or activities. They often share the dual role characteristic of norms in being the definition of an activity, as well as the regulator of action in the context of the activity.

Patterns are observed regularities, are characteristic of any system, and are basically descriptive. The continuity of patterns provides grounds for description and prediction, and might be considered definitional in the way that the pattern of play (determined by rules) constitutes a game.[2]

Guides to social conduct are called social norms, when they are generally recognised and complied with by members of a society.[3] Thus the guide must relate to an ideal or customary or 'correct' form of conduct.

PRESCRIPTIONS dictate thought or activity by command, permission or prohibition. Prescription, in the social context, is an activity of a norm-giver (an authoritative source), which indicates the authoritative status norms assume in guiding social conduct.

Regulations are a form of prescription having the purpose of regularising a certain activity (e.g. traffic regulations). They have a coordinating role in the sense that rules or directives do, but are expressions of an authoritative will concerning the activity.

Laws are the institutional embodiment of political norms. Where law deviates from widely held social norms, it is generally subject to change, but note that sanctions often accompany the promulgation of law in order that a sovereign will (e.g. of the state) is effective.

DIRECTIVES or 'technical norms' dictate the means appropriate to achieving a particular end. Thus they presuppose the necessary conditions of achieving an end (e.g. 'instructions for use' appended to some product or equipment), and are generally descriptive. A prescriptive element arises when the end is subject to evaluation.

Criteria are employed in the process of judgement, as modes of control. They are related to other norms in being controls, yet are somewhat more subjective since they refer to the judgemental process, while other norms may control the meaning of the facts judged.[4]

Standards are used to measure, and lay off a scale of, values; are prescriptive measures. The usual objective character of norms is not necessarily exhibited in standards, but any norm may take the role of a standard, and in either case relative values are judged by standards which take some objective form as their adequate judgement.[5]

The following concepts share characteristics of more than one of the main types of norms:

Customs arise in the context of social activity over time, in which customs are established patterns of common practice, and are thus similar to rules. Like prescriptions, customs exert social pressure to conform, which supports and maintains the practice.[6]

Principles are both prescriptive and technical guides to thought and action, reflecting some authority (perhaps related to law or custom or belief) and giving direction (for example, about how to achieve The Good Life).

Ideals are concerned with 'being' rather than 'doing', through their relation to notions of goodness or virtue. Virtues are the characteristics of whatever is considered good in some class of things (in the present context, political systems, laws, social relations, etc.), and are conceptually related to the ideal ('the good').

The brief discussions above provide a starting point for constructing a definition of norms. Each concept has been defined in terms of its relation to the other concepts, or partial synonyms of the general concept of a norm, and an extract of the defining characteristics will yield a reasonable definition of norms: see the main text of Chapter 1.

NOTES

1. See Georg Henrik von Wright, *Norm and Action* (London: Routledge & Kegan Paul, 1977), p. 106.
2. Avrum Stroll, 'Norms' (*Dialectica*, Vol. 41, 1987; Proceedings of the VIIIth International Colloquium in Bienna/Biel May 1–4, 1986).
3. *Ibid.*, p. 12.
4. John Dewey, in J. M. Baldwin (ed.), *Dictionary of Philosophy and Psychology* (New York: Peter Smith, 1940), p. 182ff.
5. Dewey, *ibid.*; Stroll, *op. cit.*
6. Edna Ullmann-Margalit, *The Emergence of Norms* (Oxford: Oxford University Press, 1977), p. 8.

2 Realist Assumptions

The central aim of this chapter is to show that built into realist assumptions about world politics are a host of normative considerations, and while realists have had to contend with them, these considerations are not reflected in the tenets of realist theory.

The overall argument of this and the following chapter is that traditional theories of international relations (specifically realist theory) have not only excluded values from the list of central considerations in the study of international relations, but have also constrained the development of normative theorising generally (not just about 'morality') in this area by containing it within the traditional inter-state, power-political paradigm. Thus, while the importance of values is often recognised, regret is simultaneously expressed that value considerations cannot play a part in 'serious' international political theory. It should be said that nothing about norms is inaccessible to realism, but by emphasising the distinction between 'is' and 'ought' and concentrating on the cognitive force of 'is', realism tends to ignore the influence of 'ought' in the realms of knowledge and politics – an aspect of reality.

This critique of realism highlights problematic assumptions which are more clearly evident in realist theory, but because of the influence of realism and the porosity of the classifications of international relations theory, these assumptions also crop up elsewhere as a consequence of tradition, this latter being understood in terms of disciplinary norms.

In the area of normative theory, examined more closely in the following chapter, broad and ancient origins in ethics and political philosophy, as well as early writings directly concerned with international relations (from the classics of political thought to early proposals for European federation and world government) will be considered. Subsequently, various categories of normative thought (such as just war theory, and formulations of human rights) will be discussed to show both the underlying character of normative approaches, and the traditional role they have often conformed to. Various cases of overlap between realism and normative concerns will be examined (normative commentary being quite common in realist works), as these are perhaps the most interesting examples of the constraints imposed by realist assumptions. Fundamental differences, such as that between Max Weber and John Dewey, concerning the theory/practice, fact/value and means/end distinctions, will be presented as representative of the problematic in international relations theory. From this discussion will be drawn conclusions about potential roles for normative theory in the study of international relations at large, the relationship between normative theory and traditional realist theory, and the place of the present work as an attempt to clarify these issues.

In this and the following chapter, distinctions will be made between the dominant theoretical traditions, or schools in the International Relations literature – predominantly 'realist' – and normative theory, as defined in this work. While the various approaches do not represent completely exclusive categories, and are not easily defined (although realist assumptions in general are widely recognised), there are distinctive characteristics in each case which are significant for the overall argument of the book.

In one respect the distinctions between approaches bear on the traditional role of normative thought, in relation to dominant realist perspectives, and in a second respect they bear on theoretical parameters in the study of international relations which have been determined by realist assumptions. The discussion is not intended to provide a rigorous history of thought, nor even a typology, but rather to indicate the extent to which the distinctions amount to conceptions of the international political condition and of the nature of politics in general, and consequently delimit theoretical and practical activity. In this sense, a conception, characterisation, or even apprehension of the object of study – the international system in this case – is not the prerequisite for theorising about it, but rather a consequence of theory.

In particular, the realist school will be examined to show how – as a dominant and traditional approach – it has systematically excluded value considerations from the analysis of international relations, and constrained the development of theory in the field by establishing parameters and promulgating assumptions about the subject which severely limit explanatory ability. What follows should not be taken as an entirely dismissive critique, as there is clearly merit in much realist thought (not least clarity itself), but neither are the shortcomings of realist theory to be underestimated, since the popularity of this approach among policy-makers means that a theoretical liability right away becomes a practical one as well. This latter observation points to a particular aspect of the more general question about the relation between theory and practice, held here to be an intimate and interactive relation.

Beyond a critique of realism and other traditional approaches, the following discussion (in the next chapter) will show by contrast the innovative and productive character of normative approaches, and by comparison among these latter will reveal characteristics which have made normative approaches vulnerable (to charges of idealism or utopianism, for example), and yet fundamental to the study of social phenomena, including – perhaps especially so – the study of international relations. Subsequently, the arguments employed in the present work will be justified and placed in the context of the broader concerns of international relations theory.

Even where realism has allowed particular normative issues a limited role, they have been forced into the conventional state-centric categories. For example: justice is considered in respect of inter-state war and peace, or the more mundane obligations of states to one another, and is always conditioned by considerations of the realities of power (or it is relegated to the domestic political environment); human rights are at best considered in respect of the duties between state governments, or at worst are seen as strictly a matter of internal political relations – domestic politics – insulated from external criticism by the doctrine of sovereign immunity. The same may be said of those issues for which there is ample concrete physical evidence of the global implications: environmental degradation, nuclear and other indiscriminate weapons of mass destruction, population growth, economic development, and so on.

The real significance of normative theory is thus hidden by the 'structural' constraints imposed by traditional theory, and normative approaches have felt obliged to respond to the demands of these traditions in the language of the dominant paradigm. In some respects normative theory finds points of reference in versions of liberalism, and may be seen as an outgrowth of liberal critiques. However, the great potential of normative theory is viewed more favourably against the backdrop of contemporary critiques of traditional international relations theory which have grown out of critical theory and post-modernism.[1] It is in this rather different theoretical environment that the worth of normative approaches can be more clearly seen, in part because these critiques of epistemological and ontological assumptions have forced a reassessment of political and social theory generally, and thus of the foundations of international relations scholarship in particular – here considered to be an aspect of the larger project.

This kind of critical inquiry has simultaneously revealed the frequently buried relationships between the principles of epistemology and ethics, and between political organisation and human aspirations. It is here that fundamental normative questions arise. It should be said, however, that normative theory need only partake of postmodernism (sharing some of its concerns) as a way of sharpening the focus on normative issues that arise in the context of late modernity. That is, descriptive normative theory applies to the contemporary or historical world, even if prescriptive normative theory can apply to possible future worlds.

Realist thought in its traditional forms, and the reworking of this body of thought in the form of neo-realism (or what Waltz calls structural realism), will be reviewed in light of the contemporary critiques mentioned above.[2] The provenance of realist thought in international relations will be discussed with reference to the influence of realist thinkers from 'outside the field' or predating it, including Thucydides, Machiavelli, Rousseau, and the late nineteenth-century German thought of Meinecke, Treitschke, and of Max Weber in the twentieth century. The development of the tradition will be considered through discussion of well-known international relations authors such as E. H. Carr (*The Twenty Years' Crisis*), Reinhold Niebuhr (*Christianity and Power Politics and Christian Realism and Political Problems*), Hans Morgenthau (*Politics Among Nations, Scientific Man vs. Power Politics and Truth and Power*), Martin Wight (*Power Politics and Systems of States*), George Kennan (*Realities of American Foreign Policy*), and Hedley Bull (*The Anarchical Society*). As representative of neo-realist thought, the work of Kenneth Waltz (*Theory of International Politics*) will receive some attention. Reference will be made to commentators (secondary sources) as much as to the original canonical texts, since it is the influence of realist thought on the discipline which is at issue here. In every case it will be noted that attempts to deny or diminish the importance of normative considerations are ultimately unsuccessful.

REALISM

In a survey of neo-realist thought, Robert Keohane states that

> ...it is important to understand realism and neorealism because of their widespread acceptance in contemporary scholarship and in policy circles.[3]

and subsequently that

> The danger that one will become the prisoner of unstated assumptions is rendered particularly acute by the value-laden nature of international relations theory.[4]

These two statements provide a neat synopsis of the problematic addressed in this chapter: a dominant realist approach to the study of international relations may well have imprisoned thinking in this field. The consequences of theoretical dominance are the more urgent when a single body of theory infuses general practice, and the more profound when it is recognised that theoretical activity itself is subject to the influence of value structures.

There are particular aspects of realist thought which not only define that theoretical approach, but to some extent define the theoretical endeavour itself, such that the agenda of metatheoretical issues is set by the predominance of realism as the benchmark of international relations theory.

The first of these aspects of realism is an inclination to pursue a science of international politics which is somehow analogous to the natural sciences, and hence more likely to acquire some of the prestige accorded to 'Science' in a culture which is intrigued and impressed by technological progress. This phenomenon is evidenced both in Morgenthau's traditional realism and in Waltz's neo-realism (and is criticised by the traditionalists of the 'English School', of which more later).

Waltz, for example, presents a systemic theory emphasising political structure in three dimensions: ordering principles, functions of units, and capabilities of units.[5] By assuming anarchy in the states system, and functional similarity among states, the first two dimensions of structure are controlled and the third – 'power' – becomes the significant variable.[6] This is a tidy and effective theory of international politics ('elegant', in scientific parlance), until one questions (a) the degree of anarchy in a system which exhibits many forms of cooperation and coordination (whether voluntary, or hegemonically imposed), (b) the similarity of functions among states which have widely varying political experiences and ideologies, and (c) the profound difficulty of estimating capabilities given that these are defined in terms of complex relationships, not to mention (d) the limitation of considering states to be the only significant units in a world rife with transnational forces of all kinds. Which is to say, the theory sidesteps a range of normative issues. In this case, one might argue, the goal of scientific respectability overrides the goal of understanding the subject matter: The desire to provide an explanation seems to have brought with it a forgetfulness about the reason why an explanation was thought desirable in the first place. This is odd, given Waltz's sensitivity to the purposes of theorising, but no doubt he would say it is due to his limited theoretical aims.[7]

Morgenthau's more historically oriented traditional or classical form of realism similarly evades this kind of criticism, since he is himself a critic of the scientistic behaviouralism of the sixties and a defender of qualitative analysis. However, Morgenthau is equally inclined to seek out simplifying categories, such as power, and constructs theory around the established realist assumptions about interstate relations. His focus on state power is as empirically grounded and conceptually static as the scientism he deplores.[8]

A second aspect of metatheoretical agenda-setting is perhaps less pernicious than its immediate affrontery suggests: the implication that realists are the only theorists addressing, or indeed capable of addressing, reality. The very term 'realism' amounts to a co-option of reality by those adopting this appellation, and yet the very heart of theoretical debate is the definition of reality through the act of providing an account of it.

ORIGINS AND DEVELOPMENT OF THE REALIST TRADITION

The origins of the key assumptions of contemporary realist thought can be located in thinkers of earlier centuries. For example, Rousseau's observation that wars occur because there is nothing to prevent them, is reflected in Waltz's view of war resulting from anarchy as a permissive cause with national interests providing reasoned motivation.[9] Of course, the same critique could be applied to both views as well: to use Waltz as the test case for the moment, the relationship between characteristics of the state (his 'second image') and the anarchic international environment (his 'third image') is not well developed, allowing both the impact of domestic public opinion on foreign policy and the socialising aspects of the international realm to be overlooked – in fact there is much to prevent wars, if only the costs of fighting them. (A normative critique would point to rather more constructive relations – exceptions to the 'rule' of warlike behaviour – which are readily apparent in the modern international system, and would raise questions about the notion of causation employed by Waltz in this case.) What this example illustrates is the degree to which contemporary realist theories rest on problematically simple assumptions borrowed from thinkers of previous periods, and modified only superficially to fit modern requirements of scientific respectability, but not (it should be said) the requirements of modernity.

Similarly, the definition of the realist position in contrast or opposition to idealism rests on the improbability or practical difficulty of proposals for world peace or federation (e.g., by Cruce, de Sully, Saint-Pierre, Kant, and others) and legalist interpretations of appropriate state behaviour (e.g., Bodin, Grotius, Vattel) from previous centuries.[10] The most famous attack on idealism in the younger literature of international relations is by E. H. Carr, responding with inherited pessimism to the failures of the inter-war period.[11] None of these negative definitions of realism allow escape from the Hobbesian attitude to previous events in international relations, nor can they offer a positive contribution to the future.

Among the clearest proponents of realism is Hans J. Morgenthau who (borrowing heavily, though with little acknowledgement, from Max Weber[12]) provides a convenient list of 'six principles of political realism' in *Politics Among Nations*:[13]

(1) Politics, like society in general, is governed by objective laws that have their roots in human nature.
(2) The main signpost of political realism is the concept of interest defined in terms of power.
(3) This key concept is an objective category which is universally valid, but not endowed with a fixed meaning.
(4) There is an ineluctable tension between the moral command and the requirements of successful political action.
(5) The moral aspirations of a particular nation are not identified with the moral laws that govern the universe.
(6) The autonomy of the political sphere is the profoundly distinctive intellectual and moral attitude of realism.

To locate these principles in the context of the present critique, the following are, in Thomasian style, the immediate objections or replies:

(1) 'Natural laws' no longer provide an objective standpoint, and assumptions about human nature are contentious.
(2) Defining interests in terms of an undifferentiated concept of power provides a vague signpost of dubious utility.
(3) The universal objectivity of such a concept is only possible because its meaning is indeterminate.
(4) The tension between morality and politics is created by theoretically excluding morality from a definition of politics.
(5) If there *were* moral laws governing the universe, it would be strange if particular nations did not partake of them.
(6) This restrictive attitude to, or definition of, politics limits and impoverishes realism, detaching it from broader normative consideration of the social realm.

The problems associated with these principles may already be evident, and they will be discussed at various points in the present work. For the moment it will be more useful to examine a critical assessment of realism in general, which naturally draws in broader themes than those identified by a single realist author. Michael Smith identifies 'four key components to the realist approach',[14] according to which realists assume:

(1) that human nature is characterised by 'an ineradicable tendency to evil ... among all men and women'. Views range from Niebuhr's concept of original sin, to E. H. Carr's 'search for power and security' as a fundamental human motivation, to Morgenthau's 'element of universality [which] may be called human nature'.

(2) that the 'only really important collective actor is the state' ("the state-centric assumption"). Thus, the realist view of change is that it can only be achieved by manipulation of the habits and assumptions of an existing political reality.

(3) that 'power and its pursuit by individuals and states [is] ubiquitous and inescapable ... In an anarchic milieu, states are engaged in an unending quest for power'. Thus, the important subjects of theory are the components, methods and instruments of power.

(4) 'that the real issues of international politics can be understood by the rational analysis of competing interests defined in terms of power'. Thus, a rational aspect of the national interest underlies the two ideal types of foreign policy objective – 'to maintain or to increase power'.

Among Smith's criticisms of these realist assumptions is the broad and undifferentiated concept of power, which is treated as both end and means but (as discussed elsewhere) realism provides no account of how goals are established. A further criticism is that the emphasis on the anarchic character of international society underplays the relationship between domestic and international politics: domestic politics are seen as merely one variable affecting the external efficacy of states, notwithstanding another realist theme – the durability of the unitary nation-state. Finally, significant changes in the character and agenda of international politics are not recognised by realism's reference to 'timeless laws' or 'perennial forces'. This, as Smith says, 'is not to deny the continued salience of old [factors]; but it does question a theory which denies that anything important has changed'.[15] In his gentle criticism of George Kennan, Smith states

> ... he did not go much beyond presenting an idealized balance-of-power system. And because he never seemed to recognize the extent to which such a system required at least a minimal code of internationally shared values, Kennan never considered whether, or how, the necessary consensus around those values could be built.[16]

This last observation relates to the present critique of the scientific aspirations of realism which have limited its sensitivity to the essential issues of human collective activity, of politics: not simply what is done, but why; and this question implicates values above all. Aside from absolute dictatorships, no state can define its interests without reference to the fundamental values held by its domestic society. Britain, for example, relies heavily on a broad social consensus in support of its particular form of government which, despite the absence of a written constitution and specific democratic guarantees, remains one of the world's most stable democracies.

Equally, no international system can provide interested reasons for state action unless it is able to reflect the socio-political values of the member-states. The European Union, for example, would not provide a meaningful framework for state action unless the idea of Europe somehow reflected the values of 'European citizens' – indeed, this is the substance of debate concerning the deepening of European integration – whatever the particular interests or relative power of the member states.

Interests, whether or not defined in terms of power, must be secondary to foundational value-structures, suggesting that a normative understanding must take priority over any empirical observations about interest-driven behaviour. While attempting to provide a general theory of international politics, the realists have lost sight of their goal ('reality'; a kind of truth claim) in the search for rigor, simplicity, and the means of political 'control'.

George Kennan provides a particularly interesting case in point because of his expressions of 'idealist' concern, combined with a conventional realist view of international politics. The author of the post-war policy of 'containment' (of Soviet communism),[17] he has warned against employing morality in the determination or analysis of state behaviour, and yet he has always written with a great sensitivity to moral issues.[18] Perhaps because he is among the most forthcoming of realists in this latter respect, Kennan illustrates the constraints which a realist approach puts on a normative understanding of international politics; constraints which thereby limit not just realism but the development of normative theory as well. Of his vacillation between 'realism' and 'idealism' Barton Gellman says,

> Behind this confusion of roles is a false dichotomy between facts and values, between reality and morality, as if it were necessary to choose one or the other. It is a dichotomy to which Kennan sometimes seems to subscribe...[19]

Gellman is a respectful critic, and is genuine in searching for some pattern in Kennan's argument, but finding this difficult ('Probably on no other subject are his views so confusing... puzzles me no end in his discussions of morality and world affairs'[20]) can only note that Kennan did not aspire to write systematic philosophy (though he is an historian). Perhaps the connection between the 'two Kennans', between morality and power-politics, is that to 'Kennan's way of thinking, power always creates a "moral dilemma"'.[21] No doubt this is true, but surely such dilemmas – such value choices – are just what a study of politics should address.

Gellman identifies six different themes in Kennan's writing on morality and foreign affairs: 1) morality is only possible in the absence of power struggles; 2) politics involves both underlying ideals and superimposed power relations, but the latter demand prior attention; 3) security is a precondition for a policy based on ideal principles; 4) security and principle (national interest and morality) are conflicting values; 5) agnosticism (the moral questions are too difficult); 6) relativity (only competent to judge one's own national interest and behaviour).[22]

These various themes are not easily summarised,[23] but Gellman nevertheless offers a broad and balanced critique of Kennan's position on morality – so far as it can be located – and notes that Kennan's objections to morality are prudential rather than principled. This may be the result of an unsystematic writer, as Gellman implies, but it should be noted that there is no lack of systematic argument in respect to power. It is that morality sits uncomfortably with realist assumptions, rather than that morality is troublesome in itself, that leads realist theory to exclude moral considerations – systematically.

Kennan often exhibits great common sense and insight, as indicated by a diary entry from 1949:

...dispense with those means which can stave off defeat only at the cost of undermining victory.[24]

Yet, in spite of the enormous implications of such a view, Kennan the realist was obliged to see this noble goal as one to be achieved by a 'sufficient margin' of military power. That there might be means other than power, or that the end itself might be understood in terms other than victory and defeat, does not enter easily into the realist's field of vision. (Normative aspects of strategic thought are discussed at greater length in Chapter 7).

For Kennan, as for other realists, morality is clearly an uncomfortable, if important, subject. Moral concerns clearly arise, but they bring with them a kind of cognitive dissonance for the world-view of realism, which holds that morals belong at home (in domestic society), or even that they are strictly personal. Kennan, for example, makes a clear distinction between public and private morality in an article entitled 'Morality and Foreign Policy',[25] the argument of which will be discussed at some length in the chapter on nuclear deterrence and foreign policy. This is a limited conception of morality, and reflects the views of Reinhold Niebuhr who, like E. H. Carr, was critical of utopian idealism in the inter-war period as being inappropriate in the face of real dangers. Niebuhr wrote that

> ...the 'liberal culture' of modern bourgeois civilization has simply and sentimentally transmuted the supra-historical ideals of perfection of the gospel into simple historical possibilities. ...that this kind of perfectionism is bad religion...that it is bad politics and that it helps to make the democratic nations weak and irresolute...[26]

It is not difficult to understand why such challenges to idealism were expressed, given the apparent dangers of the historical period in which they were expressed, but they do not constitute the basis of a theory of international politics or morality. These criticisms concerned practical judgement, at a time when practical judgement was everything. It does not follow that a theory can be built upon the need for action in those contingent circumstances, nor that some 'ideals of perfection' might not provide appropriate foundations for a theory which may subsequently inform (not replace) practical judgement.[27] The present argument, of course, is critical of any absolutes that lie outside human experience of politics – outside history (supra-historical) – and of any attempt to dictate historical possibilities, but this does not diminish the need to identify political goals (whether or not these are expressed as ideals). Niebuhr is symptomatic of the realist penchant for moral concern (sometimes in the form of conservative religion) combined with a view of political theory which explicitly excludes a moral component, although this does not necessarily amount to an amoral view of political life. Indeed, the concern with morality is palpable in realism, but it does not belong to its account of international relations. As Dougherty and Pfaltzgraff argue:

> In addition to their efforts to determine how nations in fact behaved, realists developed a body of normative theory addressed particularly to policy makers.[28]

But the normative/ethical component of political action is an after-thought or embellishment, conditioned by the prior concern with prudential state behaviour, and the normative/epistemological structure of political theory which provides the context for action is not accounted for. It seems we are to wait for an after-life before living out, or living up to, any ideals. Yet this is, of course, impossible: every society (even international society) is informed by some conception of the 'good', or some ideal form. In realism, such essential aspirations are reduced to the manipulation of power, devoid of meaningful content. Ideals remain necessary, but being excluded from the political, they naturally become static and absolute. Niebuhr is himself critical of the role Christianity has played in secular politics, and says that Catholicism and Protestantism have exhausted the possibilities of error:

> In either case peace and order through power were estimated too highly and the inevitable injustice of every stabilization of power was judged too leniently.[29]

How it is possible to make such estimations, or even engage with the tension between order and justice in the absence of a political theory which acknowledges the significance of such values? It is a problem revisited in the discussion of Hedley Bull, below. Underlying the insistence on a distinction between the 'idealism' of morality and the 'realism' of politics is an insistence on absolute foundations for both, such that the twain shall never meet. Again, Niebuhr recognises the problems of absolutism when he notes:

> The proponents of 'natural law' therefore invariably introduce some historically contingent norm or social structure into what they regard as God's inflexible norm.[30]

It is not only idealist absolutism of which he is wary. He is critical of orthodox realism in noting the benefits of loyalty to a value transcending national interest:

> It corrects the 'realism' of those who are myopically realistic by seeing only their own interests and failing thereby to do justice to their interests when they are involved with the interests of others.[31]

Niebuhr rightly points out that static absolutes do not provide a suitable foundation for political life – 'Good and evil are not determined by some fixed structure of human existence' – and implies relying on some abiding character in collective relations in his reference to 'love', though for him this is a divine inheritance.[32] Thus, because of a distinction between the continuity of divine qualities and the contingent reality of human experience, there is no place in this scheme for human norms (as opposed to God's) as a fundamental part of political association. Human behaviour is viewed with pessimism, as being necessarily self-interested and ultimately self-destructive, with only the prospect of divine redemption to fall back on: hardly the basis of a humanistic theory of politics. Niebuhr attempts to find a balance, but is unable to escape the assumptions of the realist position (as elaborated by Smith above):

Realistic pessimism did indeed prompt both Hobbes and Luther to an unqualified endorsement of state power; but that is only because they were not realistic enough. They saw the dangers of anarchy in the egotism of the citizens but failed to perceive the dangers of tyranny in the selfishness of the ruler. Therefore they obscured the consequent necessity of placing checks upon the ruler's self-will.[33]

THE STATE OF NATURE

It is appropriate at this point to consider the related points of the realist assumption about the state-of-nature (after Hobbes, implying 'all against all' as between states) and the distinction between the legal and the moral (the latter distinction is discussed further in Chapter 5). Benhabib's analysis of Hegel's normative critique points to the state of nature assumption of the empiricist natural rights theorists (including Hobbes, Locke, Grotius, and Pufendorf – all of whom influence traditional realist theories of international relations) as being a presupposed assumption, 'arrived at via a thought experiment'. He argues that

these theorists abstract from human life in communities those aspects and elements which seem to them to constitute human nature, while leaving aside those which they consider accidental, in virtue of originating in convention, tradition, custom, and covenant... In fact, these thinkers are guided more by their prejudices as to what is and is not part of human nature than by philosophical principle.[34]

Furthermore, the arbitrary selection of some aspects of the human condition and the exclusion of others in the state-of-nature assumption is related, for Hegel, to the destruction of the conception of the ethical life, which thus dissolves into the separate spheres of legality and morality, alienating the individual from the society (denying the ethical whole) by placing the legal medium of the state in opposition to 'personal' morality.[35] (The later Hegel argued that the ethical life of individuals was expressed through the institutions of the state as *Volksgeist*).[36] In the realm of international relations a parallel problem is the separation of a universal human community through the interposition of a system of sovereign states, although Hegel sees this as an historically contingent circumstance through which the universal mind arises out of reciprocal relations between the 'finite minds' of nation-states.[37] The states system is reified by realists' assumption of a 'natural' condition, when states need only be understood as the means of engaging – given identity and difference – in a universal dialogue about the ethical life.

Realists, in their pessimism, are unwilling to accept that those involved in political life are themselves the source of authenticity and rectitude in their relations. But the alternative, reliance on divine guidance or scientific assertion, will provide only the illusion of certain foundations and a static conception of what is inherently dynamic. There is little opportunity in the realist scheme for moral issues to be seen as part of a larger political realm, or as an aspect of the normative structure that underlies international relations (including power relations). It is assumed by realists that states are central, and relations between them bad by default. Roland Robertson, as a sociologist refering to culture, says that 'the disputed terms in which globalization has occurred and is occurring has been greatly neglected', but this does not assume anything in particular about the circumstances of the discourse in which such terms are expressed. It does not assume a state of nature.

Marcel Merle, in his study of the sociology of international relations, points to three versions of the state-of-nature theory in which conflict is logically resolved in (a) a balance of power between sovereign entities, (b) some form of world government, or (c) an historical dialectic, but he says

> The theory of the state of nature purports to be realistic, but is the radical opposition which it establishes between internal order and international chaos still well founded, if indeed it ever was? It is of course true that resort to force is legitimate between states, while it is under state control and monopoly within states. However, this is a partial and over-formal view, introducing a difference in kind when there is only, nowadays at least, a difference in degree between the two kinds of society.[38]

and later,

> The rigorous logic of the state-of-nature theory... contains a major disadvantage: it closes the debate before all its terms have been analysed.[39]

Muddled thinking about the supposed separation between the 'realities of power' and socio-political values can be seen in Kennan's discussion of means and ends in foreign policy. Kennan argues that foreign policy is a means to an end, and that the state as a sovereign entity embodies this end or over-all purpose, 'some purpose to which the total of its political life was supposed to be dedicated and by which its existence as a separate political entity was supposed to be justified', while at the same time this entity is 'not conceived as being an end in itself'.[40] Subsequently he says, 'let us not assume that the *purposes* of states, as distinct from the methods, are fit subjects for measurement in moral terms'.[41] These purposes (for the USA, the protection of certain individual rights) are thus self-evident and unquestionable. However, Kennan is unable to hold this line of argument when his concern with 'realities' actually causes him to counsel cosmopolitanism with regard to the world environment (political and natural) and the expansion of national life, and to call for a greater sense of purpose in the development of national life – indeed he acknowledges that he is here 'at odds' with the above initial justificatory purposes of the state.[42]

DISTINGUISHING REALIST PERSPECTIVES

While realist authors are by no means all of a kind, there is a common thread in the attempted exclusion of normative elements which is ultimately unsuccessful since each in turn has to admit the importance of normative theory.

Hedley Bull offers a useful example of realism, just because his work does not fall readily into the realist mold. He is a 'hard case' with respect to the distinctions and divisions in international relations scholarship, that both he and others have suggested. This is due in part to the plethora of cross-cutting categories that have been proposed, but it is important to recognise that whatever typology is used, the significance of normative theory is evident at every juncture even within the realist canon.

In his discussion of the concept of order in world politics, Bull speaks of 'a common epistemology' and 'common values' in international societies.[43] However, he is quick to point out that such common points of reference are not entirely characteristic of the modern (twentieth century) international society, which 'is weighted in favour of the dominant culture of the West'.[44] This sensitivity to normative considerations is typical of Bull (and he does not intend prescription), but equally (and more importantly) typical is his focus on the goals of the states system (preservation of the system; maintenance of sovereign independence of states; peace/ principled conduct of war)[45] which he views as the inevitable point of reference even as he entertains the possibility of its obsolescence.[46] It is easy to agree that we must begin from where we are, but Bull fails to see the consequences of defining the possibilities in terms of existing realist assumptions. That even primary goals (like order) might be established differently does not enter into the realist paradigm, and Bull reiterates the realist state-centric conception of managing human affairs through the excercise of power. Indeed he self-conciously defends the states-system, though he claims this is not at the expense of the human community, and explicitly asserts the moral priority of world order (a wider concept) over the states system.[47] Thus, like other realists, Bull is unable to tackle international relations from a normative perspective directly, and in falling back on realist assumptions his good intentions become paving stones on a road of uncertain destination.

Among the clearer distinctions to be made in realist thought is that between the American/continental 'scientific' and British/Anglo-Saxon 'traditional' or 'classical' approaches to international relations. There is substantial discussion of the 'English School', and of the dominance of American social science in this field,[48] though both approaches are implicated in the general critique of realism offered here. Chris Brown argues that the English School (including Wight, Bull and possibly Carr) 'saw themselves as students of diplomatic practice and celebrators of the creative side of statecraft; the urge to reduce action to formulae was missing, and this gives their "realism" a fluidity and flexibility not characteristic of the school of Morgenthau'.[49] Martin Griffiths argues that the American realists, Hans Morgenthau and Kenneth Waltz, are not in fact realists at all but are 'more appropriately characterized as political idealists',[50] since Morgenthau's work suffers from 'nostalgic idealism' (evaluative reification of the past) and Waltz's from 'complacent idealism' (reification of the present). Griffiths, using R. N. Berki to construct a framework for analysis, awards the title of true realist to Hedley Bull (with the assistance of Martin Wight,[51] and in spite of 'the truncated boundaries of Wight's paradigms of international thought').[52]

Although Griffiths applies the appelation differently (and disputes Bull's 'Grotian' disposition) Bull certainly falls into the 'classical' tradition by virtue of his notable attack on the scientific approach in his article 'International Theory: The Case for a Classical Approach'.[53] Stanley Hoffmann says of Bull,

... he disliked the scientific method because he thought its practitioners were obsessed by the quest for a far greater degree of precision than the field of international relations allows.[54]

American realism can be identified with the scientific approach, as Stanley Hoffmann implicitly does in describing two other differences between Bull and the realists: 'his distrust of the realist model of state behaviour' and his primary interest in international society (the international political milieu), rather than power.[55] Mark Hoffman, on the other hand, uses the same characteristics to place Bull among the realists in a discussion of 'Critical Theory and Realism' while employing Richard Ashley's distinction[56] between technical and practical realism:

An example of practical realism which more clearly [than Morgenthau] exemplifies this category is the 'English School' and in particular Hedley Bull's *Anarchical Society*.[57]

Mark Hoffman (in noting Linklater[58]) is aware, though, that Bull is usually associated with the category of 'rationalism'. Vincent notes Bull's 'occasional, even frequent, alignment with the realists' while saying that he 'stood four-square in the Grotian or rationalist tradition'.[59] The Grotian view is one in a tripartite scheme of approaches that Bull outlines in *The Anarchical Society*,[60] derived from Martin Wight's similar scheme[61] (the differing terms of which are shown below in parentheses), and reflected in Banks' three paradigms[62] {differences shown in brackets}:

Approach	*View of international politics*
Hobbesian/realist (Machiavellian)	state of war among states
Grotian/internationalist (rationalist){pluralist}	international society of states
Kantian/universalist (revolutionist){structuralist}	potential community of mankind

In many respects this typology is only notional, since there are some overlapping elements and differences within categories, but it does serve as a context for debate between views, even if it is recognised that all of these categories derive from the assumptions of Western Enlightenment rationality and methodology.[63] This three-part arrangement is not, of course, the only possible scheme. Michael Donelan points out that both Carr and Morgenthau were content with two categories (roughly speaking, realism and idealism), and provides his own five-part scheme: natural law, realism, fideism, rationalism (which he prefers), and historicism (in two aspects).[64] More recently, the debate has reverted to two categories, neorealism and neoliberalism (or neoliberal institutionalism), though it might be said that the distinction between the two is rather blurred, and indeed the advent of alternative (post-modern, post-positivist, gender) theory could indicate the decreasing relevance or importance of the interparadigm debate.[65]

The significance of adopting such taxonomies of international political thought should not be underestimated, however, since in providing

a context for debate they also proscribe the limits of discourse.
R. B. J. Walker observes that

> far from being merely one of a series of debates that have characterised
> the history of the discipline, the distinction between political realism
> and political idealism has provided the context within which other dis-
> putes about appropriate methodology or the priority of state-centred
> accounts of world politics could occur at all.[66]

Thus it is possible to say that there are certain consequences of adopting
a specifically Grotian view, and of some interest here is the distinction
between the naturalists (Grotius and Lauterpacht) and the positivists
(Vattel and Oppenheim) among the international lawyers. The Grotian
natural law foundations of Bull's view may explain both his concern with
moral issues, and his inability to properly incorporate them into a theory
of international relations. While Stanley Hoffmann says that for Bull,

> international society has a moral basis; indeed Bull's concern for inter-
> national society and his interest in moral conceptions are inextricably
> linked.[67]

he also points out that

> it must be said that Bull himself never did lay out fully the foundations
> of his own moral position...[68]

If he had addressed those foundations, no doubt it would have been
apparent that the absolutist character of naturalistic assumptions (even
when secularised) give rise to an insistence on absolute foundations which
are no more appropriate to the understanding of a varied and changing
society than the static foundations of positivism. Bull recognises that order
is 'necessarily a relative concept', and 'exists only in relation to given
goals', but nevertheless insists that certain goals are universal conditions of
social life.[69] He supports his analysis by reference to the 'good sense' of the
'simple truisms' of natural law (as discussed by H. L. A. Hart in *The
Concept of Law*), but this line of argument suggests a case of 'the naturalistic fallacy' (as discussed in G. E. Moore's *Principia Ethica*) if it amounts to
a claim that such universal conditions are a natural (observable/provable)
social 'good'. Alternatively, but equally problematically, these universal
conditions may be viewed as non-natural 'goods' which are apprehended
by the faculty of intuition, yet are still an aspect of reality 'out there' to be
apprehended regardless of the socio-political context of their apprehension.
Bull's central definition of order as 'a pattern of human activity that
sustains elementary, primary or universal goals of social life' does not

evade the troublesome question of purpose (what should those goals be?). In providing an account of a kind of 'practical association',[70] which does not require or pursue a common vision of the good life,[71] the explanation of why such an order should come about or be pursued is not provided. This shortcoming may be understandable in view of Martin Wight's distinction between classical political theory as being 'theory of the good life' and international theory as being 'theory of survival',[72] and of course Bull sees order as instrumental to survival. Robert Jackson argues that international theory is also a theory of the good life, is part of the theory of the state, since it addresses the conditions under which the good life can be pursued within states:

> International theory in both its realist and rationalist versions is a theory of survival only because political theory is a theory of the good life... If revolutionism is a variant of international theory, then that theory is not limited to the theory of survival...[73]

This passage addresses Wight's claim that 'what for political theory is the extreme case (as revolution, or civil war) is for international theory the regular case', this being the reason for the 'recalcitrance of international politics to being theorized about'.[74]

Questioning the assumption that states are the perfect form of association necessarily undermines an exclusive concern with their survival. Hegel's characterisation of the state as the highest form of political life is, after all, entirely contingent and his historical dialectic does not permit dogmatic attachment to any particular social formation or 'natural law' (setting aside any teleological determinism that may be seen in such an account). Some consequences of orthodox conceptions of the state, for the study of international relations, are suggested by Fred Halliday in his discussion of an alternative history of world society, emphasising sociological trends rather than the expansion of inter-state institutions:

> The argument is not about whether we are or are not 'state centric', but what we mean by the state.[75]

Jackson concludes that 'political and moral theorising on international relations is expanding, arguably because the good life is affected more and more by events external to states'. Ferguson and Mansbach note that normative/legal boundaries do not necessarily coincide with political boundaries, and so abandon the dichotomy between interstate and domestic politics in favour of the concept of 'authority patterns' or 'polities' in history.[76]

Bull's notion of order, as Vincent indicates, is ambivalent with respect to it being an empirical generalisation or a logical requirement: an ambivalence with respect to the is/ought question.[77] This ambivalence undermines the critical potential of Bull's argument; it is perhaps something inherited:

> Wight's attitude to the realist position, then, is an ambivalent one; and in *Power Politics* he does not so much formulate or expound it as suggest that it is food for thought.[78]

It should be said, of course, that a consequence of this ambivalence is that it does not close the argument in the way that 'scientific' forms of realism do, but the reluctance to prescribe or recommend condones the status quo.[79] It is odd that realists like Bull and Morgenthau, preoccupied with state systems and state behaviour, claim *not* to be defenders of the status quo (and indeed were often critical of state practice): Bull states that it would be an oversight 'to derive from this [defence of the states system] an endorsement of the existing society of states',[80] and Morgenthau states that 'international relations is not something to be taken for granted but something to be understood and to be changed and, more particularly, to be changed beyond the present limits of its political structure and organization'.[81] However, prescription and critique are related (in that critique is both 'negative prescription' and an avenue for change and prescription) and the creative process requires both in full measure. Thus while Bull emphasised 'society' (with its common interests, values, rules and institutions) over 'system' (the impact of states on one another), his concern with *order* nevertheless leads to a reindorsement of the states-system – implicating both study and practice. As Mark Hoffman states:

> For the English School, the central starting point is the uniqueness of the system of states in displaying both order and elemental society in the absence of an overarching sovereign.[82]

Bull introduces some latitude by saying that the states-system is 'only part' (but 'the most important part') of world politics,[83] and Vincent is able to describe a passage on the moral priority of world society over state-society as 'tantalizingly brief'.[84] The unwritten study of justice (to complement the study of order) might have clarified Bull's position in this respect. Bull must have recognised the problems inherent in delineating the normative and the political in his discussion concerning the relationship between justice and order, and which of these has priority (in the end he says that order is not a commanding value). The difficulty here is precisely the making of a distinction between order and justice as conflicting political goals: justice is the political virtue, and it both supports and depends on order of some kind (orderliness in general, but not a particular instance of order).[85] Placing these two at odds is not an appropriate starting point for understanding politics, as noted in the discussion of Machiavelli below. The question of how politics is to be ordered always remains. In spite of his realist assumptions (e.g., about the primacy of states) and because of his concern with international society (somehow 'beyond' the states-system, though comprised of it), Bull was aware of the significance of normative issues and identified normative enquiry and values as promising potential developments in his article 'New Directions in the Theory of International Relations'.[86]

Morgenthau provides another perspective on the distinctions in realist theory, both as a realist himself (primarily concerned with the category of power) and as a critic of a particular mode of theorising. As a realist, Morgenthau declares the central concept of politics to be power; as a critic of the rationalistic quantitative approach he says 'but if I want to know how much power this politician or that government has, I must leave the adding machine and the computer for historical and necessarily qualitative judgment'.[87] He argues that

> What distinguishes the reflections on international relations since Machiavelli from those that preceded them is not their concern for practicality but the intellectual mode with which they endeavored to satisfy that concern. The Greek and medieval mode was predominantly ethical and deductive; that of Machiavelli and those who followed him was empirical and inductive.[88]

The distinction Morgenthau makes is therefore one between historical and rational-scientific modes of theorising, between an aspect of political philosophy or philosophy of history and theories whose aim is 'the rational manipulation of international relations...in the interest of predictable and controlled results'.[89] However, this distinction does not address the gap in Morgenthau's own thinking between his view that the final and most noble task of a theory of international relations 'is to prepare the ground for a new international order radically different from that which preceded it',[90] and his universalisation of the characteristics of existing power politics. In identifying the shortcomings of rational-scientific theory,[91] Morgenthau remains a theorist of the state, and his perspective is not as distant from Machiavelli's as his theoretical distinctions suggest.[92]

MACHIAVELLI AND *MACHSTAAT*[93]

Machiavelli provides an obvious point of reference for realism in his notion of *necessità*,[94] the means by which *fortuna* is overcome in meeting the requirements of *virtù*. The origins of the problem of state action had, of course, been addressed in the earliest political writings – by Thucydides, for example, who said of men that 'it is a necessary law of their nature that they rule wherever they can'[95] – but according to Meinecke, Machiavelli was the first to assess the meaning of *raison d'état* in the context of a nascent 'modern' western system of states.[96] Thus Meinecke finds a starting point for addressing the essentially modern phenomenon of Machiavellism, and its influence on political thought. The theories of Machiavelli himself have been subsequently buried or subsumed by the condensation of his ideas (e.g., by Treitschke)[97] in the concept of *raison d'état* (*ragione di stato*), yet it is important to the present argument that Meinecke emphasises the

> enormous significance (and this significance is not only historical, but also philosophical) of the problem of raison d'etat [where] one sees particularly clearly the frightful and deeply disturbing difficulties, which are concealed by the juxtaposition of what is and what ought to be, of causality and the Ideal, of Nature and Mind in human life.[98]

This 'enormous significance' is disguised in realist theories in two ways. First, realism understood as a theory of state action requires no further justification of such action beyond the imperative of engaging with contingent events in order to mould them in the interest of the state. That states act in their interest is simply an aspect of reality, from this perspective. That values might be involved in the determination of interests is not considered. As Michael Smith says of the realists,

> They have instead argued unconvincingly that values do not enter in, that 'good' policy is simply a matter of following the national interest. But the national interest is not an objective datum, an amoral law of interstate existence. Rather it is defined according to a particular hierarchy of values.[99]

Secondly, realism assumes that historically contingent events or the circumstances of the moment are also an aspect of an objective and static empirical reality, from which conclusions about state interests can be drawn unproblematically. Once again, we are confronted with Morgenthau's 'perennial forces'. Furthermore, as Walker argues, the complexities of realism's intellectual history become lost when static structures are posited (by 'structural realism', for example[100]) on the grounds of unproblematic interpretations of early writers:

> In place of a history of political thought is offered an ahistorical repetition in which the struggles of these thinkers to make sense of the

historical transformations in which they were caught are erased in favour of assertions that they all articulate essential truths about the same unchanging and usually tragic reality: the eternal game of relations between states.[101]

From such a perspective, there is little chance that what Meinecke considers 'deeply disturbing difficulties' will be observed, let alone addressed.

These assumptions lead realist analysis to focus on contingent circumstances and the efficiency of state action in bringing about or managing change in them. Thus, with respect to Meinecke's juxtapositional scheme above, the emphasis will be on 'what is', on causality, and on Nature, with little or no concern for human purposes and their relationship to interests ('what ought to be', the Ideal, Mind). In terms of the Machiavellian conceptual bridging structure, by which *necessità* (*raison d'état*/national interest) forms the span between *fortuna* (chance/contingency/'reality') and *virtù* (national values/ideals/purposes), this is an emphasis on the relation between *fortunà* and *raison d'état* which does not allow a completion of the arch by consideration of *virtù*. When the assumed uninterpreted reality of contingent events permits unquestioned calculations of interests, there is no room for (need of) investigations of a state's ultimate purposes or the values which guide its actions – such inquiries are seen as either subversive of self-evident interests or as simply unrealistic. Martin Griffiths uses Berki's analysis to make sense of realist categories along similar lines: These 'three broad referents for "the real"' (immediacy, necessity and truth)[102] are each inadequate in themselves, reality as immediacy (the condition of international politics, for Griffiths) being the dialectical product of reality as necessity (abstraction of constraints) and reality as truth (abstraction of freedoms) (cf. Berki).[103] The difference in this case (that is, for Berki and after him, Griffiths) is that necessity is given, and immediacy is the constructed response, whereas in Machiavelli *necessità* is the mode of response and *fortuna* is the given – with truth/freedom/*virtù* remaining in both cases an abstraction of uncertain status. Berki's view reveals typical realist assumptions (which might have been wholly transferred to Griffiths but for the discovery of Rorty),[104] and is made clear in his discussion of:

The Dialectic of Political Understanding... or the way to the achievement of comprehending politics fully as 'practical' reality. This achievement is what I shall be calling political philosophy or wisdom. The two levels to be passed on the way are, respectively, political science or the level of knowledge, and ideology or political belief. On the level of knowledge politics is comprehended as objective reality, a world of facts and observable, empirical relationships. On the level of belief it is approached as a world of values and ideals, an area for human action, as subjective reality. Philosophy synthesizes these two partial approaches.[105]

Such clear distinctions between fact and value, even allowing for synthesis, are characteristic of realist perspectives which in the first instance engage with the problems of state practice in terms of 'knowledge' of 'objective reality', leaving 'values' and 'subjective reality' and paradoxical truths about the conflict of values and ideological clashes to the leisurely acquisition of 'wisdom'.

WEBER AND THE LIMITS OF REALISM

One characterisation of a modern policy-maker – Henry Kissinger in this case – suggests that a practioner of a state-centric Weberian 'ethic of responsibility' must necessarily exclude from consideration any substantive goals or ultimate ends, being concerned primarily with the avoidance of catastrophe in the maintenance of the status quo.[106] Problems attending such assumptions are recognised, if reluctantly, by the realists themselves.

For example, Hans Morgenthau uses a famous quote from Weber to support his own case for the primacy of interests:

Interests (material and ideal), not ideas, dominate directly the actions of men. Yet the 'images of the world' created by these ideas have very often served as switches determining the tracks on which the dynamism of interests kept actions moving.[107]

Here, as Turner and Factor argue, Weber treats value choices as a category of interests ('ideal interests').[108] The quoted passage (the book's only nod to Weber) also qualifies interests by the use of 'directly', whereas Weber elsewhere notes the significant effects of the *indirect* influence of values.[109]

E. H. Carr, in *The Twenty Years' Crisis*, also recognises the problems and limitations of realism, and provides a damning critique of it, having first made good use of realist assumptions in his arguments against utopianism. Indeed, this somewhat cynical use of a theoretical tool is an indication in itself of the seductive yet shallow nature of realist polemics. In Chapter 6, entitled 'The Limitations of Realism', Carr notes that:

The impossibility of being a consistent and thorough-going realist is one of the most certain and curious lessons of political science.

Consistent realism excludes four things which appear to be essential ingredients of all effective political thinking: a finite goal, an emotional appeal, a right of moral judgement and a ground for action.[110]

From this, it may be assumed that at least some among the realists paradoxically share the conclusions of the present work concerning the problems of realist theory. It may be felt that some of these problems have been resolved by neorealist revisions. Waltz, for example, asserts that a theory of international relations must identify what is distinctive about them – for him, this is the nature of the international system and the way it motivates state behaviour.[111] Thus any explanations not at the systemic level (i.e., concerning competition and socialisation in the anarchic states system) are reductionist confusions, and a 'major impediment to the development of theories about international politics'.[112] Consequently, virtually all political characteristics are excluded in the description of the system's natural balance of power.

The heart of the theoretical problem is that while realists sensibly point out the effects of power and the habit of pursuing interests, neither of these avenues of inquiry are especially important to the study of politics: realism simply lays out some obvious features of political experience, while setting aside the most troublesome and important (and interesting) political questions. The pursuit of power is an instrumentality, and in itself says little about underlying causes or consequences. For the most part, the fundamental political questions concern the assignment of value, hence the necessity of choice, and ultimately the embodiment of value choices in political action. Importantly, all of this must take place in the context of relationships: the exercise of power cannot take place in a vacuum, and always assumes a political framework. There is no reason to exclude practical considerations, of course, and as Schwarzenberger says, 'a realistic exposition of *what is* is perfectly compatible with constructive views on what *can* or *ought to be*'.[113] The heart of the practical problem is that realism dictates obvious forms of practice, such as the pursuit of power and interests, that are both insensitive to the complexities of its own categories and dismissive of alternative categories of thought and action. In realism, values (the very stuff of politics) are a marginal concern, eliminated or contained by problematic assumptions.

Mervyn Frost provides a useful account of problematic assumptions in reference to a 'postivist bias' in the study of international relations.[114] Making use of Richard Rorty's arguments against the 'mirror of nature' assumption about the mind[115] (it being an assumption shared by most international relations theorists), Frost presents a case for treating normative approaches as (at least) the epistemological equal of positivist theories. This critique of positivism involves the idea of a realm of social discourse, which admits certain forms of knowledge but does not endow them with exclusive epistemological validity.[116]

There are a number of significant consequences of such a view, among which is the diminished role of philosophy as determining *a priori* criteria of true knowledge, and the problem of relativism in the absence of such universal criteria. These issues have already been introduced in the previous chapter, and will be raised again in the following discussion of normative theory as an alternative approach in respect of both its focal concerns and its unique relevance to the epistemological debate. In particular, the relationship between values and theoretical and practical reasoning provides a focal point for distinctions between realism and normative theory, which can be raised here in respect to realism and later revisited in the following chapter on normative theory.

In a discussion of history and structure in international relations theory, Walker continues his remarks concerning the distinction between political realism and political idealism by pointing to its proscription of discourse and debate:

> Framed within this distinction, 'metaphysics', 'ethics' and 'ideology' have become the names for roles in an old and obviously decrepit manichean theatre. Tamed in this way, it is hardly surprising that they have been marginalised in favour of the louder and seemingly more up-to-date claims of social science.[117]

Walker observes in a footnote that Carr and Morgenthau offer formulations of dilemmas arising in early twentieth century German historicism, as mediated by Karl Mannheim and Max Weber. Weber is clearly an important figure (as Walker has said), and is both the starting point of Michael Smith's study of realism (*op. cit.*) and the subject of Turner and Factor's book, *Max Weber and the Dispute over Reason and Value*, which indicates that Weber relied heavily on (whereas Dewey attacked) the means/end and fact/value distinctions.[118]

Turner and Factor argue that 'Weber's ideas were to form the backbone of Morgenthau's work' (Morgenthau does acknowledge the influence in an autobiographical article, published in 1977) and suggest that Morgenthau reconstructed Weber's position in Anglo-American terms, since theory of German origin would not have been well-received at the time:[119]

> it is evident that the basic structure of Morgenthau's argument in this book has simply been taken over from Weber: Morgenthau argued that

a person may potentially choose various moral positions or make various ultimate choices, and that reason and rational dialogue cannot settle the questions between these choices.[120]

Turner and Factor write that Morgenthau opposed the tradition which 'misunderstands the nature of man, the nature of the world, and the nature of reason itself'[121] – that is to say, rationalism (in respect to values); scientism in social science (applying reason to values); liberalism in politics (reasoned debate about values); legalism in foreign policy (legal-rational behaviour)[122] – and supported those who 'conceive the nature of international politics as an unending struggle for survival and power'.[123] They argue that Morgenthau's criticism of legalism is not based on the obvious problem of assuming universal acceptance of Anglo-American culture, but on the blindness to the nature of politics as a struggle of interests:

For Morgenthau, 'justice' is an illusion; struggle is real.[124]

Hence there is only the struggle of valuative and material interests, and no opportunity for rational reconciliation. In contrast to liberalism, Morgenthau and Weber take the reductive, and antipolitical view (in the same sense as Marx) that the illusion of politics finds meaning in a struggle based outside of political discourse, though of course Morgenthau identifies behaviouralist reductionism with nineteenth century Marxism and liberalism, since it fails to address politics 'in its own terms, that is, in terms of power'.[125] The point is that where Marx reduces politics to economics, Morgenthau reduces it to power, and while Morgenthau makes the distinction between quantitative and qualitative methods, his insistence on qualitative methods does not translate into a specifically normative approach. Turner and Factor outline Morgenthau's positive theory, which sets itself against utopianism (also Weber's target):

Morality in foreign policy, as Morgenthau understood it, is equivalent to the intellectual integrity of the person who subjects himself to the discipline of consequentialist moral discourse and therefor limits himself to attainable ends.[126]

For Morgenthau, the 'moral blindness of scientific man' lies in failing to recognise the tragic character of human life, and the unavoidable risk of evil in political action.[127] However, Turner and Factor argue that Morgenthau developed these ideas into a theory which informed practice – something Weber thought impossible. Thus Morgenthau advised that the duty of officials is to preserve the state, but is unable to provide the grounds for any obligation to do so ('The intellectual seeks truth; the politician, power').[128] Indeed the relationship between state and civil society is not characterised, and perhaps cannot be since the epistemological foundations for justifying any duties at all, or any practice, are undermined by ignoring the centrality of values in politics. Although Morgenthau attacks theory which is uncritical of the status quo and official doctrine,[129] the logic of his representation of politics suggests that an official is free (in the context of the 'struggle') to choose any interest he or she likes, without regard for the value choices of the society which officials represent. What is missing in realist theory is the acknowledgement that politics, even its own version (power politics), is shot through with values.

The concept of interest used by Weber (as reflected in the passage cited by Morgenthau, above) is not entirely clear in its foundation, being qualified by consideration of values even though value choices are held to be irrational. This position is sometimes referred to as 'decisionism', which holds that rational value-free decisions can be made (in science and politics) once value choices have been made. Within a context, the means to an end can be determined: interests are given. Turner and Factor say Morgenthau

> treated values and interests the way Weber did, by considering interests to be dictated by value choices, material and ideal. But the institution of the nation-state creates an anomalous situation: in international politics, according to Morgenthau, interests can be rather precisely defined.[130]

This seems to take a great deal for granted about the state, and its relation to its own and other societies, including international society. As Walker implies, this is an artifact of early twentieth century German historicism, emphasising commitment to the state as the ultimate expression of political value – an untenable position in the modern world, given that even realists like Bull recognised that the states system was only one aspect of the modern world, and both he and Morgenthau encouraged consideration of new political structures. Given the imperatives of survival and national interest ('defined in terms of power', though whether this is national power or official power is now unclear), the limits of realist action are clear-cut, if inappropriate. Thus,

> for Morgenthau, an objective, practice-informing theory of international politics is possible without departing from the Weberian strictures against normative theory.[131]

Morgenthau rephrased Weber's ideas in the idiom of Anglo-American scientific culture, facilitating the adoption of Weberian language. As Turner and Factor suggest, this was accomplished in part by interpreting the term *Wissenschaft* to mean 'science', which denies it the full breadth of a meaning that includes 'philosophy'. Naturally enough, arguments for value-free science seem quite plausible in an empiricist environment, and Morgenthau criticised rationalist quantitative methods on just those grounds. However, the broader meaning implicates Weber's view that there is no rationality to moral and political choice, and indeed that it is not possible to question the meaning or value of science or the value and rational adequacy of politics or culture – 'an extremely implausible claim'.[132]

The difficulties of normative theory prompted realists of every stripe to eschew the normative elements in international politics in favour of apparently rigorous theories of state power. However, maintaining such distinctions as those between values and interests, justice and order, ethics and politics, means only that the conception of world politics employed in realist theory is inadequate. Attempts to modify the realist approach by addition of structural and systemic considerations in neorealism has done little or nothing to alter these characteristics.[133] Even realist assumptions are rife with normative content, and realist theory is unable to account for it without resorting in the end to normative theory.

NOTES

1. For example, R. B. J. Walker argues from this perspective in saying that 'theories of international relations are always destined to be the poor relation' of traditional political thought as a consequence of Wight's rendition of the subject, and that other traditional formulations similarly constrain theory in this field. See R. B. J. Walker, *The Prince* and the "Pauper": Tradition, Modernity, and Practice in the Theory of International Relations' in James Der Derian and Michael J. Shapiro (eds), *International/Intertextual Relations: Post-modern Readings in World Politics* (Lexington, MA: Lexington Books, 1989), pp. 30–32. The postmodernist literature in international relations is represented by Der Derian, *On Diplomacy: A Geneology of Western Estrangement* (Oxford: Blackwell, 1987), and for politics generally by Michael J. Shapiro, *Language and Politics* (New York: New York University Press, 1984) and *Reading the Post-modern Polity: Political Theory as Textual Practice* (Minneapolis: University of Minnesota Press, 1992). The broader post-modernist context is provided by works such as Jacques Derrida, *Speech and Phenomena* (Evanston, IL: Northwestern University Press, 1973), Michel Foucault, *The Archeology of Knowledge* (New York: Pantheon, 1972) and Jean-Francois Lyotard, *The Postmodern Condition: A Report on Knowledge* (Minneapolis: University of Minnesota

Press, 1984), which literature is in turn placed in the context of alternative theoretical approaches by David Held (ed), *Political Theory Today*. (Cambridge: Polity Press, 1991), pp. 18–19.

2. See, for example, the debate in Robert O. Keohane, ed., *Neorealism and its Critics* (New York: Columbia University Press, 1986).
3. Keohane, *Neorealism and its Critics*, *op. cit.*, p. 4.
4. *Ibid.*
5. Kenneth N. Waltz, *Theory of International Politics* (Reading. MA: Addison-Wesley, 1979), p. 73.
6. For a useful discussion of this issue see A. Wendt, 'Anarchy is What States Make of it: The Social Construction of Power Politics', *International Organisation* (Vol. 46, No. 2, 1992).
7. See the discussion of laws and theories in the first chapter of Waltz's *Theory of International Politics*, *op. cit.*, and his response to the critiques of Ashley and Cox in Keohane, *Neorealism and its Critics*, *op. cit.*
8. See for example the various essays in *Truth and Power: Essays of a Decade, 1960–70* (London: Pall Mall Press, 1970). Morgenthau is discussed further below.
9. Waltz, *Man, the State and War* (New York: Columbia University Press, 1959), pp. 231–2; 238. In this work Waltz represents the 'classical' school, in contrast to his later structural or neo-realist work, *Theory of International Politics*.
10. See the historical survey in Torbjörn L Knutsen, *A History of International Relations Theory* (Manchester: Manchester University Press, 1992), and the analysis in Daniele Archibugi, 'Models of International Organization in Perpetual Peace Projects', *Review of International Studies* (Vol. 18, No. 4, October 1992).
11. E. H. Carr, *The Twenty Years' Crisis* (London: Macmillan, 1939).
12. For views on Weber's influence see Michael Joseph Smith, *Realist Thought from Weber to Kissinger* (Baton Rouge and London: Louisiana State University Press, 1986), and Daniel Warner, *An Ethic of Responsibility in International Relations* (London: Lynne Reiner, 1992).
13. Hans J. Morgenthau, *Politics Among Nations* (New York: Alfred A. Knopf, 1948; 5th Ed., revised, 1978), pp. 4–15.
14. Michael Joseph Smith, *Realist Thought from Weber to Kissinger*, *op. cit.*, p. 219ff.
15. *Ibid.*, pp. 225–6.
16. *Ibid.*, pp. 235–6.
17. Kennan's views, and name, came to prominence with the famous 'Long Telegram' (from Moscow) of February 1946 and the (briefly) anonymous 'X' article in *Foreign Affairs* of 1947, both written while he was in the American foreign service. He was US Ambassador to Moscow in 1952, until declared *persona non grata* for his frank description of living conditions there.
18. George Kennan, 'Morality and Foreign Policy', *Foreign Affairs* (Vol. 64, No. 2, Winter 1985–86). See the further discussion of Kennan's work in Chapter 5, under 'Normative Aspects of Foreign Policy', which supports the point made here.
19. Barton Gellman, *Contending with Kennan: Toward a Philosophy of American Power* (New York: Praeger, 1984), p. 60.

20. *Ibid.*, pp. 69 and 78.
21. *Ibid.*, p. 62.
22. *Ibid.*, pp. 64–9.
23. Kennan provides a loose summary of his position in his *Realities of American Foreign Policy* (New York: W. W. Norton, 1966), p. 49 (first published by Princeton University Press, 1954).
24. George Frost Kennan, *Memoirs, 1925–1950 [Volume One]* (Boston: Little, Brown, 1967), p. 437.
25. *Op. cit.* This would seem to be a reply to Gellman, *op. cit.* (who was 22 when writing in 1984), among others: 'There have… been demands, particularly from the younger generation, that I should make clearer my views on the relationship of moral considerations to American foreign policy' (p. 205).
26. Reinhold Niebuhr, *Christianity and Power Politics* (New York: Scribner's, 1940), from the Preface, pp. ix–xi.
27. See the subsequent discussion of Bull and Morgenthau, and notes 77–79.
28. James E. Dougherty and Robert L. Pfaltzgraff, Jr., *Contending Theories of International Relations* (New York: Lippincott, 1971), p. 101.
29. Niebuhr, 'The Christian Church in a Secular Age' in *Christianity and Power Politics, op. cit.*, p. 223.
30. Niebuhr, 'Augustine's Political Realism' in *Christian Realism and Political Problems* (New York: Scribner's, 1953), pp. 132–3.
31. *Ibid.*, p. 137.
32. *Ibid.*, p. 103. See the different treatment of love in Roberto Mangabeira Unger, *Knowledge and Politics* (New York: The Free Press and London: Collier Macmillan, 1975), *inter alia* pp. 206–295.
33. *Ibid.*, p. 127. Here Niebuhr exhibits, even in a critical mode, the four components of the realist approach: (1) a pessimistic attitude to human nature, (2) the state-centric assumption, (3) the centrality of state power, (4) the rational aspect of national interest.
34. Seyla Benhabib, *Critique, Norm, and Utopia: A Study of the Foundations of Critical Theory* (New York: Columbia University Press, 1986), p. 24.
35. *Ibid.*, pp. 24–7.
36. G. W. F. Hegel, *The Philosophy of Right* (Oxford: Oxford University Press, 1980 [1821]), p. 156.
37. Merle, *The Sociology of International Relations*, trans. Dorothy Parkin (Leamington Spa: Berg Publishers, 1987), pp. 49–50.
38. *Ibid.*, pp. 51–2.
39. *Ibid.*, p. 58.
40. *Realities of American Foreign Policy, op. cit.* (Princeton, NJ: Princeton University Press, 1954), pp. 5–7.
41. *Ibid.*, p. 47.
42. *Ibid.*, pp. 106–110.
43. Hedley Bull, *The Anarchical Society* (London: Macmillan, 1977), p. 16.
44. *Ibid.*, p. 317.
45. *Ibid.*, p. 16.
46. *Ibid.*, pp. 295–6.
47. *Ibid.*, pp. 318–20.
48. See Roy Jones, 'The English School of International Relations: A Case for Closure', *Review of International Studies* (Vol. 7, No. 1, 1981), the debate

between Peter Wilson (Vol. 15, No. 1, 1989) and Sheila Grader (Vol. 14, No. 1, 1988) in that journal, and Steve Smith, *International Relations: British and American Perspectives* (Oxford: Basil Blackwell, 1985). On American dominance, see Stanley Hoffmann, 'An American Social Science: International Relations' *Daedalus* (Vol. 106, No. 3, 1977), Ekkehart Krippendorff, *International Relations as a Social Science* (Brighton: Wheatsheaf, 1982), and chapters by Steve Smith and others in Hugh C. Dyer and Leon Mangasarian (eds), *The Study of International Relations: The State of the Art* (London: Macmillan, 1989).

49. Chris Brown, 'Sorry Comfort? The Case Against "International Theory"', unpublished conference paper presented to the Inaugural Pan-European Conference on International Studies of the European Consortium for Political Research, Standing Group on International Relations (panel on 'Power and Morality in International Relations'), Heidelberg, 16–20 September 1992, p. 5. The arguments of this paper can be found in the introduction to Chris Brown, *International Relations Theory: New Normative Approaches* (London: Harvester Wheatsheaf, 1992).

50. Martin Griffiths, *Realism, Idealism and International Politics: A Reinterpretation* (London Routledge, 1992), *passim*.

51. *Ibid.*, p. 34.

52. *Ibid.*, p. 167.

53. Hedley Bull, 'International Theory: The Case for a Classical Approach', *World Politics* (Vol. 18, No. 3, 1966), which is reprinted in K. Knorr and J. Rosenau (eds), *Contending Approaches to International Politics* (Princeton, NJ: Princeton University Press, 1969) along with the article by Morton Kaplan, 'The New Great Debate: Traditionalism vs Science in International Relations'.

54. Stanley Hoffmann, 'International Society' in J. D. B. Miller and R. J. Vincent (eds), *Order and Violence: Hedley Bull and International Relations* (Oxford: Clarendon Press, 1990), p. 16.

55. *Ibid.*, pp. 14–15.

56. See Richard K. Ashley, 'Political Realism and Human Interests', *International Studies Quarterly* (Vol. 25, No. 2, 1981) and 'The Poverty of Neorealism', *International Organisation* (Vol. 38, No. 2, 1984).

57. Mark Hoffman, 'Critical Theory and the Inter-Paradigm Debate' in Dyer and Mangasarian (eds), *The Study of International Relations*, *op. cit.*, p. 71.

58. Andrew Linklater, 'Realism, Marxism and Critical International Theory', *Review of International Studies* (Vol. 12, No. 2, 1986).

59. R. J. Vincent, 'Order in International Politics' in Miller and Vincent (eds), *Order and Violence*, *op. cit.*, p. 41.

60. *Op. cit.*, p. 24. See, however, Griffiths' *...Reinterpretation, op. cit.*

61. See his 'Western Values in International Relations' in H. Butterfield and M. Wight (eds), *Diplomatic Investigations* (London: Allen and Unwin, 1967).

62. Michael Banks, 'The Inter-Paradigm Debate' in Light and Groom (eds), *International Relations: A Handbook of Current Theory* (London: Francis Pinter, 1985).

63. See, for example, the discussion in N. J. Renger, 'Serpents and Doves in International Theory', *Millennium: Journal of International Studies* (Vol. 17, No. 2, Summer 1988) and James Der Derian's introduction to that Special Issue on philosophical foundations of International Relations.

64. Michael Donelan, *Elements of International Political Theory* (Oxford: Clarendon Press, 1990).
65. See David A. Baldwin (ed.), *Neorealism and Neoliberalism: The Contemporary Debate* (New York: Columbia University Press, 1993), and Charles W. Kegley, Jr., *Controversies in International Relations Theory: Realism and the Neoliberal Challenge* (New York: St. Martin's Press, 1995).
66. R. B. J. Walker, 'History and Structure in the Theory of International Relations', *Millennium: Journal of International Studies* (Vol. 18, No. 2, Summer 1989), p. 167.
67. Stanley Hoffmann 'International Society', *op. cit.*, p. 19.
68. *Ibid.*, p. 21.
69. *The Anarchical Society*, *op cit.*, p. 4.
70. A term used by Oakeshott, and Nardin. See Michael Oakeshott, *On Human Conduct* (Oxford: Clarendon Press, 1975) and Terry Nardin, *Law, Morality and the Relations of States* (Princeton, NJ: Princeton University Press, 1983).
71. See Friedrich V. Kratochwil, *Rules, Norms, and Decisions: On the conditions of practical and legal reasoning in international relations and domestic affairs* (Cambridge: Cambridge University Press), p. 256.
72. Martin Wight, 'Why Is There No International Theory?' in Butterfield and Wight (eds), *Diplomatic Investigations: Essays in the Theory of International Politics* (London: George Allen and Unwin Ltd., 1966), p. 33. This essay was first published in *International Relations* (Vol. 2, No. 1, April 1960). It is worth noting that both Wight and Butterfield, along with Niebuhr, are characterised as being engaged in the 'search for a normative foundation for politics' while Carr, Morgenthau and others are seen as primarily interested in 'power and politics' in Kenneth W. Thompson, *Masters of International Thought: Major Twentieth-Century Theorists and the World Crisis* (Baton Rouge, LA: Louisiana State University Press, 1980). It is a reflection of Thompson's own views that those he discusses are (with few exceptions) realists.
73. Robert Jackson, 'Martin Wight, International Theory and the Good Life', *Millennium: Journal of International Studies* (Vol. 19, No. 2, Summer 1990).
74. Wight, *op. cit.*, p. 33.
75. Fred Halliday, 'State and Society in International Relations: A Second Agenda', *Millennium: Journal of International Studies* (Vol. 16, No. 2, Summer 1987), reprinted in Dyer and Mangasarian (eds), *op. cit.*, p. 43. See also responses to this article, and Halliday's rejoinder, in *Millennium* (Vol. 17, No. 1, Spring 1988).
76. Yale H. Ferguson and Richard W. Mansbach, 'Beyond the Elusive Quest: A Search for Authority Patterns in History' (a paper given at the joint BISA/ISA convention, London, 31 March 1989, p. 3. See their *The Elusive Quest: Theory and International Politics* (Columbia, SC: University of South Carolina Press, 1988) and *The State, Conceptual Chaos, and the Future of International Relations Theory* (Boulder, CO: Lynne Rienner, 1989).
77. R. J. Vincent, 'Order in International Politics', *op. cit.*, p. 48.
78. From the editors' Introduction to Martin Wight, *Power Politics*, 2nd ed., edited by Hedley Bull and Carsten Holbraad (Leicester: Leicester University Press for the Royal Institute of International Affairs, 1978),

68	*Moral Order/World Order*

p. 19. The editors distinguish Wight's approach from those of Carr, Morgenthau, and Kennan.

79. See the conclusion of Bull's *The Anarchical Society, op. cit.*, pp. 318–20.
80. *Ibid.*, p. 319.
81. Hans J. Morgenthau, 'The Intellectual and Political Functions of Theory' in his *Truth and Power: Essays of a Decade, 1960–70, op. cit.*, p. 261. This essay was first published in Horace V. Harrison (ed), *The Role of Theory in International Relations* (Litton Educational Publishing, 1964), and in it Morgenthau aligns himself with the historical perspective of Martin Wight's 'Why is there no International Theory?' (*op. cit.*), as against abstract rational-scientific theorists.
82. Mark Hoffman, 'Critical Theory and the Inter-paradigm Debate', *op. cit.*, p. 71.
83. Bull, 'International Relations as an Academic Pursuit', *Australian Outlook* (Vol. 26, No. 3, December 1972), p. 255, and *The Anarchical Society, op. cit.*, pp. 319.
84. R. J. Vincent, 'Order in International Politics', *op. cit.*, p. 43.
85. See Hugh C. Dyer, *Justice in World Order: A Conceptual Analysis* (unpublished M.A. thesis, Dalhousie University, 1984).
86. *International Studies* (Vol. 14, No. 2, April–June 1975), pp. 283ff.
87. Hans J. Morgenthau, 'Common Sense and Theories' in *Truth and Power, op. cit.*, p. 245. This essay was first published as 'International Relations: Common Sense and Theories', *Journal of International Affairs* (Vol. 21, No. 2, 1967).
88. *Ibid.*, p. 242.
89. Morgenthau, 'The Intellectual and Political Functions of Theory', *op. cit.*, p. 251.
90. *Ibid.*, pp. 259–60.
91. Morgenthau's critique of behaviouralist scientism is found in *Scientific Man vs. Power Politics* (Chicago: University of Chicago Press, 1946).
92. Howard Williams notes the modern equivalent of Machiavelli's practical experience of government (1498–1512) and his advice to princes (his views later presented in *The Prince*, 1514, as a bid to regain favour) in the advice to U.S. governments of Morgenthau and Kissinger (the latter as an agent of the state). See Howard Williams, 'Machiavelli: *Realpolitik*' in his introductory text, *International Relations in Political Theory* (Milton Keynes: Open University Press, 1992).
93. The idea of 'Machstaat' (roughly, 'power-state') is not directly addressed here, but the Weberian influence and realist concern with power is. For a discussion of 'Machstaat' in the context of international relations theory see Cornelia Navari, 'Introduction: The State as a Contested Concept in International Relations' in Cornelia Navari (ed), *The Condition of States* (Milton Keynes: Open University Press, 1992).
94. *Discourses*, I, 1.
95. *History of the Peloponnesian War*, v. 105.
96. Meinecke, *Machiavellism: The Doctrine of Raison D'état and its Place in Modern History* trans. D. Scott (London: Routledge and Kegan Paul, 1957, 1962), p. 28. First published as *Die Idee der Staatsräson in der Neueren Geschichte* (Munich: R. Ouldenbourg Verlag, 1924).

97. E. H. Carr, having criticised the view 'that a natural harmony of interests exists' as being a cause of confused thinking (*The Twenty Years' Crisis*; London: Macmillan, 1939, pp. 66–7), quotes Treitschke (on pp. 113–4) as saying that the terrible thing about Machiavelli's teaching was 'not the immorality of the methods he recommends, but the lack of content of the state, which exists only in order to exist', (*Aufsätze*, iv., p. 428).
98. Meinecke, *Machiavellism, op. cit.*, p. 5.
99. Michael J. Smith, *Realist Thought...*, *op. cit.*, p. 235.
100. See Chris Brown, 'Sorry Comfort? The Case Against "International Theory"', *op. cit.* In footnote 1 he argues: 'Some modern variants of realism are more hostile to normative theory than others: structural realism, for example, denies the possibility of real choice in international relations, and thus effectively eliminates normative analysis – see, e.g. K. Waltz, *Theory of International Politics* (Addison-Wesley, Reading MA, 1979). However, "process" realists are in closer touch with normative theory...'
101. R. B. J. Walker, 'History and Structure in the Theory of International Relations', *Millennium: Journal of International Studies* (Vol. 18, No. 2, Summer 1989), p. 172.
102. Martin Griffiths, *Realism, Idealism and International Politics, op. cit.*, p. 25. The three 'referents' are discussed on pp. 18, 20, 22, respectively.
103. R. N. Berki, *On Political Realism* (London: J. M. Dent, 1981).
104. Martin Griffiths, *Realism, Idealism and International Politics, op. cit.*, p. 172, note 8. Griffiths refers to Richard Rorty, *Philosophy and The Mirror of Nature* (Princeton, NJ: Princeton University Press, 1979), *op. cit.* in this work.
105. R. N. Berki, *On Political Realism* (London: J. M. Dent, 1981), p. 71.
106. Agnes Heller and Ferenc Fehér, *The Postmodern Political Condition* (Cambridge: Polity Press, 1988), p. 66. See also Daniel Warner, *An Ethic of Responsibility in International Relations* (London: Lynne Reiner, 1992).
107. *Politics Among Nations, op. cit.*, p. 9; quoted from Marianne Weber, *Max Weber* (Tuebingen: J. C. B. Mohr, 1926), pp. 347–8.
108. Stephen P. Turner and Regis A. Factor, *Max Weber and the Dispute over Reason and Value: A Study in Philosophy, Ethics, and Politics*, International Library of Sociology (London: Routledge and Kegan Paul, 1984), p. 173.
109. Turner and Factor refer here to Weber's *The Protestant Ethic and the Spirit of Capitalism* (New York: Scribner's, 1958), pp. 35–7.
110. *Op. cit.*, p. 113.
111. Patrick Morgan, *Theories and Approaches to International Politics: What Are We to Think?* (New Brunswick, NJ: Transaction Books, 1987), p. 251.
112. Kenneth Waltz, *Theory of International Politics* (Reading, MA: Addison-Wesley, 1979), p. 78.
113. Georg Schwarzenberger, *Power Politics: A Study of World Society*, 3rd. Ed. (London: Stevens & Sons, 1964), p. 6.
114. Mervyn Frost, 'Normative Theory and International Relations: Overcoming the Positivist Bias', *Politikon: South African Journal of Political Science*, (Vol. 12, No. 1, June 1985), pp. 3–15.
115. Richard Rorty, *Philosophy and the Mirror of Nature* (Oxford: Basil Blackwell, 1980).
116. These points are elaborated in the following chapter.

117. Walker, 'History and Structure in the Theory of International Relations', *op. cit.*, p. 167.
118. Turner and Factor, *op. cit.*, p. 166. As an indication of connections in the literature, note that Turner and Factor's work is cited in Walker, 'History and Structure...', *op. cit.* See also John Dewey, 'Theory of Valuation', *International Encyclopedia of Unified Science*, Volume II, Number 4 (Chicago: University of Chicago Press, 1939) and the discussion of his views in the next chapter.
119. Morgenthau's quite reasonable sensitivity in this respect is in evidence later, in a response to a critic: '...an attempt is being made to exploit a residual American xenophobia in order to question my credentials'. See Morgenthau, 'Truth and Power' in *Truth and Power*, *op. cit.*, p. 23. This essay first appeared in *The New Republic* (November 26, 1966).
120. Turner and Factor, p. 169. The reference is to Morgenthau, *Scientific Man vs. Power Politics* (Chicago: University of Chicago Press, 1946).
121. Morgenthau, *Scientific Man vs Power Politics* (Chicago: University of Chicago Press, 1946), p. 204.
122. Turner and Factor, *op. cit.*, p. 170.
123. Morgenthau, *Scientific Man vs Power Politics*, *op. cit.*, p. 42.
124. Turner and Factor, *op. cit.*, p. 171.
125. Morgenthau, 'Common Sense and Theories' in *Truth and Power*, *op. cit.*, p. 244.
126. *Ibid.*, p. 172.
127. Morgenthau, *Scientific Man...*, *op. cit.*, pp. 168ff.
128. Morgenthau, 'Truth and Power' in *Truth and Power*, *op. cit.*, p. 14.
129. Morgenthau, 'Common Sense and Theories' in *Truth and Power*, *op. cit.*, pp. 247–8.
130. Turner and Factor, *op. cit.*, p. 173.
131. *Ibid.*
132. *Ibid.*, p. 183.
133. See John A. Vasquez, *The Power of Power Politics* (London: Pinter, 1983).

3 Normative Innovations

NORMATIVE THEORY

Theories or statements which are called 'normative' are, in a traditional nutshell, concerned with what ought to be as distinct from what is. The present argument attempts to avoid any simplistic distinction of this sort, arguing that apprehensions of 'what is' are intimately related to understandings about 'what ought to be', whether these are understandings of norms and values in the political realm or norms in the epistemologies of systematic knowledge. Normative theory, as defined here, is based on the primacy of norms and normative systems and structures, and thus subverts the traditional distinctions of is/ought and fact/value by locating all foundations in value choice. Normative theory concerns both the structure of knowledge and the framework of political reference.[1]

In an overview of international political theory, Patrick Morgan provides a wide-ranging discussion, which includes a chapter entitled 'Do We Study Art Scientifically?'.[2] In this chapter is a very brief commentary on 'The Matter of Values', which states that there is 'a generally accepted distinction between questions of fact and value, under which science can resolve the former but not the latter', and goes on to note the traditionalist argument that 'value problems are the key problems in international politics and in all politics'. Morgan cuts short his discussion on this matter (at about a page in all), because he feels

> there is less interest in it now. This is because values refer to the *uses* to which knowledge is to be put, whereas scientists and traditionalists quarrel more over the *methods* by which to obtain it.[3]

He concludes this section by noting the danger of purposes contaminating methods, but feels that conscientiousness in scholarship is a sufficient guard. Just how methods are to be determined, or what values they might reflect, he does not say. This is an aspect of what Walker identifies as a 'quite misleading exchange in the 1960s between "scientific" and "traditionalist" approaches to international relations' (reflected in Keohane's concern with epistemology in a more recent discussion of 'two approaches'[4]) which does not recognise that 'crucial differences between the utilitarian rationalists and the historically inclined reflective school extend to prior and even more contentious problems, many of which have long been assumed to challenge the claims of modern social science'.[5]

The position outlined above (Morgan's) is indicative of a deep malaise in theoretical endeavours. Although the author is sensitive to the range of debate in the international theory literature, and to the problems of theory generally, the 'matter of values' is relegated to a brief and somewhat dismissive treatment. In particular the quoted passages reflect two unquestioned assumptions: the first is that questions of fact and value are distinct, although the same author elsewhere acknowledges the role of theory in determining the significance of facts (what determines meaning?); the second is that values are located in the choice of *uses* to which knowledge is put rather than the *method* of obtaining it, although the same author elsewhere acknowledges the role of theory in determining the acquisition of knowledge (what is to be studied?).

A further example may be taken from a work on the analysis of international relations by Karl Deutsch:

> Knowledge is different from values. Values motivate the search for knowledge and make some of its results more salient to us than others... I have tried to support all judgements and not to let my preferences deceive me. You may decide for yourself to what extent I have failed or succeeded in this search for realism and reality.[6]

This passage reiterates the fact–value distinction, and the separation of knowledge from what is taken to be the corrupting influence of value considerations: precisely the problematic assumptions of the previous position, indicating that this view is not an isolated or eccentric one but rather is widely shared in the field of international relations.

Values are not simply a means of determining what would be good to do, if only reality would permit it. Values at the same time determine what is important enough to be recognised as 'fact', and how such facts are to be gathered and organised. Science is not immune to value influence, but is rather the product of the value attached to systematic knowledge. John Dewey suggests that there is no radical methodological distinction between science and morals (in contrast to Weber's view), and that principles and general truth are of the same kind in both morals and science.[7]

Dougherty and Pfaltzgraff discuss normative theory briefly at the end of their survey of international relations theory:

> Although normative assumptions may underlie empirical research, the quest for a value-free science of politics has diminished interest over the past generation in normative theory. If political scientists choose to

emphasize empirical-analytical theory, to the relative neglect of normative theory, they will have removed themselves from a problem area which historically has been of great interest to them. They will have chosen to ignore the task of defining the meaning of 'the good life', the designing of political structures and the establishment of normative standards....[8]

Thus, while there may be some kind of distinction to be made between facts and values, it is not in any sense an absolute distinction, and least of all grounds for setting values aside in the pursuit of factual knowledge. Equally, our methods of acquiring knowledge are inevitably tied up with values which bear on its application: in adopting a particular theory, we right away know what we *want* to know, or what would be *good* to know about. Dougherty and Pfaltzgraff continue:

Indeed, despite the tendency over the past generation to deemphasize normative theory, it has been a major thesis of this chapter that normative and empirical theory and basic and applied research are by no means incompatible. Normative theory can suggest alternative goals and preferences for political institutions and can also provide propositions for testing, and empirical-theory can furnish guidance as to the kinds of political behavior which are essential for the attainment of desired goals.[9]

The euphemism 'deemphasize', in reference to the plight of normative theory, is overshadowed by stronger terms in Mervyn Frost's account of the 'postivist bias' in the study of international relations.[10] Making use of Richard Rorty's arguments concerning philosophical assumptions about the mind as a 'mirror of nature',[11] Frost argues that normative approaches and positivist theories are epistemological equals – though normative theory has some residual advantages over positivism. The 'bias', in brief, is that to have knowledge the mind must reflect (mirror) what is outside it (nature), and the task of philosophy is to determine the way in which this occurs. This view 'underpins the thinking of most theorists in international relations', says Frost. Chris Brown, also referring to Rorty in his discussion of critical and postmodern theory, points out the implication of taking anti-foundationalism seriously:

something profound has happened to Western thought once it becomes clear that the foundations upon which it rests are, ultimately, radically, insecure.[12]

Rorty's critique is, essentially, that determining the mechanism of 'reflection' – how knowledge is obtained – does not provide independent criteria for judging the truth of knowledge so obtained: we don't know a good mirror when we see one. Frost notes that this critique is echoed in the work of such modern philosophers as the later Wittgenstein, Quine, Sellars, Davidson, Kuhn, Feyerabend, Heidegger, Gadamer, and Habermas. Brown adds to the list of 'pale anti-foundationalists' like Rorty, the more radical figures of Nietzche, Heidegger and latterly Derrida and Foucault.[13] Collectively they eschew the notion of a correspondence theory of truth (such as a 'mirror of nature') and substitute the notion of a social discourse which 'allows' certain knowledge claims – but without any privileged access to epistemological validity. As Frost points out, this makes it

> 'possible to conceive of there being *knowledge* about normative issues'.[14]

Nevertheless, the nature of such knowledge may remain ambiguous: it may be either theoretical knowledge of 'allowed' value commitments (that is, knowledge of intangible thoughts or ideas), or empirical knowledge of 'acceptable' value-realising behaviour (that is, knowledge of acts or tangible artifacts defined in reference to certain values). By limiting discussion to the latter – the conditions and consequences of realising values – an orthodox empiricist position may restrict normative theory to its descriptive, as opposed to prescriptive role:

> Valuations, Dewey argued, are capable of being empirically observed, in the historical and cultural-anthropological sense. This sort of knowledge does not warrant 'value-propositions', i.e., purely normative statements.[15]

However, the introduction of a validating 'realm of discourse' opens up the possibility of assigning a similar cognitive status to both descriptive and prescriptive normative statements (value propositions) such that it is as acceptable to make truth claims about values themselves as about value-directed facts, though neither enjoys epistemological privelege. Furthermore, the discourse itself is both a social fact and an abstract conversation among those sharing a socio-political space. Of course, the problem of relativism arises as soon as universal *a priori* criteria are abandoned, but this problem always exists potentially, and is mitigated by the constraints of a discourse. The discourse provides a security of meaning without the liabilities of absolutism.[16]

In a sense we create our own reality, even if not – as Marx said of creating history – just as we please. This is an aspect of what Heidegger refers to as 'facticity': we live in a world of facts of our own making either through theory or social practice, but we can't undo our creations just as we please either, nor deny what we have already made of ourselves (facticity is finding oneself already in a given world, and being attuned to it). One is reminded of Bull's story of a person who, when asked for directions, replied 'If I were you, I shouldn't start from here'.[17] Of course we must always 'start from here', but should also be aware of the extent to which we define our location. This is why political decision-makers often find themselves having to choose between what would be the 'right thing', and what is dictated by prudence in the face of 'the facts': the solution would be to alter the facts to fit the value, but of course the facts have already been determined by previous choices made on the grounds of prudence, and the alteration of these facts by value considerations will only occur over time. Nevertheless – and this is central to the present argument – the first step in this process must be the recognition of epistemological conditions determining the initial 'location' from which a journey begins; what exactly will be changed by enacting policy depends on the definition of the status quo, and such definitions may be founded on unchallenged assumptions about political representation, economic growth or legal status, arising out of nationalism, racism or sexism. According to the view which denies any priveleged access to *a priori* criteria of knowledge, the epistemological condition is established by the relevant domain of discourse which credits or discredits particular knowledge claims: this is an essentially normative condition, common to the political realm.

As suggested in the previous chapter, the monopoly on 'reality' implied by the term 'realism' raises just such philosophically troubling issues about assumed reality: that is, the assumption that there *is* a single objective reality 'out there' waiting to be apprehended, even if the debate about which theory correctly apprehends it can not be settled. A critique of the assumption of an uninterpreted reality is provided by the 'linguistic turn' in philosophy, reflected in such varied authors as Manning, Oakeshott, Winch and Wittgenstein, and also by Richard Rorty's argument discussed above. This problem has also been addressed by deconstructionist thinkers (such as Derrida) who see all aspects of reality lying in context, such that a fuller understanding of reality can only be achieved through an unravelling of settled truths, or a peeling-back of the layers of previous 'text' which have successively sustained apprehensions of reality. Of course, this does bring with it (as Gayatri Spivak has put it) a melancholy feeling, since textuality is limitless and ultimately suggests a kind of nihilism.[18] Following such a scheme, any given theory of international relations would amount to a layer of text, somehow dependent on previous thought or theory, and itself similarly conditioning future thought.

Thus we are unable to transcend ourselves, having to start from where we are, but we may nevertheless escape the parameters of traditional theories about our world once we recognise their uncertain origins in our own thinking, or the thinking of previous generations. Hence a theory of value structures (including those of theory itself), indicating the foundations of both theory and practice in international relations, will take us as far as any other rational system of knowledge; that is, to the point at which only some form of faith could provide a greater degree of 'certainty' about the Truth. Viewing theory in this way, it may be possible to avoid or alter or 'reimagine'[19] an unwanted reality, which exists simply because of difficulty in seeing how it is (to a degree) self-generated, and how it is perpetuated by allowing 'the facts' to constrain alternative understandings through a prudential (utilitarian) rationality which is itself bounded by this same self-generated reality. This neither diminishes the importance of such a reality (contingently, it must be coped with) nor provides a ready formula for change, but simply restricts claims about reality to a domain of discourse – a normative structure – since there is no access to an uninterpreted reality. As Frost points out, there is no sense in the notion of a reality 'out there' (Sellars' 'myth of the given') for which one interpretation or another provides the most accurate description.[20]

For the study of international relations a particularly significant dimension of such self-sustaining indigenous 'realities' is their claim to universality. The demand for universals may be understood as a central problematic of world politics, and it is useful to note that universals are a feature of both scientific claims to true knowledge (where truth is indivisible) and of social claims about fundamental values (where morality is absolute). As strict rationality allows of no relativism, what is real must be real everywhere; one notable consequence of this view being that much international conflict arises from efforts to impose particular national truths and values, and discourses.

From the championship of religious creeds, to the institution of the modern nation-state, to the development of the global economy, to the proliferation of various technologies, the history of international relations has been characterised by universalising forces. In many respects these have brought a degree of uniformity to international political life through shared institutions and practices. At the same time, the division of political authority, and the division of labour (and wealth) in the international political economy, means that there will always be underlying value differences arising from different national experiences. Furthermore, international collective choices will inevitably fall short of garnering universal participation in their formation under a system of different and independent sovereign authorities, overlaid by a variety of cross-cutting allegiances and divisions.

Nevertheless, the consequences of contextual epistemologies are not necessarily relativistic; not least because there is no sense in positing a reality 'out there' in relation to which views are relative. Still, there is a degree of objectivity to be found in the need for coherence with ordinary experience – not in the positivist or empiricist mold, but in the sense that any explanatory scheme must give a plausible account of 'reality' – and this aspect of 'facticity' provides grounds for judging the merits of a particular interpretation, necessarily through the medium of a pertinent 'language' or discourse since these are the only available means of discussion.

A potent critique of interpretations of 'reality' and of dominant discourses is provided by gender theory, with its growing literature in the field of international relations.[21] The impact of reinterpretation from a feminist perspective reveals the depth of certain assumptions concerning the human condition, and this revelation is in itself an indication of the potential of normative theory in locating and criticising underlying values. By bringing about a shift in focus from the presumed value neutrality of sexual difference (sex being a biological category) to the value-laden category of gender (a socio-political construct), gender theory has been able to uncover a long-standing bias in the study of international relations. This gender bias has not only been responsible for excluding the perspectives of those called 'women' (people limited to socially constructed roles, and generally disenfranchised), but also for perpetuating political practices of a patriarchal nature which by definition do not reflect the full range of human experiences and values. Gender theory thus provides a compelling example of normative theorising which effectively challenges institutionalised assumptions and practices, provides reinterpretations, and suggests alternative and previously unconsidered political possibilities.

In some respects the anarchic conditions of world politics may be said to present difficulties for a normative approach, with its emphasis on values in political understanding. From a scientific perspective, the relative indeterminacy of values compares poorly with the universal validity of empirical observation. From a moral perspective, any degree of relativism must encourage scepticism about moral judgements and the role of values in international political analysis. Indeed variations in collective experience may be understood, from a Marxist or structuralist perspective, as the product of varying material circumstances and hence material interests. Yet these apparent dilemmas for normative theory are simply the product of dominant theoretical assumptions which have contributed to the marginalisation of normative thought – assumptions which are now being called into question.

LIBERALISM, SUBJECTIVISM, RELATIVISM, AND MORAL SCEPTICISM

The unfavourable comparison with scientific methods is less troubling for normative theory when scientific theory is revealed to have a value content, and where the reliability of empirical observation is shown to be questionable (Heisenberg's uncertainty principle) or unimportant (Lévi-Strauss's inductivist illusion).[22] Furthermore, when the possibility of reference to an uninterpreted reality is denied, the value of empirical observations can claim no special merit. The objection that interests are prior to values evades the problem of identifying or ascribing interests in the absence of any framework that gives them substance – a framework necessarily pervaded by values. Perhaps most telling is the dilemma of moral scepticism in the face of subjectivism and relativism, but this too is an aspect of critiques – commonly made of liberal political theory – which have their roots in absolutist expectations.

James Fishkin argues that subjectivism *may* be avoided 'if only we choose to think and live in the manner required', which in turn requires 'a change in moral culture'.[23] The insistence on a categorical imperative in ethics is paralleled by an insistence on an absolute objectivism in epistemology, the combination of which, through traditional ethics and traditional international relations theory (read realism), imposes such restrictions on value considerations as to rule out any significant theoretical role for them. That values exist anyway, and are acknowledged by traditional theory to have some undefined importance, is a problem which is effectively ignored in the quest for rigour.

Such rigorous expectations are not only troublesome for undermining the basis of moral positions which cannot live up to them (e.g., the inherent contradiction in liberal theory – to be liberal and yet *insist* on liberalism), but also because they call for a kind of efficiency in theoretical premises which leads to intellectual and political tyranny. These circumstances also perpetuate a culture of absolutist expectations in which there is always a demand for certainty, and no encouragement of the genuinely political activities and skills which provide the means of coping with a degree of uncertainty, and with inevitable change. As Henry Kariel observes,

Nietzsche would seem to have been alone in noting the futility of hectoring those who craved foundations and flocked to a saviour. Unable to maintain their balance under pressure, the masses would but resent the kind of political process in which they themselves might become actors.[24]

There is no doubt that some foundations are required, but they are themselves constructed by a political process, and therefore remain always political issues. The dilemma is characterised in another way by Heller and Fehér:

> Theoretical reason does not provide certainty, and yet it is certainty which morals must be based on. But certainty eliminates choice. And how can one eliminate choice without backing away from modernity to traditional norms guaranteed by divine revelation?[25]

If it is accepted that values exist, and are important in some way, the significance of normative theory in the study of international relations may then be said to rest on the perceived number and importance of shared values and assumptions – as opposed to 'objective interests' or the product of empirical science. Taking the discussion only this far, however, may still leave normative theory with the burdens of indeterminacy and relativism. When the significance of normative theory is seen to rest also on the volume and character of the intercourse which establishes values and assumptions, and normative *processes* are the object of attention, the problems of indeterminacy and relativism of values seems less burdensome, since these values are somewhat transient in their particulars even if the presence of values is a persistent aspect of the international socio-political processes in question.

Dewey's discussion of 'Valuation and the Conditions of Social Theory' suggests that the fact/value distinction is perpetuated, and the existence of values denied, when theory ignores the cultural and institutional contexts in which interests arise:

> When current theories are examined which, quite properly, relate valuation with desires and interests, nothing is more striking than their neglect – so extensive as to be systematic – of the role of cultural conditions and institutions in the shaping of desires and ends and thereby valuations.[26]

It is this failure to observe the social conditions under which interests arise and function – conditions that constitute lack or need – that permits the distinction between ends and means, between valuation and evaluation, says Dewey.[27] Theoretically, this gives rise to two extremes: one taking desires as 'original' and isolating them from any existential context, thereby making values arbitrary (relativism); the other viewing values as 'ends-in-themselves', as ultimate standards of valuation (a priori absolutism). This last,

> in its endeavor to escape from the frying pan of disordered valuations, jumps into the fire of absolutism.[28]

Dewey argues that desires give content to 'ends-in-view', which are valued as potential solutions of some conflict or need, and evaluated in terms of the means of solution (i.e., whether they will succeed). Being also causal conditions of results, desires must be appraised as potential means. The 'should be' of desires which are critically judged in relation to the actual social conditions of their attainment stands apart from the 'is' of impulsive desire; it is the former which give content to ends-in-view, thus informing value choices.[29]

A relevant example may help to clarify this view: The desire for security gives content to the end of peace; peace is valued as a potential solution of insecurity, and is evaluated as such in terms of the potential success of the means of achieving peace. As the desire for security is also a causal condition of successful peace, it must be appraised as a means of achieving peace. The desire for security may manifest itself, for example, in a violent reaction to threatened insecurity (the 'is' of impulsive desire), but it may manifest itself differently when critically judged in relation to social conditions. Where an initial violent reaction breeds further violence and compounds insecurity, the desire for security may manifest itself – if social conditions permit – in mutual restraint or some other cooperative solution (the 'should be'). It is this latter manifestation which gives content to the end-in-view of peace, and informs the choice of peace over some other end in terms of a critical appraisal of the desire for security itself as a potential means of achieving peace.

Thus 'evaluating values' is a process which depends on an assessment of the prospects for successful realisation of a given value, in view of the means of its realisation (including desires and interests) as judged in the context of existing social conditions (whether of a particular national society or of world society, or perhaps both). Because the conditions and consequences of this process of valuation change, so must values themselves: empirical knowledge of this change means that what were assumed to be authoritative values and interests are subject to revaluation, and conversely their authority will be sustained by an absence of change.

> The notion that valuations do not exist in empirical fact and that therefore value-conceptions have to be imported from a source outside experience is one of the most curious beliefs the mind of man has ever entertained. Human beings are continuously engaged in valuations. The latter supply the primary material for operations of further valuations and for the general theory of valuation.[30]

Dewey's theory of valuation grounds values in human experience, and admits that no abstract theory can stand in judgement of existing valuations. Therefore any new values cannot be dictated by such a theory, but must 'grow out of existing valuations, subjected to critical methods of investigation that bring them into systematic relations with one another'.[31] That there is no ready means of relating diverse and mutually ignorant values is both cause and effect of *a priori* theories which locate values 'outside' or 'above' actual valuations: a cause in that the need for systematic understanding is so great as to encourage grasping at such theories; an effect in that once such theories gain prestige, they 'conceal the necessity for concrete methods of relating valuations'.[32] This relates to discussions (elsewhere in the present work) concerning the inadequacy of correspondence theories of truth, requiring some external referent, and coherence theories which support various truth claims by placing them in relation to one another. Thus the impediments to establishing relational/coherence theories are largely of the practical variety, originating in persistent institutionalised practices which are uncritically accepted. Institutionalised traditions are also the source of an apparent relativism, a problem which plagues normative inquiry. Such relativism could be challenged from the perspective of a broader value context, but the institutions would have to be challenged as well. However, that the practical difficulties are great does not warrant mistaking them for theoretical obstacles.

Acknowledging the problem of relativism does not necessarily leave normative theory in a dilemma. Terry Nardin, for example, suggests that relativism may be a reasonable middle ground between 'the poles of dogmatic certainty and radical doubt'.[33] What is more, the nature of relativism is not necessarily that which is so readily assumed in international relations, as a consequence of anarchy – that is, values being relative to particular national societies or nation-states. Relativism may well refer simply to the international social context, values being conceived therefore as either historically relative or relative to interpretations of the international condition.

These circumstances are redolent of the conditions of particular cases of national life, which simply exhibit more limited forms of relativism, and do not suggest that any particular theoretical difficulties are novel or unique to the international system. The only qualification required is that the instruments of authority differ between domestic and international societies (hence the problems of applying the domestic analogy), but this does not suggest that relativism is any less problematic for national societies simply because authority has closed the debate. Writing on the domestic analogy, Hidemi Suganami describes a relevant debate in the literature of international relations theory:

from the late 1970s to the present, which, on the one hand, saw a well-articulated attack by Bull and others on contemporary institutions and proposals embodying various forms of domestic analogy, and which, on the other hand, witnessed a serious defence of cosmopolitanism by Beitz and Linklater neither of whose argument, as we noted, involves the domestic analogy as an essential feature. This, however, does not mean that Beitz or Linklater would necessarily be opposed to institutional proposals which make a selective use of domestic analogues...[34]

Heller and Fehér suggest that '... it is ill conceived to establish a direct relation between the increasing relativism of world-views (philosophies) and the relativism of morals'. The relation may be inverse: moral relativism is exacerbated by making absolutist claims for any one world-view, and the more constructive solution is an acceptance of mutual relativisation and seeking only

> a single and restricted common ground: a few moral norms and values which might be regarded as valid and binding for all of us.
> The diversity of world-views, philosophies, metaphysics and religious faiths does not bar the emergence of a common ethos, unless one of the competing world views completely determines the commandments and interdictions, and does so not only for its own adherents but also with a universalizing aspiration.[35]

THE NORMATIVE LITERATURE

The definition of normative theory employed here is, quite simply, theory which addresses norms. There is nevertheless a distinction to be made between essentially traditional theories which happen to be applied to problems connected with certain norms, and theories which take a normative perspective as their starting point. This latter type of theory represents the subject of this book: theory concerned with the origin, evolution, and dissolution of norms and normative structures, which are held to be the substance of socio-political experience rather than a product of some external determinants.[36] In some respects, those theoretical undertakings (very often hypothesis-testing, or commentary, as opposed to theory proper) which deal with normative problems from more traditional perspectives are responsible for constraining the development of normative theory proper. The literature in the field of international relations which is explicitly concerned with normative theory proper is rather limited. However – and because the term 'normative' is generally interpreted to mean moral or ethical, or even idealistic – there is a large body of theory concerned with particular normative issues (justice, human rights, arms control, peace, etc.), if not with normative theory *per se*. If normative theory is understood to address the perennial questions of politics (justice and order, authority and legitimacy, law and morality, war and peace), then we must also include in this literature the classical writings of political philosophy and early works in international relations.[37] As we will see in a subsequent chapter, a broad understanding of normative theory involves many of the abiding concerns of philosophy in general, including the foundations and transmission of ideas.

Mark Hoffman states that the 'roots of normative theory can be found in the classics of political philosophy: from Plato and Aristotle to Aquinas and Augustine, and from Grotius, Vattel, Wolff and Pufendorf to Hobbes, Locke, Rousseau, Kant, Hume, Burke and Mill'.[38] Hoffman goes on to set out four normative approaches (legal, realist, classical and cosmopolitan) which roughly coincide with developments in international relations theory: The legal approach ranges from Lauterpacht's legal reductionism (all conflicts are essentially legal rather than political), predominant in the inter-war period, to McDougall's instrumental view of law as a means of achieving shared values (law being co-extensive with politics), this latter view being especially relevant to the more recent interest in human rights; The realist approach is characterised by moral scepticism, relativism, consequentialism and the primacy of national interest (all arising from the conflict betweem morality and *raison d'état*), and various examples can be found in such realists as Niebuhr, Aron, Carr, Morgenthau, Kennan, Hoffmann, Thompson, Kissinger, etc. This continental tradition is distinguished by Hoffman (after Wolfers) from the universalistic Anglo-Saxon tradition (cf. the 'English School') grounded in natural law and the social contract, which emphasises international society (with 'common practices, customs, norms, principles and rules') and is exemplified by Bull, Manning, James, the trilogy on international political theory edited respectively by Donelan, Mayall, and Navari, and just-war theory (e.g., Walzer). Finally, Hoffman sets out the cosmopolitan approach as an attempt to depart from state-centrism and apply notions of distributive justice (e.g., Beitz, after Rawls) and basic rights (e.g., Shue) to a broader world society of individuals, to which the state is merely instrumental, or secondary (e.g., Linklater) – this implying the necessity of structural reform in the international system (note also Galtung, Burton, and authors of the World Order Modelling Project such as Falk and Mendlowitz). Hoffman concludes his survey by suggesting that 'it is impossible to have a comprehensive theory of IR which does not incorporate and account for the normative aspects of world society'.[39] For this reason no doubt, normative issues are addressed (in different ways) in all of the various approaches discussed previously.

However, the conclusion about the need to account for normative aspects would seem to fall short of cosmopolitan aspirations, and of the present argument, by characterising value-phenomena as something to be incorporated into some larger picture of the world. This view is not too far removed in its effect from realist scepticism – which does not (to be fair) ignore normative questions, but doesn't know quite what to do with them. To some degree, therefore, the marginalisation of normative issues may be perpetuated even in their defence. The role of normative theory argued for here – even without going so far as suggesting that it might constitute a general background theory for international relations – places normative concerns at the fore, both as a consequence of their epistemological priority in general and of their centrality in politics in particular. Any other starting place will naturally lead to difficulty in accounting for normative issues, having skipped the vital initial stages in which value questions must be addressed – in the foundations of a philosophy or methodology, and so in the construction of a theory of international relations. That there are always new and contingent value questions should not be surprising in any open and active society, but they may go unrecognised, be misunderstood, or be actively ignored if the prevailing conception of international society denies it a normative character, as well as content.

Of the various approaches outlined by Hoffman, the realist approach is the only one which systematically marginalises normative questions in the international political realm. The legal, classical and cosmopolitan approaches all take normative questions seriously, but the first two are caught up with state-centric structures which limit their ability to take a robust view of normative theory. Thus it is only the cosmopolitan approach which meets the more rigorous requirements demanded here, by placing fundamental values at the beginning rather than the end. The core of cosmopolitan arguments, says Vincent, is the commitment to the value of *human* life, and that

> it is not reasonable to allow this value to be diluted by the mere boundaries which human beings happen to have constructed against each other.[40]

Thus Charles Beitz writes of the tension between 'Cosmopolitan Ideals and National Sentiment'.[41] The conclusions of his earlier influential book, *Political Theory and International Relations*,[42] (which are worth quoting at some length) are that prevailing theoretical conceptions of international relations are inadequate and lead to incorrect normative principles of international practice... The refutation of international skepticism and the critique of the idea of state autonomy clear the way for the formulation of a more satisfactory normative international political theory... Such a theory provides structure and purpose for the empirical study of international relations....[43]

In making the connection between normative theory and empirical study by means of 'structure and purpose', the epistemological significance of normative theory is emphasised without diminishing the role of empirical research in locating substantive content (whether norms or some other aspect of socio-political relations).

Beitz also concludes that

It is important to distinguish moral structures from political ones, and to recognize that global normative principles might be implemented otherwise than by global institutions conceived on the analogy of the state... Thus far, such systematic moral debate about international relations as has taken place has been between adherents of international skepticism and the morality of states. However... the more pressing issues are those that divide the morality of states from a cosmopolitan morality.[44]

As elsewhere, 'normative' is used to mean 'moral' and although Beitz is clear about the epistemological role of a normative approach, when he distinguishes the moral from the political he is not as clear about the relation between normative structures and politics. This implies a distinction between normative theory and political theory which his overall argument does not suggest. Perhaps this puzzle is resolved by Beitz himself (ten years later) when he writes that normative theories are often criticized for indeterminacy, and that the criticism reflects an aspiration for mechanical precision which is to be resisted because 'it reflects a radical misconception of the nature of practical reasoning and of the role that political theories can be expected to play in it'. He suggests that theoretical reflection can clarify convictions about political ethics and 'concentrate the force of our normative commitments on the problems of practical decision', where the goal is to arrive at well-founded choices. 'Yet it is not the theory but the theorist who is responsible for these choices. Political theory should guide practical judgement, not replace it'.[45]

Thus Beitz distinguishes between practical institutional structures in the realm of politics and the moral structures which inform them. This does not do full justice to the moral assumptions underlying practical judgement, in the sense that even what is practically desirable requires some prior assignation of value: practical judgement is made in an existing socio-political context. The ambiguity about whether 'values' are a moral or practical category creates difficulties in applying the term 'normative': values can be understood as having *both* moral and practical significance, and being in both senses normative (having to do with norms) but not *necessarily* only in the sense of normative *ethics* (i.e., morality). The normative character of politics can be acknowledged and the strict delimitation of theory and practice avoided. Indeed, Beitz is quick to point out that

> the institutional problems that a theory must address help shape our conception of its subject matter, and the content of the theory informs our understanding of the issues of principle that the practical problems pose.[46]

Andrew Linklater writes, in *Men and Citizens in the Theory of International Relations*, of the tension between membership of the human race and citizenship of a state – 'between two concepts of obligation, two modes of moral experience'. He claims that Kant was the only rationalist to approach a 'coherent vision of world political organisation', but because of the historicist critique of rationalism, Linklater seeks 'a non-rationalist foundation for the traditional belief in obligations to humanity, and for the recovery of the critique of the international states-system'.[47] He states

> It is within theories which sought to comprehend the nature of man as an historical subject, as a self-developing and self-transforming being realising the conditions of his freedom, that I locate the foundations of a modern theory of international relations.[48]

Thus, Linklater employs what he sees as a uniquely human capacity – self-determination – as the basis of a cosmopolitan argument for 'a moral community more inclusive than the sovereign state'.[49] This in turn allows him to assess evolving forms of international relations in terms of their realisation of this capacity, especially through overcoming inter-societal estrangement in moving (through a history of reason) towards some kind of unity of the species.

One recent exponent of normative theory, Mervyn Frost, argues that

> the main reasons for the dearth of normative theory in international relations are to be found in the underlying philosophical and methodological assumptions implicit in the main approaches used by scholars in the discipline.[50]

He seeks to uncover in particular the positivist bias, and to challenge positivism. Distinguishing between the 'scientific' and the 'classical' approaches,[51] Frost says that these two approaches nevertheless share an empiricist methodology and have in common

> a radical distinction between the status accorded to factual judgements, to which the discipline of international relations should aspire, and that accorded to value judgements. Facts are given epistemological priority.[52]

This line of argument is carried further by pointing to the problems of interpretative social science (which might be thought 'neutral', while being attuned to subjective values), and the necessity of engagement in debate: a critical approach denies the possibility of a neutral stance, and undermines the 'assumption about the incorrigibility of people's self-understandings'.[53] On this account the subject's considered reaction to a theory about themselves or some immanent subject (their life) determines the validity of the theory. Of course, this does not resolve the problem of finding an objective or inter-subjective foundation for shared knowledge or shared values, but clearly there can be no structure without reference to normative ideas – and right away people are bound together in making reference to them, at the least.[54]

Normative issues, says Frost, arise only in the context of shared understandings, or a given practice of normative argument; within a domain of discourse. In a world of state centric practices, normative issues thus make direct or indirect reference to the state. How to act in relations with (or in regard to, or even as) a state is thus a central question.[55] Frost sets out to find a justification for such relations, and critiques various approaches (conflict of ideology, natural law, etc.) before adopting Dworkin's method of starting from settled norms, and locating a background theory (to justify social institutions as a whole) which accords with these norms. Difficult normative problems ('hard cases') can then be resolved by considerations of 'fit' with the settled norms.[56] Frost suggests there is such a body of settled norms for international relations, and provides a list of them.

The real issue in this line of argument is the nature of the justificatory background theory for those norms that are apparently settled, since this provides the basis for more general agreement. Frost examines theories invoking order (he discusses Bull), those invoking utilitarian principles (e.g., Waltz, *Theory of International Politics*), those invoking rights concepts, and those invoking contractarian principles (e.g., Walzer, *Just and Unjust Wars*). Finally, Frost lays out his own Constitutive Theory of Individualism which, by reconciling the tension between *rights* norms and *sovereignty* norms (something contractarianism promises, but can't deliver), provides a background theory justifying settled norms. This theory draws on Hegelian views of the social context of the individual, and in deriving from settled but necessarily contingent norms, is essentially anti-foundationalist.

This theme is picked up by another writer on normative theory, Chris Brown, who characterises anti-foundationalism as tending to

> deny the possibility of grounding those notions that lie at the heart of he enlightenment ideal – notions such as 'truth' and 'reason' – whether applied to scientific or to moral discourse.[57]

Brown points to Nietzsche and Heidegger as precursors of the post-structuralist thought of Foucault and Derrida. He also notes the challenge to scientific rationality of Anglo-American philosophers such as Kuhn and Feyerabend, and the radicalised American pragmatism of Rorty, but suggests that the great variety among these schools of thought should not obscure a common characteristic:

> the impact of all varieties of antifoundationalist thought on the level of confidence with which it is possible to assert the universal relevance of the values of modernity.[58]

Thus the values of the enlightenment and of modernity simply do not provide the stable foundations required by conventional views of morality. Brown suggests that post-modernists like Rorty would argue that

> new moralities can emerge based on the practices human beings create among themselves, and assessed not by reference to grounded values but in terms of the extent to which such practices pragmatically 'cope' with the world and the degree to which they promote pluralism by allowing space for the emergence of alternative practices.[59]

The important idea of 'coping' will called upon in subsequent discussion, being a distinctive feature of normative theory as characterised in the present argument, in contrast to the 'grasping at straws' of absolutist theory.

Friedrich Kratochwil approaches a similar point from a slightly different perspective, emphasising a 'problem-solving' character as a generic feature of all norms. He invokes a theory of 'communicative action' such that 'within a normatively secured framework of communication' grievances can be aired and value-choices debated, even if such debate is not only about instrumental questions.[60] Accordingly, theory which rests on physicalist observational facts, such as Waltz's *Theory of International Politics* (which attempts a systemic theory on the grounds that there is a gap between intentions and the systemic meaning of acts), fails to comprehend that action is only meaningful in terms of the rules (norms) governing interaction – and this is conceded by Waltz's own argument that decision-makers have to become socialised into a system.[61] As Griffiths points out,

> [Morgenthau and Waltz's] shared descriptions of international politics... and the prescriptive and evaluative stances that flow from them, are woefully inadequate to the complexity of the subject-matter.[62]

Kratochwil argues that 'human action is rule-governed' and that this is methodologically important, especially in reference to *action*: norms influence decisions through the medium of deliberation.[63] He suggests that a distinction between norms (as rules) and values can be exemplified by reference to two ideal-typical theories of society, one basing social order on *rights* (norms) and the other on *values* (attitudes). The latter represents an emotional attachment to communal values while the former is a rationalised expression of rules or of law.[64] (Note that the present argument holds that any rights-based theory must acknowledge that rights can only acquire meaning in the context of an existing social order, so values must be given existential and epistemological priority and rights must be seen as *ex post facto* rationalisations.) Kratochwil characterises norms as problem-solving devices, which permits viewing rules or rights as contingent solutions to acknowledged problematic value differences. Thus he attempts to show

> not only that rules emerge even in the absence of explicit communications, but that rules in explicit form are necessary in order to overcome the conflicts that are bound to arise.[65]

This, he says, involves a transition from tacit rules *of* behaviour to intersubjective rules *for* behaviour (his emphasis), which 'either shore up trust or attach penalties'.

Here the argument reflects some of the themes raised in the preceding discussion concerning the problems of anti-foundationalism, and their resolution through institutionalised forms of meaning. Once again, a distinction is drawn between descriptions of the values at play and prescriptions based on the recognition of these values. Since collective recognition is evidenced in discourse, which describes acknowledged value-structures, this becomes the tenatative foundation for prescription (subject to change). Thus Kratochwil is able to derive a characterisation of the prescriptive force of norms: a claim to validity mediated by language such that validation occurs in the context of a discourse.

Hence the possibility of discussing normative issues requires abandoning not just strict fact–value distinctions but also the view that values and norms are 'all of the same cloth'.[66] We may recall here Dewey's distinction between valuing and valuation – valuing may be reflected in the assertions of an intitutionalised society, while valuation is a process sensitive to change in the actual social conditions and therefore implicitly critical. Knowledge of such change (which is descriptive/empirical) 'would surely lead to revaluation of desires and ends that had been assumed to be authoritative sources of valuations'.[67] A similarity with Frost's view is also discernable in Kratochwil when he says

> The question of compliance with norms is part of a wider argument through which individuals act in a social context, enabling society as well as the 'self' of an actor to reproduce themselves.[68]

The next step in this line of argument is to adapt this conception of norms to more familiar theoretical practice. Lakatos is invoked to suggest that the criterion for the success of normative theory is the 'fruitfulness' of the whole research program. Kratochwil is aware of the problem of refutation (failure in a single case would be damning), but suggests that 'rules and norms can then become "causes" in that they determine, but only *probabilistically* so, outcomes (decisions)'. He infers that 'explanation involves the identification of the rules that constitute a "form of life"', though presumably these remain subject to debate.[69]

Dewey makes a related point in discussing the continuum of ends and means: He says that the *form* of an attained end or consequence (outcome) is always adequate co-ordination; both 'a *reinstatement* of a unified ongoing action' and 'an *enactment* of a new state of affairs'. In the continuous process of forming a 'co-ordinated and co-ordinating unity, a constituent activity is both an end and a means'. In this sense norms can be viewed as causal conditions of action, as well as well as the 'consummatory resolution' of previous activity with an end-in-view.[70]

Kratochwil reflects this view in using the term 'co-ordination norms', in reference to Humean rule-utilitarianism as opposed to act-utilitarianism (the latter being dependent on the conventional distinction between means and ends). He continues his argument with an elaboration of the idea of communicative action, holding it to be the source of a framework for ascertaining the conduct-guiding force of norms. Durkheim's distinction between moral authority and material or physical supremacy is introduced, to suggest that moral facts are valid because of their duty-imposing character, arising in the context of an ideally symbolised society which provides coherence and objectivity:

With its duty-imposing claims upon the individual, it is the absolute, and at the same time only a relative order, for all obligation results from the form of life that characterizes a specific society.[71]

In such an environment valuations are conducted, and values determined, in relation to the existing normative structure.

Precisely because the individual experiences a conflict with others concerning the goals, the issue arises of how such conflicts can be mediated by norms and rules.[72]

Kratochwil argues that intersubjective meaning is only attained when a 'moral point of view' emerges. He suggests that natural law provides a way of structuring the discourse on grievances. Of course, if natural law is viewed only instrumentally, the natural law doctrine is defeated (note the critique of natural law in the preceding discussion of realism), however the reference here is to Pufendorf's version of natural law which is not ontological or grounded in religion. The emphasis is on the attribution of moral status, or on attitudes toward an act rather than the act itself. The moral point of view need not be static, and it is the form rather than the specific content that makes normative structures significant.

Nevertheless, all normative structures do have a content, and it is frequently the subject of debate and analysis. This is part of the interactive relation between theory and practice, in which theory informs practical judgement, and the 'facticity' of common practice throws up theoretical problems. It will be fruitful to look at some examples of work which engages more directly with practical, substantive normative issues.

NORMATIVE APPLICATIONS

This section will briefly examine three examples of normative approaches applied to problems and issues of international relations: intervention, values in foreign policy, and human rights. These examples illustrate both the nature of normative inquiry in the study of international relations, and the limitations imposed upon it by traditions of thought which keep it at the margin of study.

Intervention

An example of a debate which addresses both the existing political condition and competing theoretical interpretations of it is that about intervention. A brief examination of this debate will bring this chapter back to the central theme by shedding light on a typical confluence of the traditional concerns of international relations theory and the more extensive demands of normative theory.

The issue of intervention has its roots in 'the old Westphalian system of a world of non-interventionist states' in which

> the absolute sovereignty of a state rested on a dual basis whereby internal authority was matched by freedom from external interference; and in this way the principle of *cuius regio eius religio*, codified in the Religious Peace of Augsburg, laid the foundation of the modern state system.[73]

Thus intervention is defined as coercive interference with the jurisdiction of a sovereign state (or independent political community).[74] Forms of intervention are various, both in character and extent, but for theoretical purposes the significant feature of intervention is that it is a matter of principle. An instance of intervention is both a violation of principles governing and defining the states system, and yet (if justifiable) an enforcement of one or another of these principles, or principles of a putatively higher order. Windsor argues that two principles or 'modes of discussion' dominate the issue of intervention: public order (internationally) and historical legitimacy (in reference to 'natural processes').[75] Naturally, the questions are then 'what order?' and 'whose history?'.

It is commonplace with matters of principle that there are various competing principles to be considered, just as it is commonplace in international relations for intervention to occur even as the context in which it occurs presents an inherent principled opposition to it. Intervention may even be a logically inherent feature of a states system. Consequently, neither the fact of intervention nor the existence of a political system founded on the principle of non-intervention provides a satisfactory basis for a theory of international relations; rather it is the common feature of reference to principles, inconclusive as it may be, that suggests the essentially normative character of these political relations and therefore an appropriate starting point for a theory which accounts for them.

This perspective need not deny an existing political condition, or even require its overthrow (in any direct sense), although it is critical and does imply reform. More specifically, a normative approach to the study of international relations enjoins all practitioners and students to reconceive the project of international relations in normative terms, as a matter of priority – a work on normative theory 'would say that' of course, and other theoretical works make their respective demands of an audience. The demands of normative theory are not, however, of the sort which necessarily undo everything else; on the contrary, the frequently hidden significance of traditional theories of politics and international relations may be revealed in the light of a normative approach which alleviates the self-imposed constraints of 'reality'.

In respect to the system of sovereign states, for example, the definitional role of sovereignty may be brought into question when, as Linklater says, 'the principle of sovereignty becomes a barrier to the realisation of the goals which it was originally summoned to protect'.[76]

Furthermore, this and other principles of international relations that do not serve the needs of particular constituencies of humanity (that is, particular states or societies) may not, by the same token, serve the needs of humanity in general: an international system which does not have universal recognition is by definition ill-founded.[77] This is not merely a question of competing interests, but of the value invested in those principles which guide the pursuit of interests.

Values in Foreign Policy

Robert C. Johansen provides a useful case study of 'policy-relevant' values, which also brings out the theoretical implications. Employing a value-framework of 'global humanism', he analyses US foreign policy to distinguish between professed values and implicit values.[78] The latter are derived from observations of state behaviour and the actual impact of policy. He employs 'a value-centered approach' to foreign policy, 'admittedly a break with the prevailing intellectual tradition' which usually focuses on the use of power without giving very much attention to the value implications of policy:

> Traditional approaches have impoverished reality and discouraged use of the imagination by excessive emphasis on the way things are and by inattention to the way things ought to be.[79]

Johansen implies a general definition of politics, and continuity between domestic and international politics, by stating that 'understanding of political events is enhanced if international politics is viewed as a value-realizing process'. Thus the particular concern of his analysis (the contradictions of U.S. foreign policy) reflects a broader awareness of the importance of normative theory:

> The value impacts of specific foreign policies then provide intellectual handles by which one may grasp the normative direction in which a changing system of world order is moving.[80]

Here, the normative approach is characterised as an investigative tool: an aspect of its descriptive role which emphasises the methodological significance of normative theory. A further example – the traditional normative topic of 'human rights' – will suggest the consequences of applying both descriptive and prescriptive aspects of a normative approach.

Human Rights

R. J. Vincent examines the place of human rights in the study and practice of international relations, pointing to the theoretical problem of particularised citizenship and universalised morality, and the practical problem of identifying or maintaining cultural differences in the face of a expanding global culture. He remarks that 'humankind is itself a project as well as this or that branch of it' and because of this, 'rights have a built-in push towards universal application' and, while human rights doctrine is not perfectly reflected in actual practice, 'there is nevertheless evidence for the existence of global norms'.[81]

In a chapter on human rights and the theory of international relations, Vincent distinguishes between moral questions (what ought to be done) and directly practical concerns (what governments should do), with the former informing the latter. This reflects the distinction he initially makes, in respect to 'the project of humankind', as between the 'normative' aspect of universal applications and the 'positive' aspect of an actual global culture. Such a distinction between morality and political practice is symptomatic of the influence of realist thought in traditional international relations theory, as discussed in the previous chapter (and being also a focal point of the present critique).

However, Vincent is clearly aware of these issues. He argues that a theory of world politics, understood 'as reflection on the public arrangements that ought to be made for the government of humankind',[82] should begin with human rights for both definitional and historical reasons: definitional because political theory is axiomatically concerned with humanity; historical because of the tradition of liberal reason, in which natural rights and natural law provide a starting point. Thus, while there is dispute about the content of human rights, there is a common vocabulary or language of human rights – as Vincent says, 'the dispute is precisely the point'.[83]

Such dispute about content can occur even as the form of political life is implicitly acknowledged, universally. Yet in noting that rights determine the political milieu in which action takes place as well as guiding action itself, Vincent remarks that there is less distance between the prescription of a moral principle and the description of a political milieu than might have been implied just now.[84]

This suggests that talk of rights depends on an existing normative structure for its meaning, a view which undermines the usefulness of rights as a starting place. Of course, from an anti-foundationalist perspective, any starting place is problematic. The point here is that a normative theoretical approach provides the opportunity of incorporating particular normative issues, such as human rights, into a conception of world politics. While disputes about the importance of particular norms (about the content of human rights for example) may continue, they do not by virtue of their intransigence diminish the political realm in which they are carried out: indeed, they are the very substance of politics. The substantive debates of politics may extend even to descriptions of the political milieu itself, and Vincent notes three views of the political world: a morality of states, cosmopolitan morality, and an 'amoral' view of rights as mere interests.

Of these three views, cosmopolitan morality is unique in its commitment to humanity – the core of the cosmopolitan argument (as described by Vincent) is noted in the previous chapter. The traditional theories ascribe to one or the other of the remaining two views: the 'morality of states' is typical of English School classicism which emphasises a 'society of states', while the somewhat different state-centrism of American-style realists ironically share with Marxist structuralism a reductionist view of rights as interests, rather than value-expressions. The similar treatment of values and interests in Weber and Marx, as noted above, is seen here in theories of international politics influenced by their ideas. Vincent cites Adam Watson's suggestion that moral ideas, like any ideas, are 'prone to the following of fashion', but he rightly responds that 'the fact of their topicality does not diminish their importance'.[85] What is suggested here is that such ideas are topical just because of their (implicitly) acknowledged importance.

CONCLUSIONS

In respect to the relation between the topical and the important, theoretical concern should not simply be with specific ideas or particular moralities (established, if relative norms) but rather with the nature and status of ideas, and with ethical and meta-ethical questions addressing the role and development of norms in international political life. Even modified realist positions lean in this direction:

Morality presupposes human choice, but also limits and channels the realm of freedom towards certain ends (the good life) and away from others (the bad life), whatever these ends may be. The realm of freedom is synonymous with the realm of morality, and this realm permeates the realm of necessity. Nothing in politics has to be accepted in a natural sense, only in a practical (or 'realistic') sense. A corollary of this understanding is the necessity of societal moral guide-lines which enable positive freedom.[86]

Broader theoretical concerns of this sort are addressed by Vincent when, for example, he concludes that

Instead of being driven out by the *moi commun*, the *moi humain* is coopted by it.[87]

Of course, the abstract, universal notion of 'humanity' is only a heuristic category if substantial meaning, including the meaning of 'human', can only be found in the context of a normative structure as provided by the collective experience of a society or community. Yet, society can exceed contrived state boundaries in many respects – what Vincent refers to as 'transnational recognition' is an external universalising condition on states and societies. These latter may only comprise layers in a *mille feuille* of norms and a hierarchy of references that give contextual meaning to both domestic and world politics. The relative position of particular cases of humanity within the global (universal) context is itself determined by the norms governing social divisions. Linklater, for example, claims that

a progressive development of international relations necessitates the transference of understandings of social relations from their original domestic setting to the international arena.[88]

In the theory (and practice) of world politics, the dominant norms remain those which describe and prescribe a system of states.[89] A normative theoretical approach reveals that these particular norms, like any others, are subject to political debate. The human purposes underwriting these norms can only be served when the ethical content of politics is acknowledged; when 'ethical life gains a foothold'.[90]

Beginning with values rather than interests also places theoretical undertakings on a sounder footing, from which we may better confront the political character of existing conditions and better cope with the abstract universal context of their existence. Uncertainty about sociopolitical foundations may leave us, as Alasdair MacIntyre states it, with a 'fundamental incoherence which is too disturbing to be admitted to self-conscious awareness except on the rarest of occasions'.[91] Yet, recognising the importance of values admits the prospect of coherence without the necessity of a universalised absolutism, whether in science or politics. It is in this latter respect that the study of international relations has been burdened and constrained by absolutist categories which limit the possibilities for self-conscious awareness.

NOTES

1. The philosophical background to normative theory is given in Chapter 4, but might be read prior to the treatment of the normative literature in the field of international relations given here. The present organisation of material is only to ensure that the main strands of the argument are not lost in extensive preliminaries.

2. Patrick M. Morgan, *Theories and Approaches to International Politics: What Are We to Think?*, 4th. ed. (New Brunswick, NJ: Transaction Books, 1987), pp. 25–47.

3. *Ibid.*, p. 41.

4. Robert O. Keohane, 'International Institutions: Two Approaches', *International Studies Quarterly* (Vol. 32, No. 4, December 1988).

5. R. B. J. Walker, 'History and Structure in the Theory of International Relations', *Millennium: Journal of International Studies* (Vol. 18, No. 2, Summer 1989), p. 165.

6. Karl Deutsch, *The Analysis of International Relations* (Englewood Cliffs, NJ: Prentice-Hall, 1978), p. vii. This passage is quoted in Mervyn Frost, 'Normative Theory and International Relations: Overcoming the Positivist Bias', *Politikon: South African Journal of Political Science* (Vol. 12, No. 1, June 1985), p. 3.

7. John Dewey, 'Challenge to Liberal Thought' in *Fortune* (Vol. 30, 1944), p. 186, cited in Stephen P. Turner and Regis A. Factor, *Max Weber and the dispute over reason and value: a study in philosophy, ethics, and politics*, International Library of Sociology (London: Routledge and Kegan Paul, 1984), p. 166.

8. James E. Dougherty and Robert L. Pfaltzgraff, Jr., *Contending Theories of International Relations* (New York: Lippincott, 1971), p. 396. A similar, though revised, passage appears in the third edition of this book (New York: Harper Collins, 1990), p. 565: 'In the current stage of its development, international relations has been marked by efforts to establish linkages between normative theory on the one hand and empirical–analytical theory on the other... Given the nature of the objects with which international relations deals and the enormously important questions associated with war and peace, normative theory can be expected to remain central to this field.' This passage, like the earlier version, reveals the typical error of separating normative theory from empirical analysis, thereby construing it exclusively in the prescriptive mode.

9.   *Ibid.*, p. 398.
10. Mervyn Frost, 'Normative Theory and International Relations: Overcoming the Positivist Bias', *op. cit.*, pp. 3–15.
11. Richard Rorty, *Philosophy and the Mirror of Nature* (Oxford: Basil Blackwell, 1980).
12. Chris Brown, *International Relations Theory: New Normative Approaches* (London: Harvester Wheatsheaf, 1992), p. 198.
13. *Ibid.*, p. 199.
14. Mervyn Frost, 'Normative Theory and International Relations: Overcoming the Positivist Bias', *op. cit.*, p. 7.
15. Turner and Factor, *op. cit.*, p. 167. The reference is to John Dewey, 'Theory of Valuation' in Neurath, et al., *Foundations of The Unity of Sciences: toward an international encyclopedia of unified science*, Vol. II (Chicago: University of Chicago Press, 1970). An earlier edition of the same work by Dewey is cited below as Vol. II, No. 4 of the encyclopedia, published in 1939.
16. The notion of a discourse arises in post-modern theory and philosophy, and is discussed in Chapter 5. See Michael J. Shapiro, *Reading the Post-modern Polity: Political Theory as Textual Practice* (Minneapolis: University of Minnesota Press, 1992), James Der Derian and Michael J. Shapiro (eds), *International/Intertextual Relations: Post-modern Readings in World Politics* (Lexington, MA: Lexington Books, 1989), and works on knowledge by the modern French philosophers Michel Foucault, *The Archeology of Knowledge* (New York: Pantheon, 1972) and J. F. Lyotard, *The Postmodern Condition: A Report on Knowledge* (Minneapolis: University of Minnesota Press, 1984).
17. Hedley Bull, *The Anarchical Society* (London: Macmillan, 1977), p. 295.
18. Gayatri Chakravorty Spivak, in televised discussion with philosopher John Searle. See the printed guide and bibliography, 'Voices: The Trouble with Truth' (London: Channel 4 Television, April 1988), written by David Herman and produced by Broadcasting Support Services, P.O. Box 4000, London W3 6XJ, and Gayatri Spivak, *In Other Worlds: Essays in Cultural Politics* (New York and London: Methuen, 1987), and her translation of Jacques Derrida's *On Grammatology* (Baltimore: Johns Hopkins University Press, 1976).
19. The idea of 'reimagining' crops up in relation to nationalism in Anthony D. Smith, 'The Nation: Invented, Imagined, Reconstructed?', *Millennium: Journal of International Studies* (Vol. 20, No. 3, Winter 1991), and in relation to feminist theory in Christine Sylvester, 'Homeless in International Relations? "Women's" Place in Canonical Texts and in Feminist Reimaginings' in Adam Lerner and Marjorie Martin (eds) *Reimagining the Nation* (London: Open University Press, forthcoming).
20. Mervyn Frost, 'Normative Theory and International Relations: Overcoming the Positivist Bias', *op. cit.*, p. 8.
21. See, for example, Jean Bethke Elshtain, *Women and War* (New York: Basic Books, 1987); Cynthia Enloe, *Bananas, Beaches, and Bases: Making Feminist Sense of International Politics* (London: Pandora, 1989); Christine Sylvester, *Feminist Theory and International Relations in a Postmodern Era* (Cambridge: Cambridge University Press, forthcoming) and her

'Homeless in International Relations? "Women's" Place in Canonical Texts and in Feminist Reimaginings' in Lerner and Martin (eds), *Reimagining the Nation, op. cit.*

22. Kenneth Waltz refers to Lévi-Strauss's 'inductivist illusion' and Pierce's view that direct experience affirms nothing, but 'just *is*', in Chapter 1 of *Theory of International Politics* (Reading, MA: Addison-Wesley, 1979), as reprinted in Robert O. Keohane (ed), *Neorealism and its Critics* (New York: Columbia University Press, 1986), p. 30.

23. James S. Fishkin, *Beyond Subjective Morality: Ethical Reasoning and Political Philosophy* (London and New Haven, CT: Yale University Press, 1984), p. 157.

24. Henry S. Kariel, *The Desperate Politics of Postmodernism* (Amherst, MA: University of Massachusetts Press, 1989), p. 148.

25. Agnes Heller and Ferenc Fehér, *The Postmodern Political Condition* (Cambridge: Polity Press, 1988), p. 48.

92. John Dewey, 'Theory of Valuation', *International Encyclopedia of Unified Science*, Volume II, Number 4 (Chicago: University of Chicago Press, 1939), p. 64.

27. *Ibid.*, p. 33.

28. *Ibid.*, p. 56.

29. *Ibid.*, pp. 32–3.

30. *Ibid.*, p. 58.

31. *Ibid.*, p. 60.

32. *Ibid.*, p. 61.

33. Terry Nardin, 'The Problem of Relativism in International Ethics' *Millennium: Journal of International Studies* (Vol. 18, No. 2, Summer 1989), p. 159.

34. Hidemi Suganami, *The Domestic Analogy and World Order Proposals* (Cambridge: Cambridge University Press, 1989), p. 164.

35. Agnes Heller and Ferenc Fehér, *The Postmodern Political Condition*, *op. cit.*, p. 50.

36. See K. R. Minogue, 'Epiphenomenalism in Politics: the quest for political reality', *Political Studies* (Vol. XX, No. 4, December 1972), pp. 462–74.

37. In addition to Chris Brown, 'The Modern Requirement? Reflections on Normative International Theory in a Post-Western World', *Millennium: Journal of International Studies* (Vol. 17, No. 2, Summer 1988), see also a useful overview of the various facets of the normative international relations literature (and the difficulty of so classifying it) in his *International Relations Theory: New Normative Approaches, op. cit.*

38. Mark J. Hoffman, 'Normative Approaches' in Margot Light and A. J. R. Groom (eds), *International Relations: A Handbook of Current Theory* (London: Francis Pinter, 1985), p. 27.

39. *Ibid.*, p. 37. Hoffman provides a valuable overview, not done justice by this brief summary of it. The authors mentioned are cited in detail in Hoffman's lengthy bibliography, itself a useful reference.

40. R. J. Vincent, *Human Rights and International Relations* (Cambridge: Cambridge University Press, 1986), p. 125.

41. Charles Beitz, 'Cosmopolitan Ideals and National Sentiment', *Journal of Philosophy* (Vol. 80, No. 10, October 1983).

42. Charles Beitz, *Political Theory and International Relations* (Princeton: Princeton University Press, 1979).
43. *Ibid.*, pp. 179–83.
44. *Ibid.*
45. Charles R. Beitz, *Political Equality: An Essay in Democratic Theory* (Princeton: Princeton University Press, 1989), pp. 226–7.
46. *Ibid.*, p. 4.
47. Andrew Linklater, *Men and Citizens in the Theory of International Relations* (London: Macmillan, 1982), p. x.
48. *Ibid.*, p. xi.
49. *Ibid.*
50. Mervyn Frost, *Towards a Normative Theory of International Relations* (Cambridge: Cambridge University Press, 1986), p. 2.
51. The 'scientific' and 'classical' (liberal historical) approaches, combined with Marxism (this last approach not well developed, as Frost says) may be seen as fitting the three-paradigm scheme of Realism, Pluralism and Structuralism in the study of international relations. For a useful development of this scheme see Mark Hoffman, 'Critical Theory and the Interparadigm Debate' in Hugh C. Dyer and Leon Mangasarian (eds) *The Study of International Relations: The State of the Art* (London: Macmillan, 1989).
52. Frost, *Towards a Normative Theory...*, *op. cit.*, p. 15.
53. *Ibid.*, pp. 22ff., and pp. 27 and 35.
54. *Ibid.*, pp. 62ff.
55. *Ibid.*, pp. 84–86.
56. *Ibid.*, p. 102.
57. Chris Brown, 'The Modern Requirement?...', *op. cit.*, p. 344.
58. *Ibid.*
59. *Ibid.*, p. 346. Brown is referring here to Richard Rorty, *The Consequences of Pragmatism* (Brighton: Harvester Press, 1982).
60. Friedrich V. Kratochwil, *Rules, Norms, and Decisions* (Cambridge: Cambridge University Press, 1989), pp. 14–16.
61. *Ibid.*, p. 28.
62. Martin Griffiths, *Realism, Idealism and International Politics: A Reinterpretation* (London: Routledge, 1992), p. 34.
63. Kratochwil, *Rules, Norms, and Decisions*, *op. cit.*, p. 43.
64. *Ibid.*, p. 64.
65. *Ibid.*, p. 94.
66. *Ibid.*, p. 98.
67. Dewey, *op. cit.*, p. 58.
68. Kratochwil, *op. cit.*, p. 97.
69. *Ibid.*, p. 100–1.
70. Dewey, *op. cit.*, p. 49.
71. Kratochwil, *op. cit.*, p. 125.
72. *Ibid.*, p. 129.
73. Philip Windsor, 'Superpower Intervention' in Hedley Bull (ed), *Intervention in World Politics* (Oxford: Clarendon Press, 1984).
74. This is extracted from the definition used by Bull in *ibid.*, p. 1, which he derives from Oppenheim.

75. Windsor, *op. cit.*, pp. 60–1.
76. Andrew Linklater, *Men and Citizens in the Theory of International Relations* (London: Macmillan, 1982), p. 194. For a comprehensive treatment of the concept of sovereignty and its theoretical implications, see Jens Bartelson, *A Geneology of Sovereignty* (Cambridge: Cambridge University Press, 1995).
77. See the discussion in Michael Akehurst, 'Humanitarian Intervention' in Bull (ed), *op. cit.*, pp. 111–2.
78. Robert C. Johansen, *The National Interest and the Human Interest: An Analysis of U.S. Foreign Policy* (Princeton: Princeton University Press, 1980), p. 22.
79. *Ibid.*, p. 23.
80. *Ibid.*, p. 24.
81. R. J. Vincent, *Human Rights and International Relations* (Cambridge: Cambridge University Press, 1986), p. 3. Note that Vincent is also involved in the debate about intervention: R. J. Vincent, *Non-intervention and International Order* (Princeton, NJ: Princeton University Press, 1974).
82. R. J. Vincent, *Human Rights and International Relations*, *op. cit.*, p. 111.
83. *Ibid.*, p. 112.
84. *Ibid.*, p. 113.
85. *Ibid.*, p. 128.
86. Martin Griffiths, *Realism, Idealism and International Politics: A Reinterpretation* (London Routledge, 1992), p. 25.
87. R. J. Vincent, *Human Rights and International Relations*, *op. cit.*, p. 151.
88. Andrew Linklater, *Men and Citizens in the Theory of International Relations*, *op. cit.*, p. 193.
89. Note a recent (though essentially traditional) work which describes the ethical code devised by states to govern their relations, but which has not yet been fully effected in political practice: Dorothy V. Jones, *Code of Peace: Ethics and Security in the World of Warlord States* (Chicago: University of Chicago Press, 1991). Jones goes to some length to point out the somewhat paradoxical connection between ethical rhetoric and political practice, but does not go so far as to recognise the immanence of ethics in politics, and thus perpetuates the traditional distinction between ethics and politics which so hobbles normative analysis, including her own. It is nevertheless a useful investigation of international norms.
90. Andrew Linklater, *Men and Citizens in the Theory of International Relations*, *op. cit.*, p. 195.
91. Alasdair MacIntyre, *Whose Justice? Which Rationality?* (London: Duckworth, 1989). The quoted passage is from an extract in *The Independent*, 4 Feb. 1989, p. 15.

4 Normative Theory, Ideas and Ideology

Among the constraints visited upon normative approaches by canonical traditions in the discipline of International Relations is the distinction between theory and ideology. When applied to the practices of interpretative social science, and the subjective and intersubjective categories which it employs, this distinction implies that any theory arising out of the interpretation of human practices is likely to be tainted with a political project, and its results mere ideology as opposed to objective description.

Because much of nineteenth and twentieth century international relations has involved ideological conflict, most theories of international relations incorporate some position on the importance of ideology as a political force, and explanations of particular phenomena such as the bipolarity of the Cold War period differ on this point. This chapter will investigate the relationship between normative theory and the role of ideas in political theory and practice. For the purposes of this book, the distinction will help to define the parameters of normative theory as applied to international relations; it will also indicate some limitations of this body of theory, but without prejudice to its import. The facile dismissal of normative approaches on the grounds of being 'mere ideology' is answered by pointing to the central role of ideas in political life, and the importance of normative theory as a means of reintegrating ethics and politics.

Knutsen places this discussion into the historical context of the early nineteenth century development of new theories and ideologies:

> This proliferation of ideas at first overwhelmed the explorers of international relations; they were expelled from a garden carefully tended by a few legal and historical authorities into a new, uneven terrain of dense, theoretical foliage.[1]

Out of this theoretical foliage grew the principal themes of radicalism, liberalism and conservatism which continue to be reflected in contemporary paradigmatic debates of international relations scholarship. Because these themes were for the most part developed in reference to states and national societies, domestic politics built around national social values could be distinguished from competitive and violent international politics, allowing a more ready separation of ethics and politics at the international level. This conception of international relations is challenged by the identification and critique of value structures, which is the task of normative theory.

This chapter will, in particular, distinguish the rational characteristics of normative theory, in respect to its definitional and regulatory roles as an interpreter of empirical data, from the transcendent rationality of those belief systems whose teleology incorporates an after-life or deity, for example. These transcendent rationalities lead to the subjective differences which are wrongly held to be the failing of normative analysis. While beliefs no doubt have a significant role in the formation of social and political values, and are central to ideologies, the purpose of normative theory in explaining the structure and dynamics of these values is distinct from explanations of their origin which refer to a transcendent rationality. As Laszek Kolakowski has said,

> There is no access to an epistemological absolute, and there is no privileged access to the absolute Being which might result in reliable theoretical knowledge (this last restriction is needed, as we may not *a priori* exclude the reality of mystical experience that provides some people with this privileged access; but their experience cannot be reforged into a theory). This double denial does not need to end up with pragmatic nihilism; it is compatible with the belief that metaphysical and non-pragmatic insight is possible as a result of our living within the realm of good and evil and of experiencing good and evil as one's own.[2]

Some care in the use of the term transcendent is necessary here because in a sense any foundation for individual or collective identity (and hence meaning) must transcend the most immediate and contingent (for example, the possibility of non-private language depends on references external to the purely subjective); it is a question of what is being transcended. The distinction should be made between the transcendent (an object of faith) and the transcendental (a rational heuristic abstraction).

Similarly, there are problems in speaking of rationality, since this too is a product of a Western Enlightenment tradition of thought which has been only subsequently universalised by the predominance of Western science – a product, in this sense, of a particular normative system functioning in the realm of knowledge. We may proceed nevertheless, but cautiously, in the awareness that even the language of the present argument is a hidden influence or constraint on our understanding.

The strength and motive of normative theory in addressing the underlying value structures in international relations lies precisely in the ability to suggest rational grounds for the adoption of coherent policy measures which conform to, rather than frustrate, these underlying values. The rational grounds for such policy lie in the commonalities of normative systems arising from their social and political functions, not from their apparently disparate origins in the transcendent rationalities of religious belief systems, or the aspirations of ideologies. Hence, the case to be made here is that normative systems are essentially (but not strictly) rational, in the Humean sense of 'conventions',[3] and that their historical, existential and ontological foundations are not to be conflated with the 'extra-rational' tenets of belief systems which may inform a normative structure.

In this context one may also wish to address the empirical foundations of normative systems, while bearing in mind that normative approaches raise questions about empiricism. These issues have been discussed in Chapter 1, but may be raised here again in the process of distinguishing between empirical observations, ideas, ideologies and beliefs, between common sense and philosophy, and between practice and theory.

The present argument will suggest that in the commonly percieved hierarchy or continuum whose categories range from the tangible to the abstract, normative theory lies rather closer to the former than conventional wisdom would allow. Having pointed to the proximal relationship of the empirical and the normative in Chapter 1, the task remains to define the limits of abstraction in a normative theory of international relations, and the purpose of abstraction.

The context of the present discussion is the broader one of social science, where 'scientific' means 'non-ideological' and international relations theory is tested against the standards of normal science.

> ... as with traditional political theory, this move towards science has reified social institutions and social relations, negating in general the active part that humans play in the production of their social world, and removing from consideration the possibilty of analysing other than the most ubiquitous *appearance* of change.[4]

In this and other chapters normative theory in the study of international relations is contrasted with other theory in the field, in the context of competing fundamental ideas: ideas about human nature, about national political life, about relations between states, and ultimately about the significance of theory in the search for 'true knowledge'. An important aspect of this investigation is defining the limits of normative theory, and distinguishing it from ideology. In the process, 'mainstream' realist theory will be similarly examined to show what its limitations are and whether it, too, can be distinguished from ideology. The contrast will allow a clearer understanding not only of the relative 'scientific' strengths of the different bodies of theory, but more importantly will focus attention on the role of theory in achieving both knowledge and political goals: being both product and source of different and often competing ideas, theories will be seen as key actors in the politics of knowledge. It will be argued that normative theory can provide a stabilising background theory for such epistemological competition, and does not readily produce an over-simplified or particularistic version of 'truth'.

NORMATIVE THEORY AND IDEOLOGY DISTINGUISHED

The principal distinction between normative theorising and ideological polemics lies in a difference of purpose. While ideology acquires its meaning in political engagement and action, in relation to political consciousness or adopted political ideas, normative theory involves questioning such ideas – no doubt a form of engagement as well, but an engagement with the play of ideas; with the politics of knowledge rather than with practical politics in isolation.

Reinhold Niebuhr, in 'Ideology and the Scientific Method', provides a useful characterisation of the relationship between knowledge and ideology, which also shows that the dogma of Christian realism it is not that of scientific realism:

> ...the field of historical observation presents us with infinite grades of engagement from the obvious engagement of the practical statesman through the observations of social scientists who stand upon some contemporary ground of impartiality to the observations of social and historical scientists of a subsequent age who have gained a perspective in time upon the scene of conflict between various interests and passions. These various shades of engagement also determine the degree to which selves rather than minds must be appealed to. If it is a self rather than a mind, no scientific method can compel a self to cease from engaging in whatever rationalisation of interest may seem plausible to it... No perfection of method can thus completely overcome ideological conflict.[5]

At the level of the self and broader collective identities, the questions of normative theory are in a sense questions about Being (ontological questions), which may subsequently shed light on the nature of world affairs and the place of national policy in them, but without simple assertions, thoughtless fatalism or mere 'problem-solving'. Although Kratochwil argues that 'all rules and norms are problem-solving devices for dealing with the recurrent issues of social life: conflict and cooperation',[6] the importance of this view is that a normative perspective emphasises the fundamental role of norms in the continuous *process* of political life, rather than the particular instances in which norms may be conciously or unconciously employed for some purpose.

Norms are not simply or only 'tools' for analysis or action: they exist in human affairs, and our challenge is to understand how they exist. A theory of normative structures intends, like any theory, to offer a general explanation; a starting place. Thus normative theory provides a context for political inquiry and understanding which is prior to political action, so that while ideologies (in contrast) provide a rallying point for political action, they cannot escape the broader political environment in which they arise.

Of course, the phenomenon of ideology itself has a broad sweep of manifestations, and the fragmentation of Western political thought into radicalism, liberalism and conservatism around the turn of the nineteenth century in themselves constituted competing ideologies whose influence remains. However, ideology is distinguished by its special relationship to political action, and political action requires political actors (nation-states, for the most part, in international relations): 'An "ideology" is a systematic body of beliefs about the structures and processes of society; it includes a comprehensive theory of human nature that sustains a programme of practical politics'.[7] The connection of ideology to the practical action programme of particular political actors undermines its wider explanatory capacity and distinguishes it from a normative theory of international politics.

The foundation of national action (according to the 'national will', or the 'national interest') is a self-understanding of the national character in relation to others, which provides meaning for the nation and its decision-makers. Of course, this is true for any who aspire to political leadership, whatever ideological position they may represent. It is also true for actors other than nation-states, who must be equally aware of their relative position to other actors in the international arena, whether or not these are nation-states. In order to be effective, such self-understanding must provide an explicit, self-critical and questioning awareness of the global socio-political environment; a world-view (to be discussed in Chapter 4). As we will see in Chapter 5, the advent of nuclear weapons, and the deterrence strategies that accompany them, forced this questioning upon us in a most profound way for the first time – and they are precisely and obviously questions of existence; of Being. With the collapse of Cold War structures, and increasing awareness of global environmental change, natural environmental problems provide a new focal point for such questioning.

While the prescriptive aspect of normative theory necessarily adopts and recommends certain values (and provides reasons for doing so), the descriptive aspect of normative theory locates and explains values in the context of the value-systems in which they arise, providing the grounds for prescription. For example, a particular ideology may reflect some set of values that appeal on *a priori* grounds, yet leave the practical import of these values undetermined in the first instance. A descriptive normative analysis would provide an explanation for (and establish the meaning of) these values in the context of the society to which they apply. Once an ideology is fully subsumed in the culture of a society (that is, in the full range of normative activity), an analysis of ideology will be coincidental with an analysis of social values. But of course, there may be several ideologies or sets of values at play within any society – or within the state – leading to political and social tensions.

This is not to say that political ideologies represent the totality of socially relevant ideas, for there are other normative features of societies which are equally important and similarly subject to the ebb and flow of ideas: aesthetics (in art, architecture, and music), ethics (in business and personal relations), and epistemology (in science, where truth and verification are at issue). No doubt ideologies are conditioned in various ways by these other aspects of social life, whose influence cannot be dismissed. Nevertheless, in the examination of international political relations and foreign policies, ideology may be considered a key area for normative analysis, while remaining distinct from normative theory.

The following sections introduce the character of ideas, the philosophical context of ideas in relation to normative structures, and the contrasting features of ideology which distinguish it from normative theory.

IDEAS: THE SUBJECT AND OBJECT

What is essential in this discussion of ideas and normative theory is that political ideas, perhaps represented in ideologies (whether well or ill-defined), are subject to the influence of other 'external' ideas, political or otherwise. Ideas find definition in their contrast with alternative ideas, or, in Nietzschian fashion, they cannot be defined if they have a history. Thus the historical collective experience of a society is employed in selecting and assessing political ideas, which may be taken up in and by ideologies, and both the process and its content (ideas) are subsequently open to normative analysis. It is the position of ideas in the broader socio-historical context that can be revealed by a normative analysis, rather than simply a cataloguing of historical ideas. (It is in this context that a work such as Knutsen's can be judged.) Consequently, ideas can be viewed as normative in character, in the way that other aspects of culture and politics are normative. Predominant ideas become intellectual norms, directly participating in normative assessments of social and political behaviour, and no more free of such assessment themselves than ostensibly empirical events. In this sense, there is no escape from normative evaluation by reference to ostensibly objective intellectual positions, since ideas are part of the experiential process by which all norms are established (whether social, political or intellectual) and partake of the same communicative, educational, consensus-building characteristics that inform perceptions of reality in all its aspects.

Ideas, however, unlike other features of accepted (normal) reality, are not constrained by the most concrete norms concerning empirical phenomena and are consequently the first to effect, and be effected by, change. Being subject (like all norms) to variations in other aspects of experience, ideas may be assessed differently as the social context changes around them, losing or gaining currency and credibility. For Marx, ideas and material social existence are inseparable – the grounds for arguing that class conciousness, class interests, and therefore class struggles are the substance of human history. And yet, since political ideas are open to broader interpretation than, for example, the colour green or the shape of a cube, they may be adapted to changing circumstances, or revitalised by finding new points of reference in a new empirical reality. For the purposes of empirical analysis, therefore, ideas may be thought indeterminate, unidentifiable, and of little importance or use. On the contrary, ideas are the most important of all aspects of experience, and for precisely the same reasons that they are often discredited by those who would found a 'hard' science of politics. Such a science may be possible, but clearly not through discrediting ideas: axioms of politics cannot be concerned with specific circumstances or events anymore than natural science seeks specific findings in preference to generalisations, and specific ideas must likewise be understood in terms of ideational or ideological processes rather than incidental content.

Once prepared to accept that ideas are not fixed or independent of one another – or indeed of the world in which they are formulated and expressed – one may readily adopt a view of ideas as being both the context and substance of an evolutionary (perhaps dialectical) process. This process may in turn be viewed as one which can be understood in normative terms; one which follows the same patterns of normative evolution, affirmation, communication, reassessment, critique, devolution, and reformulation as do other socio-cultural processes. Such evolution is not teleological or bound necessarily to some idea of progress (that is, to programmatic forms of Hegelian or Kantian philosophy), but is nevertheless bounded by the acceptability of variation or novelty. A synthesis is not arrived at by some mathematical correlation of thesis and antithesis, but rather by a political process which is itself subject to normative constraints, and whose outcome is in some way proscribed. Furthermore, because ideas play a central role they are not merely the subject or substance of such a process, but are also the medium through which all such processes function and evolve: ideas are the currency of normative systems – and ultimately, of consciousness.

Ideas, on a common-sense account, are the philosophical maxims or artefacts of theory which populate ordinary language and understanding as these latter are employed in normative interactions. That ideas may be inauthentic, misappropriated, or misunderstood on occasion does not diminish their role, though it should be said that ideas must be effective in their role in order to survive. This last point is evidenced by the testing of ideas in the form of debate and criticism, which is a feature of ordinary life, though described here in more abstract terms as being part of a normative evolutionary process. Of course, ideas may be understood in a less common-sensical way as being philosophically problematic in themselves: they are, for example, the subject (and title) of Edmund Husserl's work on pure phenomenology, which influenced the course of twentieth-century philosophy by its radical departure into philosophical methodology. Naturally enough, Husserl's ideas have not escaped criticism and subsequent development but they are nevertheless relevant to, among other things, the present undertaking.

The establishment and development of the academic discipline of International Relations, during and following two world wars and the advent of nuclear weapons, has provided a new venue – and new reasons – for debates on fundamental (usually metaphysical) questions which is well suited to departures from traditional philosophy. This is not to say that the study of international relations has modern origins, since any account of this endeavour records ancient antecedents and abiding influences from every era[8] – which only underlines the obvious point that international relations is a dimension of human affairs. However, certain aspects of human affairs become more salient in particular historical contexts, and novelty of context demands novelty of thought. For one thing, the existence, form, and meaning of the nation-state – as a principal feature of political organisation – becomes a central issue in the context of international relations, not only in respect to relations between different states and societies, but also to the relationship between state and society (in individual cases of these), as well as relationships between the state-structure of one nation-state and the society of another (and vice-versa).[9] Thus, the question of the state arises in the context of systems of states or a global society, depending on theoretical perspectives, such that the security of ultimate reference to the historical accident which is the nation-state is no longer a tenable means of grounding social values, whether for individual consciousness or collective societal consciousness. Consider, for example, the notion of a global commons,[10] or the tension between the organising principles of states and those of markets.[11]

Thus the endeavour of international relations theory itself reveals the source and dynamic of cultural and political crises: these practical developments cannot be addressed simply in terms of conflicting national interests but rather must be understood in terms arising from parallel developments in modern political theory and philosophy, which in turn inform the academic endeavour. The status of ideas lies at the heart of these developments, and the corresponding philosophical debates can be well understood in normative terms.

PHILOSOPHICAL BACKGROUND FOR NORMATIVE THEORY

Inquiry into the distinctive characteristics of normative theory requires investigation of its philosophical antecedents. Because the definition of normative theory employed here is not coextensive with the general use of the term as a synonym for prescriptivism, this investigation will make the distinction clearer by revealing its philosophical referents. The relationship between normative theory, ideas, and ideology will also be clarified by reference to pertinent signposts in the history and development of philosophy.

David Hume held that ideas are the 'faint images' of forceful perceptions, or impressions, in thinking and reasoning, but he was sceptical about the external correspondence of ideas and maintained the Cartesian dualism (as between subject and object). Immanuel Kant subsequently introduced a transcendental argument, employing the notions of *phenomena* (things perceived) and *noumena* (things in themselves), which held that there can only be knowledge of phenomena (hence phenomenology) and that synthetic (non-analytical, non-trivial) knowledge of phenomena (therefore of *a priori* truths) is necessary – because of consciousness, and not simply as a matter of habit as Hume would argue. Thus, for Kant, the world we know *is* the real world; ideas about the world constitute the world. There is a primacy of the knower over the known such that objects *necessarily* correspond to consciousness, not vice-versa. But, of course, we may still ask how free the individual is in the construction of ideas – in consciousness – and whether there are not influences of a normative character on the establishment of ideas, and hence knowledge, especially knowledge of universal and necessary *a priori* truths. (For example, the constraints imposed by the notion of *noumena*, and the denial of dualism, break down somewhat in Kant's justification of his ethics).

G. W. F. Hegel constructed a systematic philosophy to give absolute truth and knowledge which adopts an anti-dualist position with respect to truth, but changing knowledge of it through a dialectical 'becoming' of knowledge (which always 'was', in a teleological sense). This position allows Hegel to accept contradictions as a natural, even healthy, condition and to adopt a contextualist view of the world – and explanations of it – which is reflected in his notions of the 'collective idea' or Spirit of the Time (*Zeitgeist*), the national *Volksgeist* and the world-historical *Veltgeist* (and simply the Spirit or *Geist*). Thus ideas are reflections of the Spirit in logic, such that logic *is* metaphysics; logic and contradictions are both 'in the world'. This contextualism is clearly normative in character, though I use 'normative' here in the analytic/epistemological as opposed to ethical sense. Of course this contextual perspective would also apply to morality, as a reflection of the Spirit and an absolute which remains to be fully known through the becoming of knowledge and thus not yet universal or, rather, universally comprehended, interim interpretations of it being various. This contextual view of moral absolutes provides a means of coping with theoretical problems of moral relativity without abandoning the notion of morality itself as a universal feature of human relations which can be accounted for by normative theory. Of course this interpretation of the Spirit may be criticised, as in Ricouer's view that the Spirit is a totalitarian concept as opposed to being properly intersubjective since it implies everyone sharing the same view or perspective rather than engaging in a discourse about views, although this latter would have a kind of collective (and normative) outcome nevertheless.

The inherent contradictions or paradoxes of reason, which are a problem for Kant but a virtue for Hegel, are addressed in a very different way by those who criticise systematic philosophy. Soren Kierkegaard, a founder of existentialism, argues for the resolution of these paradoxes through individual *choice*, while Hegel employs reason itself in the context of collective (Spirit) being. The emphasis on the individual thinker, on 'subjective truth', and on the need for passionate choice concerning a way of life, reflects a view of philosophical questions as being concerned with what to do (practice), rather than with conceptual dilemmas (theory). The concept, the medium of systematic philosophy, is unimportant to Kierkegaard in as much as he argues that existence is not reducible to a concept but requires the application of the rule: 'cognitive reality' and 'ethical reality' are distinct, as they are for Kant, but the *only* reality for the individual is her own ethical reality. The existential dialectic – paralleling but repudiating Hegel's historical dialectic – suggests that while life must be *understood backwards* (as in Hegel), it must be *lived forwards*, and hence the 'ethical paradox' is the need for commitment under conditions of objective uncertainty. This rather strong subjectivism does not play down the significance of values, but emphasises the great burden of choice and the difficulty of maintaining a subjective justification of ethical choice.

This portrait of individuals as asocial beings, mastering their own lives and authoring their own values, places an appropriate emphasis on the responsibility of individuals, but is not fully convincing with respect to the character of human existence. It is difficult to make sense of individual life in the absence of a social context, however limited, even if individuals must in the end choose for themselves. Having accepted the need for an historical understanding of life, it is difficult to see how an individual might progress in the absence of a social context and other artefacts of collective historical experience. How is one to choose values, which concern human relationships if anything, without an appreciation of their meaning as given by social experience? How will the normative character of values be comprehended? It is one thing to emphasise the need for choice, but quite another to suggest original sole authorship of values. The role and significance of ideas, including ideas about values, is clearly diminished when they are not communicated through time and space, and such communication is by definition an interactive or relational process. Obviously, Kierkegaard does not escape the need for language in communicating his own ideas, and although making the distinction between cognitive reality and ethical reality may ironically allow values to escape the normative characteristics of knowledge, this distinction is at the heart of the 'is–ought' debate discussed in Chapter 1. Indeed the processes of systematic knowledge (science) itself exhibit normative characteristics which suggest that value non-cognitivism undermines cognition altogether. These observations do not, however, stand in the way of viewing the human experience as one of commitment to values in and through acting rather than one of acting in accordance with values – a view which is the foundation of Sartre's revolutionary theory of value – but they do suggest that values arise in the context of a broader normative system rather than being adopted by individuals through Kierkegaard's 'leap of faith'. The notion of individual authorship of values implies an unlikely originality, given that suspiciously widespread 'coincidental' agreement usually indicates some sort of inadvertent plagiarism.

In a further assault on systematic philosophy, Friedrich Nietzsche argues that every proposition should stand alone; that systems are merely subjective expressions in the guise of objective truth. His epistemological nihilism (in accordance with the 'death of God' thesis) maintains – as against all philosophies from Descartes to Kant – that there is no distinction between the apparent and real world, that there are no 'facts' but only interpretations, and that language determines metaphysics (not vice-versa). In his emphasis on self-perfection Nietzsche points to the practical value of making life a 'work of art', and in turn suggests a merging of theory and practice such that metaphysics, epistemology, and ethics are all interpretations with practical consequences. On this account reason is *necessary* but not *sufficient* for morality; passion is also required. Nietzsche argues for a balanced relationship between 'Dionysian frenzy' (passion) and 'Apollonian control' (reason): as reason is already socially derived, a social morality is unnecessary, and passion provides for individuality. This moral nihilism leaves open the question of substantiating values, and for Nietzche this is the central problem of philosophy. Thus ideas may be seen, under epistemological nihilism, to play a role in the interpretation of the apparent world (the *only* world, for Nietzsche), while under moral nihilism values must find substance in their relevance to our life in this world.

With respect to the present argument, ideas remain the currency of self-referential normative systems. The notion of balancing passion and reason can be seen as analogous to balancing self-consciousness and social consciousness, or (for present purposes) nationalism and internationalism. For Nietzsche there is no absolute truth to be had through reason (as Hegel argued) but rather reason must be the slave of passion (as Hume argued): the master creates values where the slave is given them. However, even a benign view of nihilism as a destructive force making way for new creations still leaves the creative process undirected: a problem not resolved either by Nietzsche's nihilism or Hume's scepticism. Adopting Hegel's more contextual view of the master–slave relationship might have led Nietzsche to see that the master's consciousness of his creative abilities requires the acknowledgement of the slave, and that acceptance of the given values is a necessary condition of their creation. So while Nietzsche's cleansing nihilism is enlightening it is also unsatisfying, while both Hegel, and later Husserl, are prepared to go further (in the pursuit of presuppositionless philosophy) by arguing for at least *some* necessary truths of the non-empirical sort. If these truths concern relationships, either in the abstract realm of conceptual knowledge or in human experience, then the role of normative theory comes to light once again at the most fundamental level of understanding.

Husserl introduces phenomenology as a radical new philosophical method, rejecting both scepticism and logical positivism in establishing a non-judgemental methodological position. The 'natural standpoint' and judgements about the 'external world' are suspended (Husserl's *'epoche'*) in the search for necessary truths. On this account naturalism is unsound because it confuses natural science with *a priori* science (philosophy): phenomenology allows a radical empiricism which examines the experience of objects of consciousness, not of the objects themselves. Necessary truths are truths about the *structure* of experience and the meaning or *essence* of consciousness, and the only source of truth is the 'pure experience' of this radical empiricism. For Husserl, all concepts (including Kant's *a priori* concepts) are derived from *abstractions* of experience. Phenomenology is necessarily self-justifying, resting on the validity of its concepts, but this is true of other methods: for example, where phenomenology rests on 'pure description', analytic philosophy rests on linguistic meaning. So where cognition occurs through the *cogito* for Descartes (and others), it occurs through the transcendental ego for Husserl: there are 'ideas' rather than 'one having ideas'. Of course, all of this is problematic in as much as an intersubjective transcendental community (on which Husserl insists) conflicts with the apprehension of necessary truths through a phenomenolological consciousness: the transcendence does not resolve the dualism. Husserl seeks a rationalistic 'science' of philosophy, but his transcendental idealism is perhaps too demanding. Nevertheless, the influence of the phenomenological method on later philosophy shows in the existentialists' attempts to establish a radical phenomenological ontology, in contrast to Husserl's anti-ontological phenomenology. Husserl himself went so far as to claim that he had established the only true philosophy.

What may be gleaned from Husserl's philosophy, for the purpose of supporting the present argument for normative theory, are those aspects of the phenomenological reduction which place *ideas* at the heart of true knowledge. Husserl argues that necessary truths are not merely analytic, based on a causal relationship between experience and the 'real' world, but are phenomenological truths based on the consciousness of experience. It is difficult to place traditional notions of fact and object in this scheme (because of the dominant influence of positivism and empiricism), but the emphasis on a necessary structure of experience, and an essential structure of consciousness, suggests some intersubjective stability in the apprehension of truths from the phenomenological standpoint. It is the intersubjectivity of the transcendental 'community of consciousness' that suggests a normative quality in these structures, and the issue is then the necessity of the structure. If it is the case that *some* structure is required for consciousness, then any given structure may be sufficient. This does not provide much assurance on the matter of an absolute truth, nor for the prospects of discovering fundamental genetically-given principles of mind, but it does allow for a conception of truth as being dependent on a structure of consciousness which itself is subject to normative processes, and influenced by values.

Husserl, as a mathematician, was interested not only in knowledge of necessary truths, but in the possibility of necessary truth – he held that *a priori* truths are not conventional or normative, but are *ideal laws*, requiring the new science of phenomenology for their investigation. Husserl was himself very unsystematic, being more concerned with the philosophical endeavour (method) than with attaining truth, and suggested that we must always be in doubt, always questioning, always beginning. Perhaps it is the prospect of never overcoming doubt, of never attaining the ultimate and absolute truth, that presents the best case for adopting the perpetually penultimate stage of knowledge as the foundation and starting point of a pervasive normative process. This kind of epistemological agnosticism is not nihilistic, yet reduces dependency on absolute knowledge. As we will see in Martin Heidegger's existentialism, knowledge becomes in a sense less important when the primitive relationship to the world is seen as *concern*, rather than knowing.

The problem of Being is the central issue for Heidegger, and is the focus of his principle work *Being and Time (Sein und Zeit)*. He differs from his teacher Husserl in denying an 'ego' which constitutes the world, but holds rather that there is only Being-in-the-world (*Dasein*). This Being-in-the-world is ontically distinguished by its having concern with the question of Being: while all other existence is merely ontic, Being-in-the-world is ontological. Heidegger blurs the distinction between literature and philosophy, arguing that 'Being' requires a new grammar, its own conceptual scheme. While he agrees with Kierkegaard that the self is ethical rather than cognitive, and thus attacks conceptual analysis, his concern with both Being and the concept 'Being' is so intertwined that his own ontology may amount to conceptual analysis, on a conventional understanding of these categories of thought, though Heidegger's philosophy is in fact neither of these or perhaps a hybrid of the two.

Robert Solomon points to P. F. Strawson's distinction (in *Individuals*) between prescriptive and descriptive metaphysics, suggesting that Heidegger's philosophy might be understood as being prescriptive, but that this presents problems of evaluation: Heidegger would hold that the evaluation of philosophical theory must avoid this conventional distinction and rest instead on the adequacy of a system of thought, or of a 'language', to describe the world.[12] On this account, for example, ontology is perverted without an understanding of what it is to exist; of the metaphysical meaning of Being. Heidegger makes a distinction between 'common sense' concerning practicalities and philosophy; between historicism (the cultural relativity of truth) and historicity (living in time): ignoring the question of Being enslaves philosophy to particular cultures and undermines the exposure of prejudices which are the roots of common sense. Metaphysics is related to ethics in the sense that the meaning and goals of Being inform evaluation and commitment. Thus the question of Being is the foundation of all disciplines (not just philosophy), and the source of cultural tensions. It may be seen how this account leads to the quests for values and for truth being indistinguishable, and to the blurring of the fact – value distinction. Being-in-the-world implies being in a world of possibilities, in which 'things' only become conspicuous as such when they fall out of this context of the self and world as one – otherwise 'things' are, as Heidegger argues, 'equipment' employed in the process of being which have existential meaning through use. For example, a wristwatch becomes a 'thing' when it is broken or lost, and falls out of the context of its value in use.

It is the normative framework which establishes meaning, and when the equipment in question is a social institution like the state (or a states-system) – a normative structure in itself; a set of ideas – then it too becomes a 'thing' when disconnected from social values, to be abandoned (or opposed, or changed) when it loses its value in use; when it fails to provide meaning.

One further aspect of Heidegger's philosophy which may be usefully employed here is his notion of 'authenticity',[13] based on the existential structures of *Existenz*, Facticity, and Fallenness. Existenz is the recognition of choice for every individual; the conception of the world and oneself as possibilities. Facticity is finding oneself already in a given world, and being attuned to it. Fallenness (fallenness from Being) is equivalent to alienation, in the sense of losing oneself in society, and being restricted by communal ties from recognising possibilities. Thus the 'authentic' person is one who discovers the self in the world, understands and projects this recognition, and engages in authentic discourse about this discovery and recognition. 'Inauthentic' persons live out an enforced refusal to see themselves as they really are, and thus act blindly, substituting means for ends.

As we shall see later, this confusion of means and ends is a critical problem in foreign policy formation, and may be viewed as the result of 'inauthenticity' on the part of the nation-state in generating policy – a failure to be concerned with self-knowledge, and with the global context of its existence. Once again we see how ideas profoundly influence not only self-knowledge, in the limited sense (ideas as concepts; the substance of analytic philosophy), but also knowledge of the world and one's place in it (ideas as the currency of normative systems, both theoretical and practical). Of course for Heidegger universal values are rejected as being values imposed, and his existentialism (Being-in-the-world) requires that one choose one's own mode of existence. Again, as with Kierkegaard, the issue of value authorship arises, and for Heidegger's 'authentic' person the role of normative systems must be limited to an interpretation of the character of value discourse, rather than the foundation and maintenance of values, while in the case of Fallenness, or 'inauthenticity', normative systems are in full swing as determinants of everyday Being.

The later existentialists, such as Jean-Paul Sartre, continue to reject Husserl's notion of an 'epoche' or 'bracketing' of the natural standpoint for philosophical purposes, but continue to employ the phenomenological method to disclose 'Being' (Sartre's *Being and Nothingness* is subtitled 'an essay in phenomenological ontology'). For Sartre, Being-in-the-world is revealed through a comprehension of nothingness, which allows a freedom of consciousness from 'external' causation. Nothingness in this sense is both an object of experience, and the productive or renewing activity of nihilation. Thus consciousness can be seen as 'nothing' (the state of 'nothingness'): a post-reflective intentionality directed to objects, from a non-dualist perspective in which acts of consciousness and objects of consciousness are not distinguished, nor the object perceived and the object imagined. The French phenomenologists carry Heidegger's investigation of the preontological ('primitive') conditions of experience to considerable length, and maintain an existentialist emphasis on the individual consciousness as the only source of reality. Maurice Merleau-Ponty, in emphasising self-consciousness as the essential activity of the mind (of Being), is driven to say 'I am the absolute source'. (We may discern here a refined echo of the Cartesian *'Cogito ergo sum'*.) Again we are faced with the prospect not only of eternal doubt, an epistemological and ethical nihilism, but with potential chaos in the practical activity of social existence. Inauthentic or not, there is normative social organisation. It may be that there is sufficient common experience for individuals to authentically conclude, coincidentally, that some values are shared. As with Kierkegaard, it is the emphasis on individual responsibility both for one's own existence and – necessarily – for existence in general (Being), which is the persuasive influence of existentialist thought. Late in life, Sartre confirmed in an interview that

> ... the idea which I never have ceased to develop is that in the end one is always responsible for what is made of one. Even if one can do nothing else besides assume this responsibility.[14]

Here it is useful to consider the postmodernist deconstructionist position on knowledge, which suggests that knowledge is contingent or textual – layers of text on text. This view is generally associated with Jacques Derrida or Jean-François Lyotard, but has been reiterated by others such as Gyatri Spivak.[15] We may also wish to consider the related views of such thinkers as Roland Barthes (who suggests the distinction between the written and the read) or the semiology of Umberto Eco. The key to the deconstructionist line of thought is an immanent contradiction arising from a concern for knowledge (this much being shared with other views, obviously) which yet contends that truth can never be fully articulated, and is always contextually dependent when articulation is attempted. This creates, as Spivak notes, a rather melancholy mood; a mood which philosophers such as John Searle (who once proposed an analytical derivation of 'ought' from 'is' via the institution of promising[16]) find uncomfortable, since some foundation is required. A truth referent is needed for intelligibility, and the deconstructionist view undermines the possibility of 'truth'.

Deconstructionism argues that traditional theory is too easily seduced by a simple route to truth, and compounds the ill effects of simplification until, reaching the limits of correspondence theory it rebuilds through crisis. In effect, a deconstructionist view places the limits of correspondence much closer by insisting that correspondence itself is never fully explored, and perhaps cannot be (because of the infinite realm of the 'unsaid' textuality).

A slightly different position in the philosphy of science, is constructivism, which argues that

> the world that scientists study, in some robust sense, must be defined or constituted or 'constructed' from the theoretical tradition in which the scientific community in question works.[17]

This constructivist view is reflected in Kuhn's treatment of scientific paradigms, which has had such an influence in the social sciences generally, and in the study of international relations in particular. Hence the influence of theoretical traditions and the epistemological priority of norms (as discussed earlier) follows from the requirements of 'constructing' the world in light of tradition.

Charles Pierce described philosophy as 'a theoretical science of discovery' dealing with the ordinary facts of everyday existence. He divides it into phenomenology, normative science, and metaphysics – the first cataloging the data of experience, the second judging and evaluating them, and the third attempting to comprehend their reality – in order of logical priority. Obviously, phenomenology is the prior necessity of normative science, but note that the two are interactive once normative science is got underway since normative science creates new experiences and phenomena which must be classified. Pierce's philosophy identifies (like Hegel, though from a different starting point) three universal categories corresponding to the modes of being: possibility, actuality, and law. These are related to the three normative sciences of esthetics, ethics, and logic – these in turn relating to feeling, action, and thought (aspects of the categories).[18] For the theory and practice of international relations the second normative science (ethics) most directly bears on the interpretation of the 'real' world (actuality) and on the problems of foreign policy decision-making (action). Here, the normative characteristic is not the moralising tone so often associated with ethical concern, but the dynamic of acceptance regarding judgements and evaluations in the Humean sense of 'conventions':

> Consequently virtue is merely a quality of action or mind that is generally approved. Like religion it can have a natural history but the force of moral obligation depends upon the acceptance of the propensities, the wants, the motives to action that give rise to it. No other validity is possible.[19]

What remains to be said for normative interpretations of epistemology and social experience? To begin with, although an extensive normative system would seem to impose order, and like a religion relieve individuals of ultimate responsibility for their world, individual responsibility is not abrogated under a normative system necessarily. Indeed a normative system may aid in the assumption and execution of such individual responsibilities, or, for that matter, it may be that the normative system itself (in requiring support) is an object of responsibility. Such normative systems are apprehended, interpreted or explained through normative theory.

Of course no society can maintain opportunities for authentic individual existence if the society itself (or associated structures) is permitted to overwhelm the beneficial aspects of social cooperation (examples being cases of Fascist, Nazi, Communist, racist or 'personality cult' regimes dictating political behaviour in a restrictive and exclusive manner). But this is either the result of a failure to assume responsibility, or the burden to be shouldered by those responsible (those affected – everyone, ultimately). This is not unique to despotic societies and is also a well understood problem of democratic political life: the system is only as good as those for whom and by whom it operates. Furthermore, this is as true for systems of knowledge as it is for systems of political organisation (both require vigilant questioning), and to the extent that stability is desireable in both cases it is not surprising to find normative processes at work in the functioning of such similarly cooperative ventures. Neither should it be assumed that normative systems – open to change and interpretation – are antithetical to the existentialist positions outlined above: normative systems are an aspect of the world as we find it (Heidegger's Facticity), and of the historicity of human experience (Being-in-time). In as much as ideas fall under normative systems, whether in the epistemological literature or in everyday discourse, they too are an aspect of Being-in-the-world – and equally so for the authentic person's commitment in action and the inauthentic person's acceptance of 'pre-packaged' thought.

It is here we may begin to consider the nature and role of ideology, and its relationship to normative activity and theory.

IDEOLOGY: THE FORM OF ENGAGEMENT

In the aftermath of the French Revolution, with the collapse of the *ancien regime*, a new basis of political association was required to provide a source of enlightened policies and civic virtues. To meet this need (and by happy coincidence with philosophical developments) the French materialist philosopher Antoine Destutt de Tracy coined the term ideology to describe a new 'science of ideas: an encyclopedic and authoritative form of knowledge'.[20] D. J. Manning writes that de Tracy 'claimed this science to be the fruit of the attacks on scholasticism and metaphysics led by Bacon, Locke, Helvetius and Condiallac, and he judged that the maturation of the discipline could not have been more timely', and also that he 'attributed to ideology the power to demonstrate the relationship between experience and ideas, and the relationship between truth and a well-ordered human world'.[21]

The most influential figure to make use of the term ideology (as it it now understood) is Karl Marx, who included in it morality, religion and metaphysics, and – through an inversion of Hegel's philosophy – suggested that 'Life is not determined by consciousness, but conciousness by life'.[22] Drawing on the Hegelian view that reality and consciousness meet in thought, Feuerbach (by a revision of Hegel's views on God) pointed to the falsity of religion arising from and with the alienation of true human potential (being at least partially embodied in some greater Being). Marx then pointed to the origin of this false conciousness in material existence, corresponding forms of conciousness only subsequently manifesting themselves in religious beliefs. From here it is a small step to seeing material existence as the origin of political beliefs, or ideology. Thus de Tracy's 'knowledge' becomes knowledge with a purpose, related to its origin, and directed to political choice and action. For Marx, ideology is a static representation of changing reality which belongs to the ruling (e.g., capitalist) class, and consequently all ideologies are destined for the dustbin of history (along with ruling classes). This does not mean that ideologies are not a significant feature of political life, but only that given instances of them will not survive (though, for Marx, all ideology must eventually subside in the face of universal understanding). It has been argued subsequently that, for example, all theory is 'for' something as much as 'about' something, but there is a distinction to be made between aspirations to objective knowledge (notwithstanding the attendant problems) on which to base decisions about action and a system of knowledge which is expressly purposive, calling for particular actions.[23] (In Chapter 4, an interestingly similar distinction will be made concerning purposive and practical political association). For Marx, the only objective view is that of dialectical materialism – everything else is ideological, or subjective. Yet here we are addressing the manner in which (claimed) knowledge takes on an applied manifestation in political life, and ideas become activated in practice. With respect to understanding the role of ideas in politics, it matters little whether they are ideologically contaminated, so long as they are recognised as such.

In this sense, particular ideologies may throw up political ideas and suggest political action – indeed, ideology may in some sense be necessary to political action but need not determine the outcome of political decisions, nor effect the grounds on which ideas and ideologies are judged, so long as ideologies are recognised and the normative character of political processes is understood. Furthermore, ideas and ideologies are maleable to a degree, may survive change, and may continue to be effective political forces. The potential tyranny of a single ideology masquerading as objective knowledge is always a danger, but no more or less a danger than political tyranny as conventionally understood (coercive in a practical sense), providing that the role of ideas in political life is not underestimated. Ideology remains a means of substantiating claims about the world and how to act in it.[24]

> Ideologies share two principal characteristics: an image of society and a political programme...An ideology, then, provides a coherent perspective through which to understand and act upon the social world.[25]

Again, the distinction between ideology and theory is not a clear one, since we may wish to push the meaning of ideology, as Mannheim does, from particular judgements about ideas, through collective world-views, and finally towards a sociology of knowledge – just where normative theory finds its footing.[26] Yet modern discussions of ideology tend to center on political interaction, rather than abstractions concerning the status of knowledge. The connection between these two concerns – thought and action – is important and significant in our discussion of normative inquiry (having a bearing on judgements about the relevance or applicability of normative theory) but should be distinguished from the relationship between theory and practice, for reasons discussed below.

The classical understanding of the term ideology is problematic, as Manning suggests:

> ... the use of the term ideology by de Tracy, Marx and Mannheim, in so far as it is intended to persuade us to accept or reject particular ideological commitments, could not serve as a corner-stone in any well-constructed account of what is to be *understood* by ideological commitment in political life. That to which we may choose to adhere cannot serve in an account of adherence.[27]

Equally, a modern sociological understanding of ideology (inspired by Marx and Mannheim) is also problematic for emphasising the explanation of sociological origins of ideas (in material class interests, for example), rather than addressing the effect of these ideas in politics, and for not taking adherence to an idea or belief at face value. If beliefs require explanation, in this sense, the prerequisite for explaining them is the presupposition 'that the beliefs involved have the substance and meaning which they appear to have'.[28] T. J. Robinson argues that the justification of beliefs cannot be connected with testable knowledge, and that epistemological questions about justification are inappropriate. The questions should, rather, be concerned with how beliefs arise, and how they are related to action. Robinson characterises ideology as the language of adherence. Relating ideological thinking to ideals, he suggests that 'an ideal, sincerely believed in, is an idea of how persons both *can* and *should* live', which indicates a political possibility and recommendation. These arguments are presented in the context of a general scepticism about political theory, on the grounds that the primary object of study (human nature) is without reference in political theory (it is a prior assumption), and that such incoherence makes theoretical investigations in politics impossible. Robinson further argues that the important relationship between theory and practice should not be construed as analogous to the relation of science to technology, as if theoretical knowledge of politics could provide reliable political tools.

> ... having rejected the implied relation of theory to practice found in political theory, the form of the discussion will be that primarily of ethics, and perhaps something analogous to aesthetics, and not an epistemological concern with explanation and prescriptive theory.[29]

Of course this makes the distinction between political theory and ideology clearer, but the significance of ideology for normative theory remains because of the shared 'form of the discussion' (ethical). Furthermore, the earlier discussion of the intimate relations between epistemology and ethics undermines the distinction with respect to normative theory, if not with respect to conventional approaches to political theory. What Robinson finds troublesome in political theory is the incoherence of referring to 'some logically independent knowledge'[30] in defining our identity, which can then be mirrored in political arrangements. In normative theory that identity is located in the normative structure of social and political life, and the problematic relationship between theory and practice (in politics) may be usefully understood as a relationship between a characterisation of the (collective) human condition – an 'identity of man' – and institutionalised associations, such that there are criteria for judging political action. This is just what political theory attempts to account for, according to Robinson. Indeed, such a view reflects the significance of ethics – which he claims is related to ideology rather than theory – and supports the claims made here for *normative* theory. However, this relationship between theory and practice is not static (as implied in a 'technological' understanding), but in a process of dialectic change in as much as experience of political practices provides reasons for theorising, and theory provides reasons for choosing a practice. The possibility of a knowledge of politics that is somehow 'independent' is undermined by a normative approach indicating a politics of knowledge itself. At the same time a purely ideological account of politics is undermined by the declaration of a purpose (other than understanding), and the recognition of other competing purposes.

Having examined the characteristics of ideology which make it a 'form of engagement', it will be useful to introduce at this stage a more comprehensive and subtle account of ideology which reflects the broader purpose of this discussion with respect to the book as a whole. It is an account offered by Sasson Sofer in the context of a more general critique of international relations theory as underestimating the importance of ideology:

> There are three main components to ideology that are the source of its centrality and importance for politics and international relations. First, ideology is an action-related system of ideas that provides a framework for individual and collective action and judgement. Second, ideology fills the dual function of shaping a conception of reality and interpreting reality. Third, ideology is normative in the sense that it refers or is oriented towards what is politically desireable, and at times describes the program or stages leading to ultimate goals.[31]

Thus, ideology is particularly important in understanding the motivations and dispositions of policy-makers, the nature of the political milieu in which policy choices are formed, and the conception of the world to which they are directed. Nevertheless, this does not provide, and does not aspire to, a comprehensive theory of international relations.

Ideology, as a form of engagement in politics, is itself unable to provide an objective account of political life – though it should be recognised that the very apprehension of political life may be conditioned by it. While we need reasons to act, which may in turn require individual commitments founded on ideology, these can never be disconnected from the political world functioning beyond the boundaries of any particular belief system (of course, this is particularly true of international relations). As with the existentialist position described earlier, where the need to take responsibility is emphasised, so here the need to engage is emphasised – but it is an engagement with a larger process and system, and one which is ultimately of collective (intersubjective) concern however much responsibility individuals may choose to take.

Normative theory, as a form of engagement in political understanding, provides a background for purposive engagement in political life; a means of coping with the rise and fall of particular practices, and a framework for comprehending the nature of the political processes by which these practices come to be known, accepted, and no doubt inevitably overthrown. Thus, in relation to ideology, normative theory may be viewed as a method of relating epistemology and the language of commitment – knowledge and action. As Jameson writes

[that] 'ideology' in the narrower sense is a mass of opinions, concepts, or pseudoconcepts, 'worldviews,' 'values,' and the like, is commonly accepted; that these vaguely specified conceptual entities also always have a range of narrative embodiments, that is, indeed, that they are all in one way or another buried narratives, may be less widely understood and may also open up a much wider range of exploration than the now well-worn conceptual dimension of the ideology concept. Yet it was not to replace the cognitive by the narrative that my proposal was made but rather to coordinate both by way of a definition that insisted on their necessary alternation: ideology is then whatever in its very structure is susceptible of taking on a cognitive and a narrative form alternately.[32]

CONCLUSIONS

What may be said in conclusion is that there is a distinction to be made between normative theory (essentially rational) and ideology (essentially committed), but it is a subtle one, conditioned by the elusiveness of the fundamental object of study, and by the political character of knowledge itself. Particular world-views – particular sets of ideas – cannot be discounted in the attempt to understand political life whether or not they are 'properly justified' theoretical views or 'mere' ideologies. Thus while ideology is necessarily of concern to normative theory, as a phenomena to be accounted for, normative theory is not to be confused with ideology any more than with moralism, if by these is meant some static and purposive orientation.

The potential source of confusion lies in the approach and methodology of normative theory which, being sensitive to the importance of norms in both politics and knowledge, and being disposed in some cases to prescriptive exposition, may be mistaken for an overt form of advocacy somehow disconnected from the real or objective world (the same sort of perjorative description that is often applied to ideology).[33]

On the contrary, a normative perspective assumes that norms are an intrinsic feature of both the 'real' world and our understanding of it, and consequently that ideas (as both an object of study and an aspect of subjective viewpoints) and ideology (as a basis of political action) are worthy of our attention. Ideas, and their corresponding values, lie within our understanding and are thus also part of the world; of what is to be understood.

The point here is that normative theory cannot provide an absolute point of reference to underpin commitment or belief, and its relation to ideas and ideology is at 'arm's length'. Normative theory can offer a sociology of ideas and an explanation of ideological commitment as these bear on the study of international relations, but the limits of normative theory are the limits of presuppositionless philosophy and anti-foundationalist, constructivist epistemology. Normative theory is not 'mere ideology', but a tool of systematic inquiry necessarily functioning within these limits.

NOTES

1.   Torbjörn L. Knutsen, *A History of International Relations Theory* (Manchester: Manchester University Press, 1992), p. 128.
2.   Laszek Kolakowski, *Metaphysical Horror* (Oxford: Basil Blackwell, 1988), p. 98.
3.   Hume's critique of natural law, and his observation that 'reason is and ought only to be the slave of the passions', are based on the distinction between the formal implications of deductive reasoning in parts of logic and mathematics, the more tenuous reasoning of empirical discovery, causal relationships and ascriptions of value. See the discussion of reason, fact and value in George H. Sabine (revised by Thomas L. Thorson), *A History of Political Theory*, 4th ed (Hinsdale, IL: Holt, Rinehart and Winston, The Dryden Press, 1973), p. 550ff.
4.   John Maclean, 'Political Theory, International Theory, and Problems of Ideology', *Millennium* (Vol. 10, No. 2, Summer 1981), p. 119.
5.   Reinhold Niebuhr, 'Ideology and the Scientific Method' in *Christian Realism and Political Problems* (New York: Scribner's, 1953), p. 93.
6.   Friedrich V. Kratochwil, *Rules, Norms, and Decisions: On the Conditions of Practical and Legal Reasoning in International Relations and Domestic Affairs.* (Cambridge: Cambridge University Press, 1989), p. 69.
7.   Torbjörn L. Knutsen, *A History of International Relations Theory* (Manchester: Manchester University Press, 1992), p. 133.
8.   See, for example, F. Parkinson, *The Philosophy of International Relations: A Study in the History of Thought* (London: Sage, 1977), William C. Olson and A. J. R. Groom, *International Relations Then and Now: Origins and Trends in Interpretation* (London: Harper Collins, 1991) and Knutsen, *A History of International Relations Theory*, ibid.
9.   See Fred Halliday, 'State and Society in International Relations: A Second Agenda', *Millennium* (Vol. 16, No. 2, Summer 1987), pp. 215–29, and on this last point, especially the passage about State Interests and Social Forces (p. 223).
10. See Harlan Cleveland, *The Global Commons: Policy for the Planet* (London: University Press of America/Aspen Institute, 1990).
11. See Susan Strange, *States and Markets* (London: Pinter, 1988), John Stopford and Susan Strange, *Rival States, Rival Firms: Competition for World Market Shares* (Cambridge: Cambridge University Press, 1991), and

Susan Strange, 'States, Firms and Diplomacy', *International Affairs* (Vol. 68, No. 1, January 1992) in which she addresses (p. 11) the conventions of international relations thus: 'The standard texts in the subject subscribe to the dominant "realist" school of thought, which holds that the central issue in international society is war between territorial states, and the prime problematic therefore is the maintenance of order in the relations between these states. This traditional view of international relations also holds that the object of study is the behaviour of states towards other states, and the outcome of such behaviour *for states*: whether they are better or worse off, less or more powerful or secure.'

12. Robert C. Solomon, *From Rationalism to Existentialism: The Existentialists and their Nineteenth-Century Backgrounds* (New York: Humanities Press, 1978), p. 187. I rely heavily on Solomon's clear exposition throughout my overly brief survey of modern philosophy because his chosen path fits well with my objectives here.
13. This notion is criticised by Adorno in *The Jargon of Authenticity*.
14. *The New York Review of Books*, March 26, 1970, pp. 22ff. Solomon, *op. cit.*, concludes his book with this quote, suggesting that it expresses the essence of existentialism.
15. See Jacques Derrida, *On Grammatology* (Baltimore: Johns Hopkins University Press, 1976) translated by Gyatri Spivak; Jean-François Lyotard, *The Post-Modern Condition* (Minneapolis: University of Minnesota Press, 1985); and Gyatri Chakravorty Spivak, *In Other Worlds: Essays in Cultural Politics* (New York and London: Methuen, 1987).
16. John R. Searle, 'How to Derive "Ought" from "Is" ', *Philosophical Review* (Vol. 73, 1964).
17. Richard N. Boyd, 'The Current Status of Scientific Realism' in J. Leplin (ed), *Scientific Realism* (Berkeley, CA: University of California Press, 1984), p. 52, quoted in Nicholas G. Onuf, *World of Our Making: Rules and Rule in Social Theory and International Relations* (Columbia, SC: University of South Carolina Press, 1989), p. 39. See, for examples of constructivism, Bas C. van Fraasen, *The Scientific Image* (Oxford: Oxford University Press, 1981) and Thomas S. Kuhn, *The Structure of Scientific Revolutions*, 2nd ed. (Chicago: University of Chicago Press, 1970).
18. V. G. Potter, *Charles S. Pierce On Norms and Ideals* (Worcester, MA: U.Mass Press, 1967), p. 8ff.
19. From a description of Hume's ethical critique in George H. Sabine (revised by Thomas L. Thorson), *A History of Political Theory*, 4th ed (Hinsdale, IL: Holt, Rinehart and Winston, The Dryden Press, 1973), p. 553.
20. Robert Eccleshall, Vincent Geoghagen, Richard Jay and Rick Wilford, *Political Ideologies: An Introduction* (London: Hutchinson, 1984), p. 24.
21. D. J. Manning (ed.), *The Form of Ideology* (London: George Allen and Unwin, 1980), p. 2.
22. Karl Marx and Freidrich Engels, *The German Ideology* (London: Lawrence and Wishart, 1965), p. 38.
23. Robert W. Cox states that 'Theory is always *for* someone and *for* some purpose', and goes on to say that 'There is, accordingly, no such thing as theory in itself, divorced from a standpoint in time and space. When any theory so represents itself, it is the more important to examine it as

ideology, and to lay bare its concealed perspective'. See Robert W. Cox, 'Social Forces, States and World Orders: Beyond International Relations Theory' (*Millennium*, Vol. 10, No. 2, Summer 1881, p. 128).

Note also development of Cox's point on the distinction between problem-solving theory (operating from within a perspective) and critical theory (which admits the possibility of changing the perspective), in Mark Hoffman, 'Critical Theory and the Interparadigm Debate' in Hugh C. Dyer and Leon Mangasarian (eds), *The Study of International Relations: The State of the Art* (London: Macmillan, 1989).

24. Plamenatz suggests, in reference to his discussion of class ideology, that social and political theories fall into two broad divisions: the first takes the human condition as a given starting point, the second sees man [sic] as changing or possibly 'progressing'. John Plamenatz, *Ideology* (London: Pall Mall, 1970), p. 111.

25. Eccleshall, et al., *Political Ideologies: An Introduction*, *op. cit.*, pp. 7 and 8.

26. Karl Mannheim's *Ideology and Utopia* (1929) sparked a great debate about methodology and epistemology in German social science. See V. Meja and N. Stehr, *Knowledge and Politics: The Sociology of Knowledge Dispute* (London: Routledge, 1990).

27. Manning, *The Form of Ideology*, *op. cit.*, p. 11.

28. L. G. Graham, 'Ideology and Sociological Understanding' in *ibid.*, p. 21.

29. T. J. Robinson, 'Ideology and Theoretical Inquiry' in *ibid.*, p. 69.

30. *Ibid.*, p. 63.

31. Sasson Sofer, 'International Relations and the Invisibility of Ideology', *Millennium: Journal of International Studies* (Vol. 16, No. 3, Winter 1987), p. 491.

32. Frederick Jameson, from the Foreword to Algirdas Julien Greimas, *On Meaning: Selected Writings in Semiology* (London: Francis Pinter, 1987), pp. xiii–xiv.

33. See *inter alia*, Sasson Sofer, 'International Relations and the Invisibility of Ideology', *op. cit.*

5 Moral Language and Normative Concepts: From Ethics to Epistemology via Discourse

With the limits of normative theory in view, it is nevertheless possible to show that international politics are rife with normative features that can be systematically revealed and examined by the application of normative theory. These normative features appear at all levels of international life, but most importantly, they can be identified in the cornerstones of social interaction and systematic knowledge, and in the very means of communication about both.

This chapter is concerned to locate the function or role of language in international politics, and subsequently to show the influence of moral language on the development of normative concepts. The importance of language in political life provides grounds for arguing that these normative concepts are an intrinsic part of our understanding of politics, such that what is often judged to be purely ethical – and consequently uninteresting to the study of the 'real world' of international politics – should be understood in relation to epistemologies that provide the foundation of our claims to political knowledge. As Kratochwil says,

> we have to understand how the social world is intrinsically linked to language and how language, because it is a rule-governed activity, can provide us with a point of departure for our inquiry into the functions of norms in social life.[1]

Among the functions of norms is to provide a stable point of reference for meaning in language, for principals in ethics, and for fundamental assumptions in epistemology.

There are a few preliminary considerations which require attention. First, in the following discussion of moral language and normative concepts a distinction is maintained between moral language proper, as it will be discussed here, and the misappropriation of moral language in ordinary discourse and politics.[2] Similarly, a distinction is maintained as between normative concepts proper and the misapplication (or invention) of normative concepts. Of course, in both cases the latter exception is dependent on the former rule, in the way that the success of a lie depends on the convention of truth-telling. The distinction that is made here is consequently a difficult one to maintain, since the 'authentic' and 'inauthentic' versions of discourse share commonly recognised features, and yet the distinction is important since we are concerned to discover which features are significant for theoretical purposes as opposed to those which are merely convenient for practical purposes.

Secondly, we will wish to distinguish between language and discourse, especially when trying to understand the role of language in politics. This distinction is important to the overall argument, and is the subject of a separate section below, since the normative consequences of language are to be understood in terms of social or political meaning. A related difficulty arises in distinguishing moral language from language in general, since there may be nothing to distinguish the two in terms of linguistic performance, although there will be characteristics which indicate moral significance.[3] The distinction concerning authenticity is not dissimilar to that made between ideas and ideology, for example, in the sense that the latter is a practical and purposive application of the former (this dependency relationship may be reciprocal, but for clarity's sake this possibility will be left alone for the present). While both 'authentic' and 'inauthentic' versions of discourse are aspects of experience, understanding the meaning of 'inauthenticity' requires an understanding of what it is to be 'authentic'.[4] Trying to make the distinction may in itself amount to a simplistic assumption (that it is possible to have stable authenticity), but we would be hard pressed to do without it, as we would to do without morality (see Hare's remark below), and so the following discussion will engage with issues that follow from observations about epistemological foundations in the preceding chapter.[5]

THE COMMUNICATION OF IDEAS

The play of ideas in the normative activity of establishing epistemological foundations entails further problems of judgement. These latter are not simply problems concerning the selection of criteria for assessment, but more fundamental problems concerning the description and communication of such criteria. This chapter will investigate the nature of these descriptive and communicative activities, the logical requirements of form and content which attend them, and the necessity of normative structures which underlie them. That is to say, ethical and epistemological structures exhibit a similarity of form, and appropriate content for each is conditioned by the structural form in the way that grammar influences the content of linguistic communication. Because of the ubiquity of language on the surface of international relations (in both theory and practice), language provides an avenue of approach to the deeper issues of ethics and epistemology. Furthermore, since form and content are in this respect related to a world-view, the outcome of this discussion will be a perspective on the role that normative concepts play in the formation of world-views and the theories which support them.

At one level, morality requires a particular use of language in order to be effective. At another level, normative activity in general – including language itself – requires the communication of underlying agreement on principles: language requires 'morality', or some such normative structure. As R. M. Hare has said,

> If we tried to do [without morality], we should have to reinvent it under another name. The same holds for moral language; for it would be hard to practice morality without some way of expressing moral opinions'.[6]

Anthony Holiday claims that

> just as the existence of certain minimal natural regularities is an external prerequisite for the possibility of human language, so the existence of certain moral regularities is an internal precondition for the realisation of that possibility.

He continues his argument for normative necessity, pointing to an

> overlap between moral, semantic, and historical necessity, enabling us to identify the 'ought' of morality with the 'is' of the publicly accessible realms of linguistic coherence and historical change.[7]

and draws support for his case from the works of Wittgenstein and Marx. Once again the 'is–ought' debate which is so central to moral philosophy comes to bear, and it is worth examining some aspects of the debate once again (but without entering into the debate proper) in order to show the significance of moral language, and of language in general, in theories of international relations. These theories inevitably take up, and produce, normative concepts.

It is worth considering what it is about language that makes it such an important feature of political life, even if we are already content that it has importance in human affairs generally (a common sense appreciation of the ubiquity of language). An immediate response is this: if language is important in human affairs, it must be important in politics, since politics is the medium by which order of some sort is brought to human affairs. However, this observation does not bring much clarity to the phenomenon of language beyond what most people already understand from everyday experience. Indeed, it is just because language is so commonplace that it is necessary to consider its uses and influence.

LANGUAGE AND DISCOURSE

Here we would do well to once again bear in mind the distinction, such as it is, between language and discourse. For the moment we may adopt the view that language has formal structures while discourse has a social content (though of course, this begs some questions about language). It is clarifying to quote Michael Shapiro on this point:

> Textualist or poststructuralist modes of analysis emphasize 'discourse' rather than language because the concept of discourse implies a concern with the meaning and value producing practices in language rather than simply the relationship between utterances and their referents.[8]

Here we wish to pursue comparisons with ethics and epistemology respecting governing principles, so it is perhaps best to remain (notionally) within the realm of language for the present. Subsequent developments in the discussion which indicate normative features in language will, of course, bring us closer to the perspective of discourse analysis. If one peals back the layers of political life, revealing the levels of normative interaction, one will see that discourse, and then language, are among them.

At the most fundamental level, language may reflect those yet to be discovered principles of mind which dictate the logic and categories of human perceptions and experience. A less reductionist, and more readily comprehended conception of language would be: that medium of communication (not yet considering content) into which the young are indoctrinated and in which the mature participate. Because there are variations in the use of language – and, indeed, different languages – it is clear that while language is a universal phenomenon, the *use* of language is a participatory activity intimately related to particular societies and culture. This latter feature of language need not effect the general application of the present argument, however, any more than the investigation of normative structures is hindered by variations in these.[9] It is the universal features of language, of any human language, which interest us here. This is obviously true in respect of our interest in discovering generalisations about language, but also true about the normative features of political life that may be revealed by an examination of the use of language in politics – what grammar is to language, tradition is to international relations (both in practice *and* in theory). For example, Noam Chomsky distinguishes between 'functional explanations' and 'formal explanations' (concerning grammar) of the properties of language, suggesting that the latter offer principles which being

> not essential or even natural properties of any imaginable language... provide a revealing mirror of mind (if correct). Such principles, we may speculate, are *a priori* for the species – they provide the framework for the interpretation of experience and the construction of specific forms of knowledge on the basis of experience.[10]

Thus Chomsky is led to a humanistic conception of man by the observation that even such simple features of human activity as the ordinary use of language seem to be founded on 'unknowable' principles – principles of mind, in this case – not unlike the unobtainable absolutes discussed in the previous chapter. Chomsky carries his argument so far as to say that:

> The principles of mind provide the scope and limits of human creativity. Without such principles, scientific understanding and creative acts would not be possible.[11]

The point of making a comparison between the underlying principles of language and the absolutes of morality and knowledge for this discussion is that the close relationship between ethics and epistemology is necessarily mediated by language, since our conceptions of morality and knowledge are not aspects of sensory experience that might be represented by primitive responses or signals but are products of thought which require the use of word-concepts. All three – morality, knowledge and language – are characterised by a tension between the functional demands of the public domain (where changing normative features are most obvious) and the intrinsic formal requirement of an ultimate referent (where determinism and dogma lie in wait).

The principles to which Chomsky refers are interesting to a discussion of normative theory particularly since normative activities are 'rule-governed' (as discussed in Chapter 1), and principles are rules *par excellence*. To apply the game analogy, principles – like rules – both describe and prescribe (saying what the game is, and saying how to play it). Setting aside the problem of discovering fundamental principles and focusing instead on the common-or-garden efforts of individuals and societies to approximate such principles in their life activity, it becomes clearer that description approaches prescription as the certainty of ultimate foundations recedes and apprehensions of reality become a matter of 'debate', however subtle.

In developing a new conception of human psychology in his book *The Society of Mind*, Marvin Minsky provides a number of clearly stated insights in both knowledge and language:

> Naturally, we'd prefer to think of knowledge as more positive and less provisional or relative. But little good has ever come from trying to link what we believe to our ideals about absolute truths. We always yearn for certainty, but the only thing beyond dispute is that there's always room for doubt. And doubt is not an enemy that sets constraints on what we know; the real danger to mental growth is perfect faith, doubt's antidote.[12]

Minsky's thesis is that the human mind consists of many small processes ('agents') which, interacting according to the scheme he calls 'society of mind', lead to true intelligence. The import of this thesis is that 'the power of intelligence stems from our vast diversity, not from any single, perfect principle'.[13] Resourcefulness and versatility arise from interactions in the 'society of mind' processes.

With respect to language, and in contrast to Chomsky, Minsky suggests that we can scarcely even speculate about underlying processes and early language-learning steps since we know so little and have no coherent theories. While both authors alude to some undiscernible prior entity (whether 'principles' or 'underlying processes') they differ on the significance of grammar (as a phenomenon), Chomsky suggesting that the formal explanations of grammar reflect principles of mind, and Minsky arguing that there are so many similar language-like processes in the mind that the acquisition of speech is not surprising. Of course, Minsky's argument may fall into Chomsky's 'functional explanation' category when he says, for example, that 'in the course of learning language we accumulate various processes and tactics that enable us to partially reproduce our own mental operations in other speakers'.[14]

What is not surprising is that neither author is prepared to push his argument as far as identifying *a priori* principles, but rather they are content to suggest the presence of such principles for theoretical purposes – perhaps as far as anyone would wish to go. To fall short of such principles, however, is to remain in the realm of normative discourse, and it is here that language describes and prescribes, caught up in the very processes which it mediates.

ETHICS AND EPISTEMOLOGY

In this chapter we are interested to see how criteria of judgement are apprehended, and then communicated in such a way that a relatively rigid normative structure is built up (in the manner of morality) such that reference to it could carry some of the weight of principles – even if going so far as to establish or discover absolute principles seems impractical. As Minsky says, '...in mental realms, we make up countless artificial schemes to force things to seem orderly'.[15] It is not surprising that when such schemes are widely accepted, forming the basis both of our social world and our perceptions of the physical world, that their artificial and contingent origins should be forgotten:

> When growing up in such a world, it all seems right and natural and only scholars and historians recall the mass of precedents and failed experiments it took to make it all work so well.[16]

Minsky points to the great complexity of 'natural' worlds, which is only overcome where we impose rules of our own making. This is certainly as true of the social world as it is of the physical world, and our theories of both are impositions of self-made rules, however well they may represent 'reality'.[17] As such, theories not only describe the world, but in doing so prescribe how the world should be understood, and ultimately, how we should act in order to correspond best with the accepted truths about our world – that is, how to behave rationally.

We are concerned to make choices on rational grounds, in order to be successful in achieving the ends to which our choices are directed; to make the means of their achievement accord with the rationally structured world in which they are to be achieved. In ethical matters we are concerned to make the 'right choices', on rational grounds of course, but not only on rational grounds (such as pure self-interest, for example) since the distinguishing feature of moral choice is some reference to moral grounds, or principles. Thus G. J. Warnock argues that the analysis of linguistic performances, even those with moral content, is an exercise in the philosophy of language and 'has nothing in particular to contribute to moral philosophy'.[18] The concern of moral philosophy is to enquire about what content makes a linguistic act (or any other act) a distinctly moral act rather than, say, a practical act. This is the sense in which the distinction at the beginning of the chapter is made between moral language proper and moral language which is significant only for its expedient practical effect. The point made more immediately above concerning the common feature of reference to principles (in morality, knowledge and language) is that language and knowledge are no different from morality in their need for stable references, nor are their points of reference any more secure. Furthermore, it is only by removing the more contentious aspects of knowledge and language to the realm of morality that we are able to maintain the illusion of the fundamental soundness of the former pair in contrast to the essentially elusive grounding of the latter. It is this relegation of overtly normative aspects of human (social) experience to the category of morality that leads to the marginalisation and relative devaluation of morality, which now qualifies as a case of Foucault's 'subjugated knowledge',[19] and permits an evasion of value considerations in pursuing otherwise practical affairs, as though values were never a part of practical life, or of systematic knowledge:

> The loss of memory is a transcendental condition for science. All objectification is a forgetting.[20]

Here Adorno is concerned that the great progress brought by the Enlightenment is at risk when we lose sight of our aspirations and fail to live up to the values which we struggled to establish.

It is the assumption of knowledge – that is, that we can have certain knowledge – which leads us away from value considerations, when in fact it is the adoption of values that provided the foundation for knowledge (such as it is) in the first place. Hence a degree of scepticism brings an awareness of the value content of epistemological arguments. The problems of first principles are similar in both ethics and epistemology; so much so, indeed, that it has beeen argued that epistemology amounts to a special branch of ethics.[21] At the very least, there are close parallels in the kinds of justifications sought for both types of principles – these not being self-justifying. For example, three main views on the meaning and verification of principles apply equally well to both ethics and epistemology:

Naturalism holds that ethical and epistemic terms are meaningful, that statements employing them are true or false, and that these terms can be explained by empirical and logical concepts.

Non-naturalism holds that while the terms are meaningful, and the statements true or false, they can not be confirmed empirically. Hence knowledge of them is *synthetic a priori* knowledge.

Non-cognitivism holds that such terms and statements are not true or false, and can not be empirically confirmed. They nevertheless have a function in language and perhaps an indefinite descriptive meaning.

Of course, confusion about the 'truth' of ethical and epistemological statements does not prevent them from being widely employed in social activities (including science, and naturally international relations as well). The question remains, however, of how they are and should be employed – for what purpose, and to what end. The assumption, or rather illusion of certain knowledge simply buries these issues. Certainly, social existence requires an answer to questions about truth, whether in ethics or epistemology, and not asking a question is no substitute for answering it, but where a question is unanswerable there is great temptation to do just this. Here lies the heart of the matter: where the question is unanswerable, or unaskable, an answer must be assumed. The issue is how deeply the assumption is (or should be) buried in culture, and what the consequences are of exhuming it for reexamination or replacement.

In as much as the principles of ethics and epistemology are maintained and transmitted in language, language may be seen as the soil in which these principles are buried. Thus Umberto Eco writes that

> we must not be amazed then to hear people say that the given language is power because it compels me to use already formulated stereotypes, including words themselves, and that it is structured so fatally that, slaves inside it, we cannot free ourselves outside it, because outside the given language there is nothing.[22]

To the question of how the constraints of language can be escaped, Eco answers: 'By cheating. You can cheat with the given language. This dishonest and healthy and liberating trick is called literature'.[23] Indeed it may be only through literature, and other cultural activity, that intellectual liberation can be achieved – that is, from within culture, but at its margin. But if literature allows an 'internal' escape from the problems of language, how are their close relatives, the problems of ethics and epistemology, to be resolved in thinking about international relations where the questions are compounded by a multiplicity of cultures? Even when it is liberating to recognise what Foucault calls a 'regime of truth', which may be challenged, the sense of liberation is tempered by the prospect of entering into another such regime;

> ...the mechanisms and instances which enable one to distinguish true and false statement, the means by which each is sanctioned; the techniques and procedures accorded value in the acquisition of truth.[24]

If we view theory as the language of scholarship, it is easy to see how a given theory is power, and that in as much as theory is necessary (as language is), we can only choose which theory will exercise its authority over our thought. Being unable to escape theory in general we can choose only to exchange one set of constraints for another in adopting a particular theory. The questions about truth in ethics and epistemology serve to alert us to the nature of these constraints, which allow considered and self-conscious selection, but carry with them always the risk of undermining our faith in theory generally. Here it must be noted that the illusion of certain knowledge has another aspect: the illusion that certain knowledge is necessary for the general possibility of knowledge. The greatest liberation from the constraints of a given theory of morality or knowledge is the recognition that in all that has gone before certainty was not requisite, and that the illusion of it was only a device to secure what can not be secured.

With the constraints of this illusion removed, the foundations of theory remain indefinite but may still be described systematically. Such systematic description can be achieved by employing a coherence theory of truth, by which experiences and judgements are true to the extent that they cohere with one another, forming a coherent system. This theory of truth was preferred by Post-Kantian idealists (Fichte, Hegel, Bradley) but it need not be entirely unsympathetic to the motives of a correspondence theory of truth as accepted by the British empiricists and early Vienna Circle positivists (Schlick, et al.), since coherence itself may be conditioned by what Heidegger refers to as the facticity of being-in-the-world.[25] That is to say, it would be difficult to accept a coherence theory of truth where there is contradiction of facts, but then correspondence to fact depends on what the facts are taken to be, and this may already be determined by coherence. As Foucault says, 'the world is not the accomplice of our knowledge'.[26] With this view in mind, we may proceed to examine the means of justifying a theory without capitulating to the power of a theory once justified.

When the close relationship between ethics and epistemology is understood in terms of comprehensive normative theory, the necessity of incorporating (rather than excluding) value considerations can be seen as blurring the demarcation between science and speculative metaphysics intended by Popper's theory of falsifiability. This latter theory holds that since scientific generalisations are not, by their nature, verifiable, falsifiability is the only means of constraining the conditions of truth. Since metaphysical propositions are neither verifiable nor falsifiable (though still significant as the origin of what is today science), they may be imposed, while propositions of science proper win ground 'through argument, demonstration and discussion'.[27] The issue here is whether argument and discussion leading to agreement on a scientific proposition is any less of an imposition than positing a metaphysical proposition. That is, having shed the constraining illusion of certain knowledge we are still vulnerable to the imposition of metaphysical knowledge by convention; by normative agreement on justification. Yet the weight of normative convention concerning appropriate knowledge seems to be different only in degree from the more restrictive but nevertheless conventionalist conditions of normal science.

Understanding the general possibility of knowledge from a normative perspective shows that value considerations are not to be relegated solely to ethics, but belong at the heart of epistemology too. (The debate concerning value-free social science seems to have gone quiet in the postbehavioural period).[28] In attempting to establish knowledge of international relations, reference to 'objective data' is to be viewed with suspicion, especially where these data are treated as objects independent of a political context. Greimas points to the nature of the Epistemic Act (the transformation from unknowing to knowing) as involving Interpretation (an interpretive 'doing') which in turn requires Recognition (of truth) and Identification, using the knowing/believing universe of the judging subject, and not some referential 'reality'.[29] The significance of such an approach to political understanding is the necessity of considering the normative character of human relations, rather than seeking references in an objective world in which humans (and their politics) are mere epiphenomena. In particular, language is the medium through which human relations can be seen as qualifiers of empirical reality:

> Georges Dumzil helpfully brought to our attention the fact that formerly the Latin *credere* at the same time covered the now separated domains of signification of belief and confidence. This means that an established and maintained trust between persons founded a trust in their speech about things and, finally, in things themselves.
>
> This unseemly turning back to ancient sources teaches us at least one thing: If we want to found our certitudes, then before seeking an adequation between words and things we should examine open communication between human beings.[30]

NORMS IN REALISM

Those theories of international relations which attempt to emulate the natural sciences by adopting the epistemology of 'realism', empiricism and positivism (naive versions of the latter thought to be long dead in philosophy) in the hope of more secure claims to truth are simply adopting the well-recognised epistemological troubles of these positions while at the same time moving away from the essentially political human experience they intend to address. The product of such theory is not only unconvincing on its own grounds – though perhaps no worse than other theory in this respect – but also fails to acknowledge, and often sytematically excludes the value considerations that attend the normative process by which we are convinced at all. That such realist theories are sometimes successful in predicting the behaviour of decision-makers who share the theory is simply an example of the normative character of their epistemology, but does nothing to suggest that the theory has any self-consciousness of this characteristic, nor that it does anything to address the fundamental issues of global politics beyond the superficial 'management' of problems; problems, it should be said, that are often of its own making. As Smith says of realist theory,

> International institutions, networks and norms are considered significant theoretically only to the extent that they structure or affect the competition for power, for the prevailing relations of power between sovereign nation-states ultimately determine the character of these institutions and norms.[31]

To the extent that this latter kind of theory enters into our language, and into theoretical debates, it tends to subvert a self-consciousness of normative activity in ethics (and not just morality), epistemology and indeed language itself such that value considerations are not addressed. This expression of the desire for security in knowledge is understandable in terms of human frailty, but the illusion is maintained at some cost, and perhaps at our peril; in a world of nuclear weapons we cannot afford to be self-assured. We might still wish to be secure in knowledge, having abandoned conventional approaches to international relations, but through a more enlightened view of knowledge and politics which is implicitly self-critical. As Kratochwil argues,

> our conventional understanding of social action and of the norms governing them is defective because of a fundamental misunderstanding of the function of language in social interaction, and because of a positivist epistemology that treats norms as "causes".[32]

Indeed, it is the search for empirically measured causes that leads the study of international relations away from the study of *politics*, of human relations, as mediated by language in discourse.

LAW AND MORALITY

In practical terms, the linguistic transmission of normative concepts and the establishment of a political discourse is reflected in moral and legal codes. The ethical foundations arising from moral language and the episte-mological foundations arising from theoretical concepts, even as they are contested, are given stability through institutionalisation. It follows from the existence of discourses that institutions are subject to constant (re)evaluation.[33]

Taking into account the tension between ethics and politics in the realist understanding of world politics, it is instructive at this point to consider Michael Oakeshott's careful distinctions concerning the character of 'The Rule of Law'.[34] By clarifying the relationship between law and morality, it may become clearer how morality impinges on foreign policy (and ethics on politics) and what the realist effort to maintain the distinction between them in international relations amounts to in the end.

The key distinction Oakeshott makes is between the common purpose of an 'enterprise association', and a mode of association which is not instrumental to any goal beyond association itself. This latter mode of association is abstract, and characterised by the acknowledgement of mutal obligations among *personae* who may have no relationship (let alone a shared purpose) other than their recognition of these obligations, which is without regard to future contingent circumstances in which these obligations might arise, or the particular consequences of observing them – the rule of law.

For Oakeshott, the rule of law is compromised as soon as the mechan-isms that maintain the association (legislation, adjudication, administra-tion) are endowed with purpose (policy, interpretation, enforcement). Oakshott is not unaware of the (at least) minimal qualifications necessary to ensure that association is maintained under adverse circumstances (for example, the imposition of subventions to finance the necessary foreign policy – largely defence), but he insists that these do not bring the associ-ation closer to the desired condition but rather away from the restricted and negatively defined (hence, liberal) terms of the association, which are without any imbued purpose (not even defence, since this involves exter-nalities). However, because it is necessary to qualify the rule of law in practice, the full range of political questions concerning justification and purpose creep in right away. Here, his discussion of moral association is informative.

Moral association is not the same mode as association in terms of the rule of law, but it is significant (given the necessity of qualifications to the rule of law) that moral association suggests qualities which underlie the success of association. In particular, Oakeshott notes that both *lex* (law as enacted), and *jus* (the rather indeterminate conditions of justice) must be involved in an association in terms of the rule of law. This is because, as in our broader discussion of foundations, there will always be questions of the authenticity and 'rightness' of rules. Authenticity can be determined by reference to the 'rule book' (*lex*), and 'rightness' by reference to conceptions of justice (*jus*) – which refers back to the terms of moral association.

Oakeshott argues that considerations of justice are a particular kind of moral consideration, which requires a discerning moral sensibility which is able to distinguish between questions of 'virtue', 'good conduct', and justice (only the latter determining what should be enacted as law). What he does not mention in the possibility that a conception of justice may well extend to broader considerations, and this is precisely the point of arguments for economic rights and distributive justice, which go beyond the limiting concern with political rights that is associated with orthodox liberalism. Thus the content of law becomes an issue, in addition to its form.

In moral association, where the rules of association and notions of justice are inevitably ambiguous, these fundamental questions can only be settled by reference to (respectable) informed, considered public opinion – which must take some norm as a guiding principle. For Oakeshott, this is not the nature of an association under the strict terms of the rule of law (the only purpose of which is inherent in the recognition of law), but it is nevertheless the necessary condition in which the rule of law arises, and it is the only means of testing 'rightness' (if not authenticity). Oakeshott himself goes to some lengths to show how seldom anything approaching a pure version of the rule of law is realised, which raises the question of whether it is possible. In short, a changing and evolving normative structure underlies even the most rigorous, 'value-free' construction of political association.

All political association therefore contains elements of a purposive enterprise association, even if the purpose is simply the maintenance of the 'technical realities' of that association. Political life is by definition without absolute foundations (or it ceases to be political), yet requires some foundation, and such foundations as may be established are necessarily contingent human norms. We would thus do well to understand them, in both character and content.

CONCLUSIONS

In the context of the relationship between ethics and epistemology, the language of moral and legal association reflects realist assumptions about the norms governing association, seen as 'practical' structural causes or foundations. When the element of purpose in any structure is acknowledged norms can be seen as embodying the politics of association, and reflecting the ethical discourse which underwrites the epistemology of association. When ideas are transferred from epistemologies of domestic society to the international or global realm (as they often are, in spite of the problems of making such analogies) it is essential that the ethical basis of association is broadened to account for social differences, and that the terms of interaction are not assumed to rest on an absolute foundation. A normative approach to international relations allows the play of values to be revealed such that norms are understood as points of reference in the political world – a world that is always changing. Clearly norms have influence, but they are not to be understood as 'causes', or 'ends', but as qualifiers which provide meaning in political life. The study of international relations cannot be complete without taking into account this normative character of international relations, or global politics, and the place that values hold for individuals or nations when they seek to define and pursue their interests through political action.

NOTES

1.   Friedrich V. Kratochwil, *Rules, Norms, and Decisions: On the conditions of practical and legal reasoning in international and domestic affairs* (Cambridge: Cambridge University Press, 1989), p. 6.

2.   This can be understood in terms of right and wrong rhetoric, as elucidated in Plato's dialogues on the subject: the *Gorgias* and the *Phaedrus*.

3.   See G. J. Warnock's argument in 'Ethics and Language', in his *Morality and Language* (Totowa, NJ: Barnes and Noble, 1983), pp. 147–58.

4.   We may be content to accept Heidegger's or Adorno's definition of 'authentic', if a definition is required at this stage in the discussion. Oakeshott also offers a definition in the section on law and morality below.

5.   See, for example, Marvin Minsky's discussion of 'genuine' thoughts, and beliefs (the latter being conditional). He suggests that making such distinctions is vital to our moral and legal schemes, but they seem less absolute when beliefs reveal ambiguities under closer inspection. Marvin Minsky, *The Society of Mind* (London: Picador, 1988), p. 302.

6.   R. M. Hare, 'Why Moral Language?' in Philip Pettit, Richard Sylvan and Jean Norman (eds), *Metaphysics and Morality* (Oxford: Basil Blackwell, 1987), p. 86.

7.   Anthony Holiday, *Moral Powers: Normative Nececessity in Language and History* (London: Routledge, 1988), pp. xi, xii.

8. Michael J. Shapiro, 'Introduction II (or I): Textualizing Global Politics', unpublished paper presented to the IGCC/ADIU Summer School, University of Sussex, 1988, p. 6. This paper is reproduced as Chapter 2 in James Der Derian and Michael J. Shapiro (eds), *International/Intertextual Relations: Post-modern Readings in World Politics* (Lexington, MA: Lexington Books, 1989), where the quote appears on p. 14. See also Shapiro's *Language and Politics* (New York: New York University Press, 1984) and *Reading the Post-modern Polity: Political Theory as Textual Practice* (Minneapolis: University of Minnesota Press, 1992). The post-structuralist or post-modernist context is provided by works such as Jacques Derrida, *Speech and Phenomena* (Evanston, IL: Northwestern University Press, 1973), Michel Foucault, *The Archeology of Knowledge* (New York: Pantheon, 1972) and Jean-François Lyotard, *The Postmodern Condition: A Report on Knowledge* (Minneapolis: University of Minnesota Press, 1984).

9. Of necessity this work is in the English language, hence a part of Anglo-Saxon, Judeo-Christian, Western culture. In acknowledging the inevitable and often hidden constraints this must impose, it is hoped that extrapolation of the arguments beyond this culture will not be confounded by cultural diversity.

10. Noam Chomsky, *Problems of Knowledge and Freedom* (London: Fontana/Collins, 1972), pp. 41–2.

11. *Ibid.*, p. 45.

12. Minsky, *op. cit.*, p. 301.

13. *Ibid.*, p. 308. It is tempting to turn this notion on its head, to suggest by analogy that there is a 'mind of society' (a collective world-view, or 'world of thought' as Minsky says) and to raise the possibility of changing society in much the same way that we change our mind – not all at once, but on reflection – as is our prerogative.

14. *Ibid.*, p. 271.

15. *Ibid.*, p. 65.

16. *Ibid.*

17. For an enlightening discussion of reality, and how this troublesome notion is made and remade in the very communication of it, see the delightful book by Paul Watzlawick, *How Real is Real? Communication, Disinformation, Confusion* (New York: Random House, 1976) or Edgar Roskis' translation of it, *La réalité de la réalité: Confusion, désinformation, communication* (Paris: Editions de Seuil, 1978). Watzlawick prefers metaphoric and illustrative (and entertaining) examples, but for those who prefer the use of examples as proof he suggests Peter L. Berger and Thomas Luckman, *The Social Construction of Reality* (New York: Doubleday, 1966). For a relevant work on international relations, see Nicholas G. Onuf, *World of Our Making: Rules and Rule in Social Theory and International Relations* (Columbia, SC: University of South Carolina Press, 1989) which views language as social performance.

18. Warnock, *op. cit.*, p. 157.

19. Michel Foucault, *Power/Knowledge: Selected Interviews and Other Writings* (New York: Pantheon, 1980), p. 82.

20. Theodor Adorno, 'Le prix du Progrès' in *The Dialectic of Enlightenment* (London: Verso, 1979), p. 230.

21. For example, by R. M. Chisholm, taking a noncognitivist position. See Richard Brandt, 'Epistemology and Ethics, Parallel Between' in the *Encyclopedia of Philosophy*.

22. Umberto Eco, 'Language, Power, Force' in *Travels in Hyperreality: Essays* (London: Picador, 1987), p. 241. In this essay Eco is addressing the views of Barthes and, indirectly, Foucault.

23. *Ibid.*

24. Foucault, *Power/Knowledge*, *op. cit.*, p. 131.

25. Heidegger also employs a coherence theory of truth: facticity requires being 'tuned in' to the world around one, and is the counterpart of angst or dread – the fear of nothingness. See Robert C. Solomon, *From Rationalism to Existentialism: The Existentialists and their Nineteenth-Century Backgrounds* (New York: Humanities Press, 1978), pp. 213–4 and p. 236.

26. Michel Foucault, 'The Order of Discourse', in Michael J. Shapiro (ed), *Language and Politics*, *op. cit.*, p. 127.

27. D. E. Weston, *Realism, Language and Social Theories: Studies in the Relation of the Epistemology of Science and Politics* (PhD thesis, University of Lund, Sweden, 1978), pp. 60–1.

28. For useful discussions of this issue see Sheldon Wolin, 'Political Theory as a Vocation', *American Political Science Review* (December, 1966), Sheldon Wolin, 'Paradigms and Political Theories' in Preston King and B. C. Parekh (ed), *Politics and Experience* (Cambridge: Cambridge University Press, 1968), and the broader surveys of Richard J. Bernstein, *The Restructuring of Social and Political Theory* (Oxford: Basil Blackwell, 1976), who in sympathy with Sheldon Wolin says, 'the very reality with which we are concerned in the human sciences is itself value-constituted, not an indifferent value-neutral brute reality.' (p. 104), and David M. Ricci, *The Tragedy of Political Science: Politics, Scholarship, and Democracy* (New Haven, CT: Yale University Press, 1984).

29. Algirdas Julien Greimas, *On Meaning: Selected Writings in Semiology* (London: Francis Pinter, 1987), p. 168.

30. *Ibid.*, p. 166.

31. Michael Joseph Smith, *Realist Thought from Weber to Kissinger* (Baton Rouge and London: Louisiana State University Press, 1986), p. 221. In the quoted passage Smith is commenting on the realist assumption about 'ubiquitous and inescapable' power relations, and he subsequently discusses the problems of treating power as both end and means. The assumption about power are further complicated if one applies the radical view of Steven Lukes, particularly when he says ' any view of power rests on some normatively specific conception of interests'. Steven Lukes, *Power: A Radical View* (London: Macmillan, 1974), p. 35. Lukes, in turn, makes good use of W. B. Gallie's seminal 'Essentially Contested Concepts', *Proceedings of the Aristotelian Society* (Vol. 56, 1955–6), pp. 167–98.

32. Kratochwil, *Rules, Norms, and Decisions*, *op. cit.*, p. 5.

33. See Cornelia Navari, 'Introduction: The State as a Contested Concept in International Relations' in Cornelia Navari (ed), *The Condition of States* (Milton Keynes: Open University Press, 1992), p. 16.

34. Michael Oakeshott, 'The Rule of Law' in *On History and Other Essays* (Oxford: Basil Blackwell, 1983), pp. 119–64.

6 Values and Interests: The Formation of a World View

Previous chapters have addressed the philosophical foundations of normative theory, its role in the play of ideas and its limitations in light of ideological belief, and the fundamental normative structures in language, morality and knowledge which underpin the practical activity of global politics. Here, the role of normative theory will be shown to extend from addressing philosophical foundations to addressing the conditions of political action at the global level. In particular, values and interests will be shown to be instrumental in the formation of world views.

The absence of secure and certain knowledge generally, and of undisputed theoretical foundations for global political life in particular, leaves the possibility of a 'correct' world view an open question. Naturally, when political action is necessary the question can not be left open, and this chapter will examine the various ways in which it is or may be closed.

One way to close the question, of course, is ideological commitment, but the distinction has already been made (in Chapter 4) between ideology, with its twin characteristics of 'an image of society and a political programme',[1] and the role of ideas. In its descriptive mode, a normative theoretical account of world views addresses the formation of an image of society – in this case, of international society or the global political condition – and is not concerned with political programmes as such. In its prescriptive mode, normative theory may nevertheless properly provide guidance with respect to the formation of political programmes, since it is not possible to entirely separate political choice from the analysis of political life: in separating the wheat from the chaff it must be acknowledged that they first grew as parts of a whole – a whole, in this case, which defies the 'is–ought' distinction such that what 'is' (as discovered by analysis) results from previous choices made on the grounds of what 'ought to be', or 'ought to do' (as affirmed by commitment).

The task at hand, however, is to uncover the origins and foundations of our political conceptions, or world views: the starting point for claims about political knowledge, and choice. Specifically, the following discussion will address the theoretical implications of invoking, in policy formation, what are held to be objective interests as a means of determining 'correct' action. In examining interest-based theory and practice, underlying value assumptions will be exposed in order to assess the role of values in determining interests. It will be argued that values are prior to interests in theoretical significance, and that attempts to understand global politics must take into consideration the value structures underlying world views as the key to comprehending what is superficially presented as objective reality, hence grounds for rational action based on interest calculations.

Initially, the problem is one that has been addressed earlier: the attitude of positivism to the apprehension of reality, or knowledge of 'what is', which restricts the social sciences to falsifiable propositional statements concerning empirically observable facts. A logical-hermeneutic approach to the same reality sees 'what-is' as something more than simple empirical factuality:

> Social reality is *constructed* by means of presuppositions (global, all-inclusive conceptions of social reality of a religious, ethical, political etc. kind), assumptions (epistemological and ontological) and rules (constitutive and regulative)... 'what ought to be' and 'what is' belong to the same order of reality...[2]

Where traditional positivist views in epistemology, and non-cognitivist views in ethics, deny the possibility of knowing reality in this comprehensive way, there is naturally a predisposition to explain socio-political phenomena in terms of objective interests which can be empirically observed. Yet this view of knowledge clearly restricts 'the conditions of possibility for all understanding of the social world'. If the activity of politics is to be properly understood, it is 'important to emphasize the decisive importance of the action of the subject as the provider of contents which condition his interpretation of reality'. Actions are thus comprehensible in the context of a shared system of meaning, or language, which nevertheless expresses subjective contents:

> ...if we employ subjective categories such as intentions, ends, rules, values, norms...[action] may be explained in terms of the contents of the consciousness of the agent which are linked with his vision of the world. The sense of his actions depends on these contents, and they contribute to the construction of the social world.[3]

It follows that perceptions or interpretations of the world may vary with these contents of consciousness, and that knowledge of reality derives not only from sensory experience of it but also from such general interpretations, or world views. A further consequence is that values figure prominantly in political understanding from both internal and external perspective, since both observer and observed are engaged in the valuation of experience. Finally, the significance of interests is thereby reduced if these rest ultimately on valuations provided by a normative structure.

In the last of eight lectures given at Oxford in 1908,[4] William James concludes with a discussion of the 'will to believe', and the 'faith-ladder' used in reaching decisions (in this case, about the relationship between pluralism and monism). He describes the latter process thus:

> A conception of the world arises in you somehow, no matter how. Is it true or not? you ask.
>
> It *might* be true somewhere, you say, for it is not self-contradictory.
>
> It *may* be true, you continue, even here and now.
>
> It is *fit* to be true, it would be *well if it were true*, it *ought* to be true, you presently feel.
>
> It *must* be true, something persuasive in you whispers next; and then – as a final result –
>
> It shall be *held to be true*, you decide; it *shall be* as if true, for *you*.
>
> And your acting thus may in certain special cases be a means of making it securely true in the end.
>
> Not one step in this process is logical, yet it is the way in which monists and pluralists alike espouse and hold fast to their visions. It is life exceeding logic, it is the practical reason for which the theoretic reason finds arguments after the conclusion is once there. In just this way do some of us hold to the unfinished pluralistic universe; in just this way do others hold to the timeless universe eternally complete.[5]

While James' position seems a strong one, the direction of his thought is suggestive of the importance of considering values as an integral part of practical reasoning. It also raises doubts about the autonomy of logical systems, as traditionally conceived in logical-positivism and in the emotivist view of ethics (the 'is–ought' problem once again).

ASSUMPTIONS

What is referred to here as a world view encompasses both theoretical assumptions about the essential nature of international relations, of politics more generally, and consequently assumptions about the 'real world' as well. It is this 'real world' in which individuals, groups and organisations (including states) must act, and for which theories must provide an account.

Thus for understanding what is presented here as a world view, it is necessary to consider the range and character of theoretical assumptions about international relations which are the basis of world views. For example, Hidemi Suganami suggests that ideas about world order are 'clustered around five basic positions'. The first two are the legal school (internationalist, *not* cosmopolitan) and the diplomatic school, both of which support the idea of a system of sovereign states. The third, democratic confederalism, emphasises representation. Federalism, the fourth position, reflects a cosmopolitan view. The fifth position, welfare internationalism, is functionalist. Each of these theoretical starting points give rise to different conceptions of, and hence prescriptions for, world order.[6]

It is also necessary to consider the character of political theory itself, and to recognise international relations as an integral part of political life at all levels (in both theory and practice), and thus a proper locus for posing political questions.[7]

In political theory generally, fundamental assumptions concern human nature in the first instance – since this conditions both the formation and efficacy of political association – and subsequently conceptions of the good life to which political action is directed. Assumptions about human nature are thus commonplace in theories of international relations, although the interaction of theory and practice means that human nature and human practices are 'constructed' in part by the theoretical discourse which legitimates them. This discourse, in turn, is in part a product of the form of political association in which the discourse arises. Hence 'image' and 'reality' are intertwined; world views and possible forms of political association are interdependent. On the matter of political association it is useful to consider again the distinction made by Michael Oakeshott as between 'enterprise' and 'civil' association,[8] and a derivative distinction made by Terry Nardin as between 'purposive' and 'practical' association.[9] The distinction is between association for the purpose of achieving a particular goal decided or adopted in advance, and association which provides the social conditions for achieving any goals at all.

In the first case ('enterprise' or 'purposive' association) a common goal or common particular interest must be attributed to the participants in a political system. In the international political system such common interests seem rare (alliances and treaties notwithstanding), and a political theory explaining international politics would be obliged to account for competing interests and suggest means of resolving competition and conflict, if any meaningful claim to 'association' is to be made. Of course, traditional interest-based realist theories of international relations play down the notion of association (preferring the notion of anarchy) for just this reason.

However, in the second case ('civil' or 'practical' association) no particular goal or interest in common is attributed to participants, but rather a set of norms by which the political system may function in support of any goals, collective or individual (*pacta sunt servanda*, for example). Theory explaining international politics thus conceived is obliged to account for the normative structure governing the pursuit of interests, rather than simply the conduct of such pursuits, and consequently addresses questions about the values represented in the very fact of political association:

> ... the common good is recognised not as a set of aims to be achieved through cooperation among those moved by a common wish to achieve them but as a set of values...[10]

It is perhaps no less difficult to locate common values (a commonly held conception of the good life) in international politics than to locate common interests, and yet such constructive interaction as there is indicates some acceptance of common procedures and standards which may be taken to represent a nascent international value structure.

It is not insignificant that a similar dichotomy of terms exists in the debate about 'is' and 'ought' as it arises in the philosophy of language, where the notion of a 'regulative rule' is distinguished from that of a 'constitutive rule' or 'institutional fact' (notably by John Searle).[11] Regulative rules are antecedent or independent of the activity they regulate (e.g., in manners or in driving), while constitutive rules actually define or create an activity as well as governing it (e.g., in games or in political representation). Brute facts may be accounted for independently from regulative rules, but institutional facts must be accounted for by the conceptual framework established by a set of constitutive rules – there is no other intelligible context for such facts. This theory of language is also a theory of human institutions in general (including science and politics), and while there have been criticisms of it, none are dismissive.[12]

This account does, of course, require taking certain qualifications into consideration. For example, institutions may be viewed from an internal or external perspective, and it is only from the internal (where the observer 'belongs' to the institution) that constitutive rules are both known and accepted, and therefore have prescriptive force. From the external perspective, rules may simply be known, being therefore only descriptive. The latter may be said to have resonance in a specifically inter-national view of the world as a states-system, but the former (internal) perspective applies when all actors are implicated in global politics by a cosmopolitan view. In this case, any global value structure is prescriptive as well as descriptive, and must be reflected in policy.

Where such a value structure can be said to exist, at least to the extent of providing grounds for communication, there may still be differences about the nature of the values concerned which can be considered differences in world views; as Adda Bozeman argues, 'ideas are not transferable in their authenticity... The world is a manifold of political systems as it is a manifold of cultures'.

To begin with, experience of political association and of values so established is no doubt generally more parochial than what is implied in speaking of international relations, yet it must be emphasised again that international relations is an integral part of political life as a whole, and national and local politics are equally a part of international relations to the extent that they are a source of political values. Secondly, there may be considerable differences concerning human nature, giving rise to different aspirations for political community.

Nevertheless, talking about international relations at all requires some universal claims, whether moral or epistemological (the close relation between these two was discussed in the previous chapter), and hence a central difficulty is contending with the relativism implied above – which is undeniable in some respects – while at the same time locating and characterising those features of global political life which are universal.

It is argued here that such universals lie in the common objective of human betterment, which may be pursued by diverse means; a similarity of form with respect to ends, represented by the assumption of values in the face of ultimate indeterminacy, but with a diversity of means, represented by contingent expressions of value in political life and in the pursuit of particular interests. As L. T. Hobhouse says:

> We consider laws, customs and institutions in respect of their functions not merely in maintaining any sort of social life, but in maintaining or promoting a harmonious life.[13]

We all live in different realities, holding different views of our world. If there were perfectly shared perceptions of social, political and economic reality, the coordinating functions of communication would be redundant, and we would enjoy a common world view. However, even in the simplest relations (interpersonal) variations in experience make such perfect sharing impossible, and communication essential. In international relations communication is the principal feature, with other cooperative and coordinated activity still less commonplace than in intra-national relations, in spite of increasing interdependence among nation-states (and other actors). Communication, if effective, may lead to shared perceptions (or at least awareness of differences) but perfect communication, perfect sharing, cannot be achieved.[14] Consequently, different world views are endemic, and interactions both positive and negative revolve around such differences. Positive interaction may involve coming to terms with differences, while negative interactions may involve conflicts as one or another world view is imposed in order to resolve differences.

INTERESTS – REALIST WORLD VIEWS

To a large degree conventional or traditional theories of international relations (principally versions of realism) assume a shared world view in the form of a power-oriented, interest-based, rational technical system susceptible to political management – including the management of conflict, in the event of opposing interests, by means of the rational application of technical sources of power. In the absence of value considerations the possibility of incommensurable world views is not entertained (a universal rationality being assumed), unless this can be readily translated into conflicts of interest (which would allow power to settle the issue). The assumption of a unitary world view of reality in which interests are key does not allow the contemplation of alternative world views, nor of political options which might arise from such contemplation. The presumption of universal interests does not acknowledge the different realities that are experienced by those with different world views in spite of how much a dominant (realist) world view dictates the terms of discourse. As Onuf points out, international relations are 'pervasively heteronomous' and the asymmetry of circumstances restricts the possibility of global comparisons – which might underlie symmetric interests – to hegemonic powers.[15]

In this way, the governing assumptions of Western political thought – which suggest that politics is to do with power, and that power is to do with mastery – tend to dictate a particular kind of world view which then limits the range of possible interpretations of international political life:

> Supreme political power thus comes to be viewed – very much in the manner of Max Weber – as a capacity to deploy a monopoly of legitimate violence.[16]

The normative significance of this image of political life is generally lost among the deeply imbedded assumptions of traditional theory.

> This is not – in spite of what we sometimes like to think – because we analyze our political arrangements in such a hardheaded fashion that the element of imagery never intrudes at all. On the contrary, the terms in which we habitually talk about the powers of the state are densely

metaphorical in texture. The point is rather that the metaphors we favor all tend to support the idea of politics as a realm of domination, subordination, and the exercise of force.[17]

Of course, this also means that in traditional 'value-free' theory there is no explicit self-conciousness of value content expressed through a world view. It also means that, in the way discussed above, the imposition of the implicit world view is perpetuated by policy based on such theories, and unmediated conflict (or capitulation) results. Using an example from the literature on ideology, it may be that a lack of political controversy suggests 'less the end of ideology than the prevalence of an oppressive ideology',[18] serving the interests of a dominant political group or actor.[19] Hence, opportunites for coming to terms with the diversity of world views in a positive and constructive way are not pursued. To the extent that conventional foreign (international) policy does take value considerations seriously, they are presented in interest-language which which does not threaten conventional theoretical foundations. It is precisely the intimate relationship between values and interests that allows this surreptitious manoeuvre.

The shortcomings of traditional power-and-interest theory may be characterised in another way, still emphasising the absence of value considerations: no structure of meaning is provided by prescriptions to act out of interest; interests are assumed, or (mysteriously) 'defined in terms of power'.[20] Power may well be the currency of politics, but it is only paper money, and must at some point rely on reserves of substantial value. Hobhouse, in discussing democracy, suggests that while true political power – rather than the locus of legal sovereignty – is the proper political question, the 'determining power is elusive...'.[21] As argued previously, any interest requires an expression of values to provide a meaning. Values provide a 'house of meaning' (as Jung said of his psychological archetypes); values provide an archetypal explanation and rationalisation of a political system, without which interests are indeterminate. Thus, a given explanation or understanding of politics is buried in a society's political culture, which underwrites political claims, justifies interests, and provides dramatisations or representations of socio-political relations that maintain and perpetuate a system of essentially mythical political 'realities'. Living in the midst of culture, we are hard pressed to see the fragility of political assumptions, and are inclined to reify political ideas, thereby closing debate on the most fundamental political questions.

As Weston argues, there are insoluble philosophical problems (universals, infinitude, etc.) which are nevertheless solved for practical purposes, through politics and culture, in every successful society.[22] Yet it is a common political conceit to universalise practical solutions, being unable to acknowledge their subjectivity from the sheltered position of a given political culture, and such universalisation leads to alienation when the grounds for political action require recognition or justification from without the relevant political culture.

VALUES – NORMATIVE WORLD VIEWS

In international relations, the global political system (however conceived) provides an objectifying framework in which the intersubjectivity of particular political cultures may be recognised, but also presents the problem (both in theory and practice) of relativistic definitions, not simply of politics in a given society, but of the global political system itself. Here lies the significance of world views for explanations or understandings of international relations. In the absence of agreed solutions to insoluble philosophical problems, in the absence of a global political culture, the traditional solution has been a pseudo-scientific claim to the empirical reality of power relations; that this conception of international politics provides no framework of meaning has not troubled those who continue to discuss the protection of national interests or the maintainance of a stable (imposed) international order. No doubt this provides justification for the activities of some state actors, but it does not provide a theory of international relations. To pretend either that there is an objective political reality (which is revealed by realist theory), or that there is a universally relevant culture (a Western modernist culture of rationality, for example) to provide a locus for the resolution of insolubles, is simply to evade the most interesting and important political questions – questions which are brought to life in international relations just because they have no cultural solution there.

Hence the problem in international politics is not simply the location of objective interests – these are indeterminate. The problem is locating political values that can ascribe meaning to global political life, and can provide grounds for selecting practical solutions to insoluble philosophical problems. In locating these values, however, contrasting or contradictory national cultures may stand in the way of agreed solutions. However, asserting cultural relativism is no answer to this problem, nor does it close debate: this problem of clashing views and opposing wishes is the apogee of *political* problems, and requires nothing more nor less than a political solution. To abrogate political responsibilities just because the traditional boundaries of political organisation have been exceeded is to abandon our collective fate to the vagaries of historical accident; a dangerous weakness in view of the globalising forces of late modernity.[23] The challenge, consequently, is to construct theory which can account for shifting, changing (and exchanging) values, and theory which can address the manipulation of values. The place that values hold in political understanding is, nevertheless, often ignored since the location of values remains problematic – particularly so in international relations.

THE GLOBAL CONTEXT

Since we are speaking here of social values (rather than individual choices), values may be located in any social context. The relevant social contexts for international relations, traditionally conceived, are nation-states. Yet as the history of international relations (in both practice and theory) has increasingly exhibited systemic characteristics, distinct from the characteristics of national societies, values may also be located in this larger social system. Increasing transnational and global dimensions add new characteristics which are less territorially oriented, but they are nevertheless social dimensions which provide a new locus of values.

Globalisation is a feature of international relations which presents the issue of local perspectives on global phenomena. These perspectives are here called world views, but it is important to note that globalisation implies a context in which local world views are formed under the influence of global processes and intensified interconnectedness among states and societies.[24] World views are therefore necessarily *from* a perspective, but *of* the global condition. Furthermore, the various local strategies for establishing identity while engaging with the world as a whole must come to terms with the values expressed in global relations and processes as well as those values arising out of contingent local experience.

Consequently, a world view is not likely to be uniquely identified with any given local perspective, but rather a shared world view drawn from the paradigms and policies of the global vocabulary. It is also possible, of course, that this vocabulary may be determined by the most 'literate' (read powerful). Roland Robertson indicates

the problems occasioned by globalization and the dangers inherent in attempts by particular societies, movements or other entities to impose their own 'definition' of the global circumstance.[25]

It may be clarifying to refer to Greimas once again, and to note a parallel between our problem of values in international relations and his examination of ethnic literature where he distinguishes between two different kinds of manipulation of values. The first is the 'circulation of constant values (or equivalent ones) between equal subjects in an isotopic and closed universe'. We might consider this to be the case in domestic or national societies. The second, following from the first, involves 'the problem of the introduction and removal of these immanent values to and from the given universe, and it presupposes the existence of a universe of *transcendent values* that encompasses and encloses the first in such a way that subjects who possess the *immanent values* appear as receivers vis-à-vis the subject-senders of the transcendent universe'.[26] We might view this latter, then, as the problem of value exchange in international relations, where the prospect of a shared system of values depends on such a system being related to the distinct value structures of the participating societies. Yet transcendent belief systems were introduced earlier as exceeding the limits of normative theory, so any universe of transcendent values for international society must not be a universalised reflection of a particular value system, but rather a product of a collective understanding of international political life as that which 'encompasses and encloses' the particularities of national political life. In this sense the advent of global (rather than properly inter-national) social dimensions suggests the possibility of localised values participating in, and being understood in the context of, global values.

IMPLICATIONS FOR THEORY

International relations theory must, therefore, be viewed as an integral part of political theory generally. Indeed, it is in international relations that the explanatory power of political theory is put to the greatest test, as national political traditions become less influential. Nevertheless, political traditions do resurface in the history of international political thought: theory itself does not lie outside history. As Walker argues, many of those political categories that we take for granted are reifications of traditional notions – the state, sovereignty, etc. – now perpetuated by neo-realist theories.[27] These are, of course, notions originating in the context of a European states system (and thus in European political thought) – whether the origins of the system are in the fifteenth, seventeenth or nineteenth century is a matter of debate – and subsequently globalised through the hegemonic processes of colonialisation and subsequent decolonialisation, war and military alliance, economic dependency, and so on. This is not to say that there are not other and older cases of states-systems, but their influence has waned, and it was European expansion that unified the globe, even though this process was itself subject to foreign influences.[28] While the dominant national actors may have changed (some being outside of Europe – e.g., US, Japan, China), the categories of international political thought have been maintained, especially the notion of 'insiders' and 'outsiders'. While there are competing paradigms of international relations, some emphasising global economic structures (relations of production, the international division of labour, a world market) or cosmopolitan pluralism (relative autonomy, world society), traditional realist or neo-realist theories of power relations remain dominant, especially in policy-making.

Yet international politics is becoming more resistant to simplistic accounts of power relations, and indeed the problems of modernity force us to ask how politics is to be discussed at all, let alone how and where to locate 'power'.[29] No doubt power, however defined, conditions political choices by establishing the 'facticity' (to use Heidegger's term) of political life, but the meaning of genuinely political power (as opposed to mere force capability) is highly elusive, and not clearly related to the traditional political categories that power-political theory relies on.

Furthermore, this confusion is not aided by the accounts of realist theory provided by its proponents. Robert Gilpin, in his article entitled 'The Richness of the Tradition of Political Realism', attributes to realism an interest in constraining excesses of elites and advocacy of national interest (in contrast to elite interest – though it is not clear just how the distinction is to be made), under rules of prudent behaviour, to protect national interests and minimize international violence. None of this provides any insight into the theoretical importance of realism, but rather suggests that it is simply a set of guidelines for political behaviour: as Gilpin says,

> realists study international practice and theorize about it in part to add to the list of 'do's and dont's' of Thucydides, Morgenthau and others in the tradition of 'advice to princes'.[30]

It is interesting to note that Morgenthau himself chooses to support his arguments with the following quote from Abraham Lincoln, who, not knowing the will of providence, felt he must

> study the plain facts of the case, ascertain what is possible and learn what appears to be wise and right.[31]

For Gilpin, an underlying assumption is that 'perennial forces of political struggle limit human perfection', from which follows a summation of the realist position:

>...this moral skepticism joined to a hope that reason may one day gain greater control over passions constitutes the essence of realism and unites realists of every generation.[32]

This stands in contrast to the notion of balancing passion and reason (in Nietzsche), and the notion that reason must be the slave of passion (in Hume), and offers no account of how values might be generated or interests defined. Nevertheless, realism clearly comprises an influential, or at least widely shared world view, and consequently establishes one possible set of parameters for engaging in political thought and action, which in turn amounts to a definition (regardless of adequacy) of such undertakings.

Thus the formation of a world view can be seen as the process by which the possibility of discussing politics is articulated, and by which theoretical political categories are justified – and in cases of dominant world views, sometimes reified. Analysis of this formational process, then, provides a means of exposing reified political categories (and static theories), opening the way for rearticulations of political life. Even within traditional approaches to international relations, such analysis can provide greater clarity.

In order to characterise the process by which world views are formed, it is necessary to bring out the relationship between underlying social and political values and those putative political interests which provide the substance of conventional approaches to international relations. In particular, the assumption that interests offer a universal language of politics that avoids value relativism is challenged on the grounds that any political system must rest on a system of values (manifested in culture, approved political and economic practices, assumptions about knowledge, etc.), and that interests arising from a political system are only as universal as the underlying values: either universal values are possible, or there is no possibility of a universal foundation for politics, and we must look elsewhere for political meaning when denied the resort to traditional political communities (e.g., sovereign nation-states). In effect, the interstices of a system of states are treated as apolitical: as relations between self-sufficient entities rather than politics, as an administrative no-man's land where talk of political values is baseless and confusing. Yet the interactions that take place in this space are conditioned by the values underlying participants' actions, and the greatest problems arise when interests are assumed without corroborating reference to values. Furthermore, the precise location of this no-man's land – a notionally extrajurisdictional political space, inhabited by parties to any 'international' exchange – is not clear, given questions about the status of the sovereign state, its relationship to other such entities, and to civil society (whether conceived as national or cosmopolitan). Thus comprehending world views is essential to comprehending intentions in any international exchange, and to assessing the link between expressed interests and the values that support them, as will be discussed later in the context of defence and foreign policy. In all of this, an understanding of value structures – hence the role of normative theory – is fundamental.

CONCLUSIONS

In considering the formation of world views it is clarifying to draw parallels with political thought and philosophy in general. That is, the formation of world views is tied up with the evolution of thought about the human condition in all its aspects; influences on our thinking about the world begin with historical influences on our thinking about ourselves, and subsequently about ourselves with respect to others (political awareness). In brief, the search for universal values requires a reconsideration of all that which has made us different, in the evolution of conciousness and politics. If there is some common end, some shared fundamental value, it has long since been buried under the diverse development of cultures and civilisations.

There are, then, two possible consequences of this archaeology: the first is the possibility of discovering commonality in our origins; the second is the possibility of seeing more clearly the hopelessness of our quest. The second possibility suggests a new enlightenment concerning our plight to be achieved by clearing away the debris of history, of the many follies and grand designs which were intended to resolve the indeterminacy of human existence. What remains after such a dig is complete may not be very satisfying, but no doubt it would provide a more solid foundation for modern political tasks (and anyway a better shield against modern political dangers than any technological device). As modern philosophy finds itself returning to the pre-Socratics, so the study of international relations must look to the foundations of political association. It matters little whether this labour is rewarded by a rediscovery of universal political ends, or simply by a clarity of vision concerning the political condition. Wishing to know what to do in politics, we must know better *how* to do politics, that is, how to cope with political values other than by asserting interests – something which assumed interests cannot tell us, and unarticulated values cannot teach us.

International relations theory partakes of political theory in the sense that its problems are problems of political association on a grand scale. Where values are inherent both in the origins of association and in the continuing life of any association, there are no value-free interests which substitute for the political fact of value-laden norms at all levels of associative existence. Where the political domain exceeds the traditional confines of association by incorporating the global dimension these norms are inevitably tied up with universal discourses about theory and practice, and norms reflect and dictate this global domain of politics. The manifestations of such norms have been characterised here as world views.

NOTES

1. Robert Eccleshall, Vincent Geoghagen, Richard Jay and Rick Wilford, *Political Ideologies: An Introduction* (London: Hutchinson, 1984), p. 7.
2. Giuliano di Bernardo (ed), *Normative Structures of the Social World* (Amsterdam: Editions Rodopi, 1988), from the editor's introduction. The synoptic idea of reality being socially constructed was popularised by Peter L. Berger and Thomas Luckmann in *The Social Construction of Reality* (Garden City: Anchor Books, 1967), but for a more extensive treatment see Nicholas G. Onuf, 'Constructivism', in his *World of Our Making: Rules and Rule in Social Theory and International Relations* (Columbia, SC: University of South Carolina Press, 1989).
3. *Ibid.*
4. Published with the title *A Pluralistic Universe*, Hibbert Lectures at Manchester College on the Present Situation in Philosophy, by Longmans, Green and Company, 1909.
5. William James, *A Pluralistic Universe* (Cambridge, MA and London: Harvard University Press, 1977), p. 148.
6. Hidemi Suganami, *The Domestic Analogy and World Order Proposals* (Cambridge: Cambridge University Press, 1989).
7. See R. B. J. Walker, 'Ethics, Modernity and the Theory of International Relations' (forthcoming), esp. the last paragraph (p. 45).
8. Michael Oakeshott, *On Human Conduct* (Oxford: Clarendon Press, 1975), pp. 112–122.
9. Terry Nardin, *Law, Morality, and the Relations of States* (Princeton: Princeton University Press, 1983), p. 4ff and p. 9ff.
10. *Ibid.*, p. 17.
11. See John R. Searle, *Speech Acts: An Essay in the Philosophy of Language* (Cambridge: Cambridge University Press, 1969) and *Expression and Meaning: Studies in the Theory of Speech Acts* (Cambridge: Cambridge University Press, 1979). Note the above quote about 'Social reality...' from di Bernardo.

12. See the detailed discussion of these issues in Ricardo Guastini, 'Constitutive Rules and the Is–Ought Dichotomy' in di Bernardo (ed), *Normative Structures of the Social World, op. cit.*

13. L. T. Hobhouse, *Elements of Social Justice* (London: George Allen and Unwin, 1922, reprinted 1958), p. 27.

14. Consider, for example, the argument that translation is always possible between human languages, but that understanding of the cultural context, the nuances and the hidden assumptions of another language requires direct experience.

15. Onuf, *World of Our Making, op. cit.*, p. 282.

16. See Quentin Skinner's review of Geertz in *The New York Review of Books*, 16 April 1981, *op. cit.* Skinner also notes the revealing discussion of traditional conceptions of power in Steven Lukes' Power: *A Radical View* (London: Macmillan, 1974), which I discuss elsewhere.

17. Skinner, *ibid.*, p. 36.

18. Eccleshall, et al., *Political Ideologies, op. cit.*, p. 11.

19. See, for example, Herbert Marcuse, *One Dimensional Man* (Boston: Beacon Press, 1964), in reference to US political culture.

20. See Hans Morgenthau, *Politics Among Nations* (New York: Alfred A. Knopf, 1978), p. 5, where he describes the concept of interest defined in terms of power as the 'main signpost that guides political realism'; it is the second of his six principles of political realism.

21. Hobhouse, *Elements of Social Justice, op. cit.*, p. 197.

22. D. E. Weston, *Realism, Language and Social Theories: Studies in the Relation of the Epistemology of Science and Politics* (PhD thesis, University of Lund, Sweden, 1978), *op. cit.*

23. Roland Robertson, 'Mapping the Global Condition: Globalization as the Central Concept' in *Theory, Culture and Society* (Vol. 7, Nos. 2 & 3, June 1990 – Special Issue on Global Culture), reprinted in Michael Featherstone (ed.), *Global Culture: Nationalism, Globalization and Modernity* (London: Sage, 1990).

24. Globalisation is a relatively new term in the international relations literature, although the word 'global' is often used to avoid a state-centric bias. Useful recent works on globalisation include Roland Robertson, *Globalization: Social Theory and Global Culture, op. cit.*, and Andrew G. McGrew and Paul G. Lewis, et al., *Global Politics: Globalization and the Nation-State* (Cambridge: Polity Press, 1992): Definitions of globalisation are more complex than the following summaries indicate: 'Globalization as a concept refers both to the compression of the world and the intensification of conciousness of the world as a whole' (Robertson); 'Globalization refers to the multiplicity of linkages and interconnections between the states and societies which make up the modern world system' (McGrew). It is worth noting that nothing in these definitions necessarily suggests the demise of the states-system or the founding of a world society, or that globalisation is unique to modernity.

25. Roland Robertson, *Globalization: Social Theory and Global Culture* (London: Sage, 1992), p. 6. See also Anthony D. King, *Culture, Globalization and the World System* (London: Macmillan, 1991).

26. A. J. Greimas, *On Meaning*, p. 93, *op. cit.*

27. R. B. J. Walker, remarks made in discussion at a session of the ISA/BISA Annual Convention, London, April 1989.

28. See the introduction to Hedley Bull and Adam Watson (eds), *The Expansion of International Society* (Oxford: Clarendon Press, 1984).

29. Again, R. B. J. Walker notes 'the difficulty of speaking about politics in the late twentieth century', which may 'seem abstract to those who have learnt to treat the abstractions of an earlier era as the very stuff of common sense and brute reality'. 'Ethics, Modernity and the Theory of International Relations', *op. cit.*

30. Robert Gilpin, 'The Richness of the Tradition of Political Realism', *International Organization* (Vol. 38, No. 2, Spring 1984), reprinted in Robert O. Keohane (ed.), *Neorealism and its Critics* (New York: Columbia University Press, 1986), p. 320.

31. Hans J. Morgenthau, *Politics Among Nations*, 5th Ed., revised (New York: Alfred A. Knopf, 1978), p. 263.

32. Gilpin, *op. cit.*, p. 321.

7 Normative Aspects of Deterrence, Foreign Policy and Environmental Change

> The principal weakness in modern understandings of the significance of the operations of state powers …comes from our more or less panic-stricken imaginative incapacity to face up to the stunning cognitive intricacy of the political universe that we need to grasp.[1]

This chapter attempts to demonstrate the essentially normative character of the discourses governing deterrence theory and foreign policy analysis, in order to make out the case that in the most important and challenging areas of traditional disciplinary concern normative considerations are central to the study of international relations. A further examination of the implications of global environmental change for the study (and practice) of international relations illustrates that in an area of relatively recent and particularly acute concern, the importance of these normative considerations is increasingly evident.

NORMATIVE ASPECTS OF NUCLEAR DETERRENCE

The issue of nuclear deterrence, and its attendant problems and debates, provides an ideal substantive policy area for the elucidation of normative characteristics in international political relations. Because this issue area is peculiar to modernity, and qualitatively different from its closest relatives in the area of military policy, it provides an opportunity to examine the role of normative dynamics in policy formation in the absence of precedents or historical exemplars of the sort that generally guide policy choice. Policies of nuclear deterrence rely heavily on theory and underlying assumptions, having little or no empirical data (excepting Hiroshima and Nagasaki, and weapons testing) to draw on.

Western strategic thought has been based on the assumptions of earlier thinkers (largely relating to the Soviet Union and the Cold War) concerning purely rational actors and a technological revolution. That is to say, the discourse of strategic thought is essentially normative, being grounded in

163

certain key assumptions or theoretical norms.[2] Furthermore, strategic theory is essentially normative in the sense of being prescriptive, both in respect to definitions of the strategic problem and in respect to the appropriate policy response.[3]

Consequently, the role of normative structures is emphasised, relative to the more commonly understood parameters of policy formation provided by 'objective' experience. Furthermore, the substantive aspects of nuclear policy-making are overtly moral to a far greater extent than other military-political issues, since the objectives and methods are not clearly limited to considerations of victory, self-defence or other conventional measures of success: Indeed it is ironic that the measure of success in nuclear policy is the avoidance of its implementation.

> What policies a society should adopt for its nuclear weapons is a profoundly moral question. ...there is no moral question of any significance that is not fact-drenched and no facts' of any importance that are not inextricably embedded in particular ways of looking at the world.[4]

As for the broader concerns of strategic studies, it may be said that a general problem is the concept of 'security', and the security dilemma: Whose security should take precedence, and need the security game be 'zero-sum'? What kind of security, and at what cost to the social resources which are being secured? Security from what? These questions are not properly dealt with in the mainstream of strategic studies literature, and as Hugh Macdonald says,

> recent 'mainstream' work has been subjected to a persistent barrage of criticism, especially on the morality of deterrence, the nuclear emphasis of the superpowers' confrontation, and the preoccupation with military-technological refinements at the expense of political trust and alternative resource claims. There have also come voices insisting upon the wholeness of the international system, and hence the indivisibility of North from South or of societal well-being from the narrower conspectus of military security, implying that 'defence of the realm' should no longer be the first duty of societies.[5]

We may wish to consider what, then, is the duty of international society (such as it is) with respect to security. There have been a number of significant attempts at 'collective security' in the past (notably failures), but little attempt to transcend the conventional notion of security as being properly the business of governments acting for individual societies (*pace* general references to 'global peace and security'). As we will see, this has something to do with conceiving of the international system as being isolated from those normative social and political features that are well understood in national societies.

In order to address the character of this shortcoming in conceptions of international society, as well as some of the related issues mentioned above, the next part of the chapter will focus on the particular issue of ethics and deterrence. Subsequently, the role of political purpose in strategy will be discussed to indicate the necessary reliance on normative referents.

Strategies of Ethics

Questions of ethics and nuclear strategy have, for the most part, been posed and answered with the implicit or explicit intent of justifying either the strategic status quo or the movement to denuclearise international relations. Despite the familiarity of this simple and artificial dividing line in the ongoing nuclear debate, there is in fact a remarkable diversity of opinion. In short, there are ethical arguments available to support every position along a spectrum ranging from 'first use' to abolition. That there is such an active moral debate about the nuclear condition is evidence of our difficulty in coming to terms with it. That there is such a diversity of ethical positions is indicative of our predipositions about the matter.

In this chapter I suggest that nuclear strategy presents an array of issues which are, like the weapons themselves, qualitatively different from anything we have had to deal with in the past (hence our difficulty). I further suggest that the nature of the debate, while quantitatively different in respect to its scope, is not unique in social discourse but merely highlights political aspects of ethics (hence our predispositions). It may be that questions about ethics and strategy collectively represent a microcosm of the political realm, and if that is the case, it is not surprising that we are presented both with a great problem and with deeply held convictions about the solution. In his concluding remarks, Philip Bobbitt characterises the existing circumstances of nuclear strategy, but without ascribing any necessity to them:

> Precisely because nuclear strategy has not arisen from actual conflict, with the fresh recurrence to (and re-evaluation of) first principles that war precipitates, it has become ideological, and is unable to cure itself. Because it has lost its connection to strategic reality, it is in fact not disengaged from but at the mercy of public opinion.[6]

A brief and incomplete survey of the issues and the nature of the debate (regretably restricted, here, to debate in the West) will allow us to deal with the propositions introduced above. The questions in this area are the subject of study by, predominantly, ethical philosophers and military strategists. According to Hardin, et al.,[7] the two groups take different approaches to the central question of nuclear deterrence: the strategists, in general, adopt a realist perspective in which the Soviets figure as opportunistic adversaries, and the chief problem is arms control;[8] the philosophers are principally concerned with the morality of various nuclear postures and policies, the chief question being whether evil may be threatened or done that good may come. Among strategists there is diversity of opinion ranging from the status quo to war-fighting, counterforce, or strategic defence capabilities to denuclearisation (but not abolition, on grounds of existential deterrence and 'technological recalcitrance'). The philosophers can be grouped into deontologists (with an interest in the nature of actions, *per se*) and utilitarians (concerned with outcomes of actions; with consequences).

As one author suggests, even arguments that are concerned strictly with what one does, rather than with what happens, can be challenged by an appeal to consequences.[9] Similarly, there are limits to what may be justified by a consequentialist (means to end) argument. There is room for moral calculation at the margin, where both perspectives are strained. Another author argues that deterrence can not be properly addressed in the abstract, from either a strictly moral or strictly military perspective (the first requiring agreement on premises, the second ignoring the subtleties of managing competing interests), and describes deterrence as a 'real' issue.[10] Regardless of how one understands the phrase 'real issue', it is apparent that deterrence presents problems that are not easily categorised; perhaps not easily conceived of. That ethical and practical considerations are conflated in the analysis of deterrence points to the underlying significance of morals in human affairs, and to the political component of morality.

No doubt there is a 'strategy of ethics' as well as an ethics of strategy. While strategies of ethics may be employed in politics generally, here it will suffice to explore it in the context of deterrence policy. This exploration need go no further than the nuclear debate, as found in the literature, by which one or another of a wide range of ethical positions is employed to support predispositions and intuitions about deterrent strategies. Such a view accounts for the often incongruous battles for 'moral high ground' in the politics of defence, by which various interest groups attempt to couch their objectives in ethical terms. Unfortunately, this leads to the cynical conclusion that interests determine values, and does not allow us to recognise how greatly values affect interests, and ought to. It is just this issue which is so clearly brought out in the nuclear debate.

The fundamental role of values in social and political groups is uncovered when we find ourselves debating, as we always debate conventional political issues (who gets what, when, where), about our values: These values are a matter for collective agreement. Those who have some interest in one or another solution to the deterrence dilemma recognise the need to validate their interests in terms of social values; in terms of morality. By rejecting the moral content of political issues (as Kennan does in the case of foreign policy),[11] this inherent dynamic of the political process is overlooked. When the state and civil society are clearly distinguished, and the latter concept is relegated to the field of 'domestic politics' or sociology, the function of social values in the field of international relations can be ignored. In spite of indications to the contrary (from Clausewitz, for example) the conventional wisdom seems to opt for a more sanitary and convenient comprehension of political reality which excludes value calculations in favour of 'interests', narrowly defined.

It may be that the unprecedented problems of deterrence will force the abandonment of such conventional understandings in favour of a conception that has, after all, always been a part of our political experience whether we have chosen to acknowledge it in the study and practice of politics or not: Value structures are an integral component of civil societies, and state apparatuses reflect these values in their policy choices and in their calculation of national interests. In the context of the nuclear debate it becomes apparent that our 'apolitical' beliefs about morality are effecting our 'amoral' views of politics. What is most significant about nuclear deterrence is not the novelty of the problem itself, but how it has forced an impoverished conception of international relations (perhaps of politics in general) to its limits. Under conditions of nuclear threat, the notion of 'national interest' loses clarity, and as we will see in the next section this is also a difficulty for the study and formation of foreign policy.

Political Purpose

...at least one important lesson can certainly be drawn from the history of serious political thought. It is that virtually every human being or assemblage of human beings at any time has good reason, often overwhelmingly good reason, not merely to check carefully whether some of their current factual beliefs are in fact valid but also to reconsider whether all their current desires, hopes fears and commitments are in fact well-advised or morally decent.[12]

Beyond the truism of 'technological recalcitrance', we may well be suffering from the more profound affliction of 'normative recalcitrance' – having learned to 'Stop Worrying and Love the Bomb', or at least live with it, we may find ourselves unable or unwilling to re-educate ourselves or to withdraw from this addiction.[13] Having constructed adequate justifications for perpetuating the conditions of deterrence, we may find ourselves lacking both sympathy for, and understanding of, any variations or alternatives which may be presented. Lacking the normative foundations for reassessment or introspection, we may find such alternatives not simply idealistic and utopian, but incomprehensible and surreal. In the absence of normative reference points, such alternatives may fall victim to cognitive dissonance before their merits can be considered. Of course, even those alternatives which are granted their day in the court of public debate will face the fierce cross examination of status-quo assumptions. This is not to say that deterrence can or should be immune to the process of social and political change, which sweeps all other issues before it, but simply that as a recognised dilemma the condition of deterrence should not be allowed to achieve the status of an historical necessity in the way that technological progress (and perhaps even Enlightenment) has slipped beneath (or beyond) our critical gaze.[14]

The lesson to be drawn from rapid change in Eastern Europe and the Soviet Union in 1989–90 and after is that what seemed to be an immutable fact of international life – overt confrontation between East and West – has all but vanished, leaving us with the idea of deterrence but little reason to employ it now that European security is being redefined. Having backed the rather traditional notion of deterrence so heavily, we lack the critical and innovative approaches which changing circumstances require. A normative approach provides a suitable platform for addressing changing political values, in this case the range of values and purposes implicated in considerations of security, such that the contingencies of change need not present insurmountable obstacles or destabilising uncertainties.

Being sensitive to the normative development of global politics and society is not just a means of estimating what is accepted, or how to engineer such acceptance – in the sense that Adorno's Culture Industry leads us to choose 'sameness' – but is also an opportunity to reflect on what it is that is being accepted: Even if we are prepared to condemn ourselves to sameness, preserving only the illusion of choice, we may still (before losing conciousness altogether) wish to be sure that we can live with the self-imposed sentence. Living under conditions of deterrence is a troubling matter not only because of the potential effects of the irrational acts which the rationality of nuclear deterrence demands for its realisation, but because of the active effects on the collective psyche of being committed to irrationality. Of course, it may well be that human existence is characterised by irrationality, but for the most part it is possible to seek refuge in the delusion of rational choice. Nuclear deterrence offers no such solace.

Perhaps the most obvious point about nuclear deterrence policies is that they represent a technical solution to a political problem; a technical means to achieving a human purpose. Certainly, the history of human development has often been measured by the employment of new technology, but there is some room for suggesting that political rather than technical skills are required to resolve political problems, and that the application of technology is sometimes dysfunctional. Among strategic thinkers there is little doubt that the key to making and understanding strategy is the recognition of the predominance of *political purpose* as the first and last justification of any strategy. This view is invariably supported by reference to the famous philosopher of war, Carl von Clausewitz (who, in crude summary, held war to be an extension of politics), or to other prominent figures who have reiterated his argument, and added their own evidence by way of example.[15] Definitions of strategy have usually emphasised the difference between strategy and tactics, and although Clausewitz's 1805 article in *Neue Bellona* criticised Bulow's superficial distinction based on range from the enemy, his own definition makes a distinction to emphasise the idea of purpose:

Tactics constitute the theory of the use of armed forces in battle; strategy forms the theory of using battle for the purposes of the war.[16]

The 'purposes of the war' are, by definition, political purposes.

A more modern strategist, Basil Liddell Hart, defines strategy as

...the art of distributing and applying military means to fulfill ends of policy...[17]

Having emphasised the place of politics in strategy, it should also be said that many strategists have concerned themselves for the most part with strictly technical (sometimes tactical) considerations; no doubt they are significant considerations, but nevertheless they are the minutiae of strategy and far removed from the underlying political aspects. This has the unfortunate effect not only of reducing awareness of the pervasive political questions, but also of distancing (through esoteric discourse) strategic decision-making and discussion from non-specialists whether in political office or among the general population. In particular, some fundamental issues have slipped past the public domain in the rapid advance of nuclear technology. Indeed, even the 'experts' are hard pressed to keep up with new developments in technology, and this has masked the need to consider political advances.

Aside from the question of political aims as the justification of strategy, a further question has been posed by the advent of nuclear weapons and their essentially political attributes, as distinct from notable practical attributes. The question is whether a 'nuclear strategy' is logically possible at all, since what political purpose could be served by using these weapons is unclear, and it would in any case be difficult to control their use under the likely circumstances of nuclear conflict (of which there is, happily, no empirical knowledge in the first place). The most consistent theme in nuclear strategy has been deterrence, which by definition is not concerned with 'battle' and 'military means' – at least, not in the first instance. The deterrence debate often pivots on what is to be deterred, and how (for example, can nuclear weapons deter the use of conventional weapons?), and whether the deterrent will be credible (seeing is believing, and believing is everything), so clearly tactical considerations creep in, but only with respect to implementing a deterrent and not necessarily in order to effect a war-fighting strategy (as in the doctrine of 'Mutual Assured Destruction'). There is the further complication of preparing for war as part of a deterrent (as in 'Flexible Response'), but again this does not bear on the conceptually distinct notion of deterrence as a means of *avoiding* war, not engaging in it. Thus deterrence does not amount to a strategy at all, if what is meant by strategy is a planned application of military means (and this is exactly what is left unattended by deterrence): the real strategic problem is about what happens if and when deterrence fails. Since the political significance of nuclear tactics cannot be judged in advance, should deterrence fail, there are no guidlines for action; the elements of time, irrationality and uncertainty deny the foundation of a politically directed strategy for the use of nuclear weapons, and as Lawrence Freedman says:

> The study of nuclear strategy is therefore the study of the nonuse of these weapons. Suppositions about their actual employment in combat may influence their peacetime role, but historical experience provides minimal guidance.[18]

What this tells us about nuclear strategy is that we are entirely guided by the norms inherent in our theories of international political life, and in our assumptions about the adversarial character of relations between states or societies.

Philip Bobbitt cites Freedman as being exemplary of an older school of modern history, 'concerned with how political events influenced strategic ideas'; His own view is that certain intellectual patterns, or ideologies, determine the shape of strategic doctrine and his approach to the subject, therefore, is to

> look for connections between events and ideas, without assuming that historical reality is the mold for our strategic concepts – assuming, one might say, the reverse.[19]

As we have no concrete, empirical, 'objective' grounds for strategy (a partisan interest in survival is not objective), it must rely on value structures in our strategic thinking rather than in overt and tangible interests. This does not resolve the problem, of course, but it does suggest caution, and perhaps even a way of seeking to understand the strategic assumptions that we rest so heavily on. In his *Introduction to Politics*, Harold Laski concluded that

> A generation, in fact, like our own, whose feet lie so near to the abyss, has no right to optimism about its future; the fact that it knows the way is no proof that it will choose the way. In this, paradoxically enough, there lies perhaps our greatest hope. The dangers about us are so tangible and immediate that we are driven to experiment and innovation. We have learned by tragic experience the fragility of civilised habits…[20]

Though the reference is to the international community, it might well be to to the fragility of our habits of mind. Being aware of this shortcoming in our understanding of the world, we may be less likely to destroy that world out of an ignorance which is attenuated only by the values we collectively adopt, or live with. When security depends on values, both as the basis of strategic thought and the substance of that which is to be secured, it behoves us to approach the issue from a normative perspective that is overtly concerned with the origin and evolution of such values.

Having employed deterrence (reliant on political values for meaning) as an example of the normative character of central problems in international relations, it should not then be assumed that the lessons of the problems of nuclear strategy can be applied in their particulars to the problems of international relations in general. Indeed, Bobbitt makes this point, while noting (in the same passage) that deterrence theory arises from general assumptions about national behaviour and human nature:

> Nuclear deterrence is, we may be reminded, an extraordinarily limited theory that relies on extraordinarily broad assumptions. The theory is

limited to those conflicts in which the fundamental security of the state is put at risk. Thus the theory is of limited value in international relations.[21]

At the same time, deterrence strategies reflect general assumptions about the nature of international relations, and reveal the tenuous relationship between these assumptions and that 'knowledge of reality' they aspire to represent. It should also be recognised that some aspects of the 'zero-sum' thinking characteristic of Cold War strategy may have spilled over into the foreign policy-formation in general.

Through the employment of a normative approach to the study of international relations, it is possible to address the value structures which are the foundations both of this social realm and of our systematic knowledge of it. An appreciation of the contingency of existing political practices and epistemological assumptions is the starting point for a more subtle and flexible theoretical account of the international realm, including such central problems as nuclear deterrence.

An example of such contingency is the significant change in European security relations following political reform in the Soviet Union and Eastern Europe, and Western responses to this reform, most notably during 1989–90. What had long seemed a truth about East–West relations crumbled along with the Berlin Wall – witness two contrasting graffitti painted on the Wall, the first shortly after its erection, the second after the beginning of its demolition:

VARHEIT IST KONKRET (TRUTH IS CONCRETE) – Brecht

DIE MAUER IST WEG (THE WALL IS DOWN/GONE)

The undoing of this truth is incomplete and uncertain, of course, since the loss of one truth demands the creation of another, and this process is only beginning.

Some cling to old and reliable ideas until the last moment, or longer, indicating that it is often the domain of values rather than the concrete circumstance that determines 'correct' behaviour: following the reunification of Germany in October 1990, officers from the Bundeswehr went to inspect equipment newly inherited from the disbanded Nationale Volksarmee (NVA) only to find that in spite of recent cordiality in inter-German relations there were row upon row of army vehicles fully loaded with ammunition, ready to move at a moment's notice in the event of invasion from the West – oddly enough, this was still thought to be a real possibility until the final moments of reunification, indicating 'a military machine whose procedures, attitudes and expectations differed fundamentally from those of its Western counterparts'.[22]

A contemporaneous book reviewer notes that in the aftermath of East–West confrontation 'there exists much talk of new security, but little consistency on the concept, its goals or prescriptions', while at the same time there is an underlying concern with the discovery of commonality, which 'must be discovered, exposed and detailed, not simply invoked or alluded to, as is current fashion'.[23] Another reviewer notes a speculation concerning perspectives on deterrence 'that norms of international behaviour and perceptions of legitimacy that derive from these norms substantially affect behaviour, and points to the 'immediate relevance of research into the institutionalisation of belief systems'.[24]

For the purposes of the present argument, these statements and observations about changing security relations in Europe after the end of the Cold War confirm the general case about the significance of norms in international relations, and support the claim that a normative approach to the study of international relations has a unique contribution to make. One writer goes so far as to suggest that:

> If nothing else, 1989 has demonstrated beyond any doubt that the study of politics is an art form; it is by no means a science, even of the 'social' variety.[25]

This refers, of course, to the unpredictability of events in that year. It is, however, possible to pursue 'science' in the sense of systematic knowledge, providing the contingency of both the subject matter and our knowledge of it is recognised and accepted. Within those parameters, it is possible to account for the values which inform both the political relations under scrutiny and understandings of that political 'reality' in such a way as to avoid the crisis of truth that must otherwise accompany radical change.

NORMATIVE ASPECTS OF FOREIGN POLICY

Having shown the tenuous and indeterminate character of nuclear strategy, as a particular and no doubt unique aspect of policy which is highly dependent on a normative framework, we may now consider the extent to which foreign policy more generally is influenced by values in the process of its formation. If values can be considered significant in foreign policy formation, the analysis of this process – and of the product (policy) – must take account of the norms which govern it. To begin with, it is worth considering the traditional 'normative' question of ethics as it applies to the analysis and formulation of foreign policy. There is a fundamental premise to any discussion of ethical problems in policy formation: policy is not amoral. This premise is not universally accepted, and indeed the contrary position is part of the traditional realist view of international relations (although there is clearly a long and honoured tradition of concern with moral issues such as, for example, just war theory, or the implied morality of a balance of power in the tradition of Vattel). In order to contend with the view that foreign policy is not primarily concerned with moral questions, I will provide a brief critique of such an argument.

George Kennan, in his article entitled 'Morality and Foreign Policy', maintains the position that foreign policy is the responsibility of governments ('not of individuals or entire peoples') and that governments must act on considerations of national interest, which has no moral quality. In excluding individuals and peoples, Kennan separates state and civil society, denying the moral agency of the state. This is a position which may be convenient, but is problematic at the margin (in times of war, for example). He argues that governments must protect 'tangible and demonstrable interests', clearly distinguished from moral principles. In the event, he recognises that moral principles have some role (at least where a government has the power to choose between policies), but that expediency is a common motive for practical reasons. By this recognition he detracts from his own position, but without providing an account. He suggests that resources be employed to advance 'the national interest and the interests of world peace', but does not raise the possibility that the two may conflict. He states that 'the renunciation of self-interest, which is all morality implies, can never be rationalised by purely secular and materialistic considerations'. He further recommends 'a policy founded on recognition of the national interest, reasonably conceived, as the legitimate motivation for a large portion of the nation's behaviour', but does not acknowledge the connection between 'national interest, reasonably conceived' and the 'renunciation of self-interest'. The question of enlightened self-interest is begged, as it is precisely the rationality of a conceived national interest which is at issue here. The necessity of conditioning short or medium term self-interests by considerations of long term collective interests cannot be denied – indeed, this is the logic of domestic sources of 'national interest'. Kennan also points to the risks of nuclear war and the abuse of the natural environment as being overriding concerns, for which past experience has not prepared us. He asks if there is not a moral component to addressing these problems. I believe there is, obviously. He is unsure.

Kennan concludes by referring to the great force of 'true moral behaviour', and the risk of losing it through a diminished ability 'to distinguish between the real and the unreal'. It is, I argue, the preoccupation with subjective interpretations of national interest that has been largely responsible for diminishing our comprehension of reality in the realm of international relations, and Kennan unwittingly makes an argument for normative approaches in raising the issue. I contend that Kennan still has it wrong, as do many in the realist school, and that no useful separation of enlightened interest and moral sensibility can be made (absent a naive understanding of morality).

The Current Study of Foreign Policy

As consideration of values has not been a significant aspect of foreign policy analysis in its traditional manifestations, it will be useful to discuss the present state of this area of study.

The study of foreign policy has retained many features of the behavioural revolution in social science, concentrating on quantitative analyses of empirical events; of the 'inputs' and 'outputs' of the foreign policy making process. A comparative method is often used, having the advantage of revealing differences and exposing assumptions, but also the disadvantage of generalising the conditions of policy formation over different social and political systems. An historical perspective may also provide a critical distance from the subject matter – 'a temporal rather than spatial distancing'[26] – but again the disadvantage of conflating different historical circumstances undermines the scientistic goal of objective observation which a comparative approach aspires to. This is not to dismiss comparison out of hand, as there are clear advantages to the method, for example, over a strictly discriptive account of a single policy decision. Comparison itself provides a means of relative or ordinal evaluation.

Nevertheless, there are shortcomings in the conventional approaches to foreign policy analysis, which are to some extent reflections of the formation of policy (or, perhaps, vice versa). Recent authors have pointed to the character of these shortcomings, and it is no surprise to see that they bear on our discussion of normative theory. Michael Dillon has pointed to the danger of an overly abstract comparative analysis 'removed from ... human communities with specific histories and cultures'.[27] Elsewhere, Harold Saunders has argued that it is necessary to look beyond abstract state sytems to human beings.[28] The importance of these remarks is both practical and theoretical, having significance for both the formation and analysis of foreign policy. Saunders argues that there are forces at work in global politics other than the traditional tools of rational statecraft, these latter being predominantly instruments of power. There are also instruments of persuasion and cooperation which have 'organising and directing power' through the formation of ideas and perspectives: 'organising power as they become widely accepted ways of understanding events and directing power because of the actions that flow from them', which can revealed by paying 'more attention to the larger political environment in which peoples reach fundamental judgements about peace, war, negotiation, and economic change'.[29] Thus Saunders emphasises political action over contests of force as a means to influence change, and suggests that the concept of 'relationship' be used to encompass the interactive political process.

Similarly, Neil Richardson argues for a 'dyadic' approach which views the state not simply as an independent monadic actor, but is sensitive to the interdependence of decision making processes which requires examination of at least 'two state decision-making leaderships simultaneously'.[30] Further, Charles Kegley suggests that what is needed 'to include human beings and their decisions and motives in accounts of foreign policy is an integrating concept' – the one he offers is 'decision regime' – and goes on to say that 'the field has suffered from the absence of such a concept'.[31] The above concerns, arguments and proposed concepts point clearly to aspects of normative inquiry which have already been discussed here, providing not only support for the present argument, but examples of normative theoretical approaches in application.

In an article surveying the area of foreign policy studies, Steve Smith outlines

> five main ways of studying foreign policy: through a domestic politics perspective; international relations theory; comparative foreign policy theory; case studies; and middle-range theory.[32]

Of the first, being governed by the particular normative system of the society in question, there is no guarantee that resulting observations of policy formation will provide any more than some insight into national bureaucratic structures and political practices. Smith says that 'by stressing choice and decision, they ignore or downplay constraints and nondecisional influences on behaviour; as such they hinder the task of explaining the dynamism of international relations'.[33] Perhaps more pertinent to the present argument is Smith's suggestion that international relations theory is too general to stand as '*the* theory of foreign policy', due to the contingent circumstances of its formation and 'different empirical content'.[34] Of comparative attempts to combine internal and external causes, he says that the epistemology is too 'firmly rooted in positivism' to take alternative approaches into account.[35] Case studies, or historical analysis – the most prevalent form of foreign policy analysis – are, claims Smith, idiosyncratic and an unsuitable basis for theory building, and are less than forthcoming about the theoretical assumptions of these individual accounts.[36] Finally, middle-range theory offers a middle ground between general theory and historical analysis of particular cases. These theories tend to focus on a specific aspect of a general feature of foreign policy (not unlike the present approach). Smith concludes that the principal difficulty about forming a theory of foreign policy is that 'all of international relations seems to be about foreign policy'.[37] This suggests that most insights on the nature of foreign policy are from without the specialised study, or sub-discipline, and gives weight to Kratochwil's observation about the dangers of 'an unwarranted narrowing of focus in regard to international relations'.[38]

In the context of this book, the problematic in foreign policy formation concerns the basis of policy choice the assumptions upon which policy-makers must rely as being shared foundational points of reference for the state or society on whose behalf they are making policy decisions. Traditionally, reference is made to the 'national interest' as the determining objective of all policy, and yet this concept of national interest is notoriously problematic, being defined only in vague terms. The sources of this interest, and consequently the grounds for claims about its representativeness, are highly elusive – are the interests concerned those of the government or state apparatus, those of a political elite or of particular interests groups, or are they genuinely shared interests common to the entire society?[39]

In his discussion of European integration, Paul Taylor notes the significance of two differing views on the need for a socio-psychological community to underwrite sovereign authority, which 'profoundly affected attitudes on the status of the decisions of the existing European institutions'. Neofunctionalists, such as Haas, initially regarded national governments' recognition of an international institution's competence as sufficient, only later considering the problem of 'authority-legitimacy transfer'. Taylor then considers the view that Federalism provides 'a political solution, a way of managing different interests'; a view, he says, of which Mitrany and Rosentiel are suspicious. The older Functionalist view 'insisted that the development of socio-psychological community was the essential precondition of sovereignty', while at the same time emphasising that a high level of capacity – the ability to receive, understand and act authoritatively on demands – is required of an institution to ensure stability and maintain legitimacy, especially in a disparate community.[40]

These reflections on the problems of political integration, and especially the question of legitimacy as opposed to mere efficacy, reflect the tension arising from the differing points of reference in either 'interests' or 'values'. The matter of institutional capacity described above refers to the accomodation of interests, in the first instance, although clearly these interests may be either conditioned or determined by an overriding value attached to the 'idea of Europe', or to ameliorating the stigma of recent national political history (e.g. fascism) by complementing it with a broader political identity, or to future prospects of a united Europe in the context of the global political economy. Indeed, the Functionalists felt elite expert opinion, operating through international institutions, would influence broader public opinion and build the necessary sense of community. Similarly, the emphasis on a socio-psychological community 'as the precondition of sovereignty' clearly reflects a recognition of the importance of norms or values in the achievement of political goals such as integration, though it does not ignore the connection between these values and the successful pursuit of particular interests. The relevance of this discussion for the present argument is the implication that values have primacy over interests in respect of their role in determining the framework in which interests are to be pursued (in this example, a shift to 'a European focus for group interests') whether or not this framework itself is comprised primarily of shared values or a constitutional community of competing interests.[41]

Values and Interests in Foreign Policy

It has been argued earlier that reference to interests is problematic just because they are not self-justifying or even self-evident but are, rather, dependent on value systems which are inherent in any factual or empirical referent that may be paraded to garner confidence in a policy. In discussing interest as a guide to foreign policy, Vernon Van Dyke observes that 'particularly in the writing of Hans Morgenthau concerning the national interest much of the trouble is definitional rather than epistemological'. Van Dyke critiques Morgenthau's infamous formulation – 'interest defined in terms of power' – claiming that 'he does not himself advance a definition explicitly, whether or not in terms of power. In truth, he seems almost deliberately to accentuate the vagueness of the key terms'.[42]

For Van Dyke, it is clarifying to distinguish between 'dependent' and 'independent' interests and between 'goal' and 'instrumental' values, but the distinction between values and interests is not vigorous in his hierarchical scheme and he admits to the similarity of meaning of these terms in common usage. Nevertheless, the problem with conventional assumptions about interests is brought out well, especially in the sense that the relationship between values and interests is denied when values are held to be simply confusing, and thus something not just to be ignored but actively avoided in the policy-formation process. It may be that this process itself, being largely the business of a professional elite, has been somehow disengaged from the mainstream of political activity. Van Dyke notes that

the well known distinction has been made between "politics" and "administration," the suggestion being that politics is the realm of choice among values and that administration is (or should be made to be) the realm where technical expertise is relied upon to promote the values that have been politically selected.[43]

Further to this problem of defining the national interest, even when acceptably defined, is a problem peculiar to a foreign policy which purports to reflect this interest: the policy (and interests) must be projected into an international forum where the contingent origins of the policy in the society which generates it will become all too obvious when compared to other competing interests and policies of equally contingent origins. There is nothing external to the policy-generating society which will guarantee the acceptance or even the comprehension of that policy by others in the international sphere. As a matter of logic, any foundation for such policy must consequently refer to some internationally accepted frame of reference if it is to be properly considered foreign policy, as opposed to something labelled 'foreign policy' which is in fact intended only for domestic consumption, and indeed only valid for domestic consumption since it has no international currency.

In many respects this sort of problem has been overcome by a wide range of international institutional values, or normative systems (international law, intergovernmental organisations, policy cooperation or international regimes, etc.), including the most general form of these: common practice. That is to say, to the extent that the foundations of political choice and action are to be found in the values of the society to which they apply, this must be as true of international society (whatever conception of this one may hold) as it is of national societies. The ability to comprehend and to function in the international realm is coincidental with the development of normative systems emulating the social structures that are more familiar in particular societies.[44]

Returning to the European experience once again, as an obvious example of political cooperation in action (not forgetting Caricom, and other similar cases), the development of European Political Cooperation (EPC) provides a clear indication of the normative processes influencing foreign policy formation: 'EPC has created some habits and methods of problem-solving which have been taken up by other government circles'.[45] EPC is an international normative structure 'under construction', so to speak, but it simply reflects the normative character of international political life that is everywhere, if nowhere so obvious as when manifested in the overt language of political cooperation.

In the context of international relations theory, problems arising from traditional political and epistemological conceptions arise once again in respect to the example of the European experience:

> Many of the early theories imposed a highly positive value judgement on any kind of integration (as a reaction, naturally to World War II). With a general decline of the pro-integration mood integration theories were often perceived as 'ideology' which was harmful to practical ventures like EPC.[46]

This aversion to 'harmful ideology' reveals the inability of traditional international relations theories and concepts to distinguish between a cynically purposive ideological position and the ordinary – indeed, definitional – political activity of identifying and pursuing collective goals. When politics are viewed as nothing more than the competitive pursuit of particularistic interests, any subtlety in conceptions of the political is lost. When the political realm is recognised as the realm of changing or developing values, the importance of theoretical endeavours becomes evident: theories provide a normative structure of knowledge which is similar in form to the normative structure of the political events under examination. If theory is reduced to mere descriptive typology or doctrinal statements, it is no wonder the value of theory is questioned.

> In the critique of theory there is often a confusion as to its claims. Theory is not a blueprint for action: it is decidedly not a doctrine and above all it is not an ideology: While avoiding the rich theory as to the nature of theory itself, we may simply state that its main attempt is to provide a coherent account and explanation of a phenomenon (which it often defines itself). Tangentially, it might have a predictive capacity.[47]

NORMATIVE ASPECTS OF ENVIRONMENTAL CHANGE

The normative features of international relations illustrated above may be further illuminated by consideration of the impact of global environmental change (GEC) which, it should be said, represents consequences as grave and disturbing as nuclear warfare and is clearly a central preoccupation of foreign policy everywhere, even if for some developing countries environmental protection is a *quid pro quo* for development assistance. Of particular significance to the overall argument of the book is the contrast between the obvious empirical nature of environmental change, which is nevertheless virtually impossible to translate directly into useful political data (e.g., political interests) because of the uncertainties of environmental science and environmental economics, and the notable differences in political priorities among actors (e.g., political values). It is thus a useful example of an area which can benefit from the application of normative analysis in respect of the relevant knowledge and value systems. The normative effects and implications of GEC will be examined here, as will the challenging notion of 'environmental security' as a case of conceptual tensions between traditions and innovations in the study of international relations. Our general concern here is to see whether and how environmental values reflect the broader circulation of values in the global context.[48]

Both natural scientists and policy-makers have, respectively, examined the origins and extent of environmental change and debated appropriate policy responses – sometimes swapping their roles, which raises questions about sources of empirical data and the interpretation of it (i.e., epistemological issues).[49] 'Megascience' projects of global sweep are underway, seeking to unravel the complexities of deeply interconnected ecosystems which are the subject of modelling exercises.[50] Policy-makers have responded with scepticism about the degree of change and its consequences, or applied 'the precautionary principle' in acting to limit environmental degradation regardless of the uncertainties.[51] The economic costs of GEC have introduced shifts in market behaviour and calls for regulatory intervention, typically on a 'level playing field' basis, though there are competitive advantages in environmental technologies and economic adaptability.[52] Increasingly, international trade is influenced by environmental considerations and both products and processes are now scrutinised for environmental impacts.[53] Similarly, the potential risks of investment in non-sustainable activities has led to selectivity and conditionality in international finance and investment. Social movements of every stripe, from environmental activists to political parties, have taken up the green banner and introduced ever-widening publics to the ecological consequences of their lifestyles (as an example, green social movements are influential in post-communist Eastern and Central Europe and the former Soviet Union, being sometimes decisive factors in political coalitions, and may even have precipitated revolutionary change).[54] It is perhaps easiest to identify particular local social norms with these latter dimensions of ordinary human concern, but of course our lifeways are inseparable from the larger institutional activities that support and reproduce them. In fact, it is not unusual these days to hear industrialists speak of the need for a new industrial culture,[55] or bureaucrats of an environmental imperative, although too often values expressed as a concerned individual are not admitted to the professional discourse of institutional functionaries.[56]

The widely used term 'the environment' might be understood as an overarching concept representing a shift in values, since it encapsulates many interrelated issues which are prominent in (perhaps definitional of) late twentieth century public discourses. Clearly, there are *differences* among local experiences, but the broad terms of environmental concern provide a common point of reference, if not a universal value. The environment, as an issue pursued by international governmental and non-governmental organisations (IGOs and NGOs), is characterised by global-local relations: witness the green slogan 'think globally, act locally'. While there are obviously specifically *global* environmental problems such as ozone depletion, biodiversity, climate change, etc., there are also local problems of particular salience for local communities, countries and regions, and importantly there are differential consequences of global environmental change for the various localities and hence local differences in attitude to or understanding of the global condition.[57]

Naturally, many differences exist independently of environmental issues, the international system being established largely on the basis of historical patterns of identity and difference, but here we are concerned to see how these differences may be understood as normative factors conditioned by the politics of global environmental change.[58]

Normative Effects

Normative effects of GEC are not restricted to such global historical trends as western industrialism, although this is widely held to be responsible for much of what ails the planet, but may also include local non-industrial practices which have led to deforestation, desertification, pollution and other forms of environmental degradation, and to current public and policy responses or lack of response as contributing causes of environmental change which reflect value bias. Of course the local–global nexus renders the two interdependent, since as Ulf Hannerz points out:

> ...today's cosmopolitans and locals have common interests in the survival of cultural diversity. For the latter, diversity itself, as a matter of personal access to varied cultures, may be of little intrinsic interest. It just so happens that this is the principle which allows all locals to stick to their respective cultures. For the cosmopolitans, in contrast, there is value in diversity as such, but they are not likely to get it, in anything

like the present form, unless other people are allowed to carve out special niches for their cultures, and keep them. Which is to say that there can be no cosmopolitans without locals.[59]

Hence a global value system should be understood as organisation of diversity rather than replication of uniformity.[60] Diversity is found in examinations of particular communities or societies, such as those collected by Jeffrey McNeely and David Pitt, which are of particular interest since they deal with traditional methods of managing fragile ecosystems in order to provide for the basic needs of a local society.[61] Since both physical and cultural survival are at stake, one can see how very different local circumstances nevertheless share common features with one another and with the global dimension of environmental change. For example, inherited agricultural techniques (or detailed knowledge of food sources in the case of the few remaining hunter-gatherer societies) and land management skills may be essential ingredients of sustainability, yet where new technologies are introduced, or local conditions are changed by development, this knowledge base is put at risk. The normative dimension is apparent in the introduction of inappropriate technology from an alien context, which not only undermines traditional indigenous sources of knowledge but may well disrupt the ecological balance. The political dimension in such cases is represented by the relative empowerment (or lack of it)[62] of local groups or sub-cultures in relation to dominant social forces at the national, regional, or international level – note just one expression of the perspective of indigenous peoples, which might easily apply to experiences in many parts of the world where environmental degradation has given rise to resistance: 'For many of us, however, the last few centuries have meant a major loss of control over our lands and waters. We are still the first to know about changes in the environment, but we are now the last to be asked or consulted'.[63] Conceptions of property and patterns of land ownership reflect the normative dimension of environmental economics, since these are by no means universally shared assumptions. Western capitalist conceptions of property rights do not fit easily with societies where property rights have been conceived differently, as in for example the intergenerational group ownership of land, with conditional possession rights for individual users.[64] A typical consequence of such a clash is the development, by modern industrial techniques, of apparently unused and unclaimed (i.e., untitled) land which was in fact only temporarily unoccupied due to the seasonal migration of a nomadic population, allowing a cyclical recovery from grazing and other uses.[65] A more specifically 'social' normative dimension arises from the preceding considerations, since it is intimately tied up with traditional knowledge, political institutions and economic systems of production and distribution, all of which depend on relative autonomy if social relations with the natural environment are to be sustainable. For example, local social values are instrumental in regulating population growth, so as not to exceed the carrying capacity of land. The natural environment is also a source of social identity, either through association with a geographic location or with a particular species, and often has a spiritual role.[66] None of the foregoing denies the possibility or even desirability of change, nor does it posit a fundamental distinction between relatively marginal traditional societies and mainstream western societies since these are connected through a global political economy and other aspects of the 'world system', but it does indicate the complex relationship between human activities and the environment and suggests that the implications of environmental change may be best understood from a normative perspective.

In industrial societies the process of industrial development itself has led to environmental degradation, not only as a by-product of productive techniques but also as a result of social demands increasing in line with the prospect of these demands being met (economic growth and rising expectations). The spill-over of industrial development on a global scale introduces environmental degradation outside of industrial societies through the location of industry in cheap labour markets or the export of waste, and by altering patterns of consumption and demand. Non-industrial societies, when pressed by famine or disrupted by conflict, find their traditional solutions are ineffective and not readily adapted to changing circumstances: increasing the population is a common group survival strategy, but it generally results in exceeding the carrying capacity of the land and increases dependency on external inputs which further undermine autonomy. Enforced migration or displacement rends the social fabric, and places unwelcome pressure on host populations. Soil erosion and deforestation are commonplace, as populations struggle to meet the need for food, fuel or export earnings. Developed capitalist societies, facing different but parallel pressures in the form of consumer demand and international competition, respond by increasing production to meet already inefficient and now enhanced patterns of consumption, and increase the demand for raw materials and fossil fuels, thereby furthering the degradation of the natural environment. Potential efficiencies in a global market are denied by relatively protectionist policies, and the pursuit of comparative advantage in raw materials leads to unsustainable rates of extraction. A notable difference between developing and developed societies is the latter's technological and economic capacity for adaption to and mitigation of environmental change, but there are obviously limits to this:

note the 'Limits to Growth' debate initiated by the Club of Rome and picked up by the Brandt and Brundtland Commissions,[67] and the challenging criticisms of environmentalists everywhere. This is not to say that there are not significant differences between developed western societies, just as there are between so-called traditional societies, since there is evidence of different attitudes and priorities concerning the environment even among comparable economies.[68]

In any society, including international society, value change occurs over time, and this includes the predominant view of nature. Note, for example, Fritjof Capra's critique of the Cartesian world view and his call for a more appropriate, ecological, perspective.[69] The key point here is to note that environmental change is intimately related to human activities, and social capacities and predispositions, all of which reflect normative characteristics such that a connection can be made between values and environmental change.[70]

Normative Implications

The normative implications of GEC are rather underexamined. The reference here is to societal responses to changes in the environment, whether man-made or 'natural' – a distinction which may be viewed as characteristic of modernity.[71] That is to say, the inquiry turns at this point to consideration of the impact that experience of environmental change has had on normative systems. One such implication of change is the increasing salience of the category of 'risk'. So for example, if modernity is characterised in part by rapid change in political, economic and social conditions, and corresponding practices, the response to such change may be encapsulated by what Ulrich Beck calls 'risk society'.[72]

Douglas and Wildavsky note in their book *Risk and Culture* that there is disagreement about perception, estimation and management of risk – including fears for the environment. They note that the problems of risk hinge on knowledge about the future and consent about the most desired prospects – where these are uncertain and contested, respectively, there is no obvious solution. Most interestingly, they note that 'any form of society produces its own selected view of the natural environment' and that 'common values lead to common fears'.[73] There are also those who suggest that an aspect of rapid change, or what Paul Virilio calls 'speed', raises the prospect of our values and practices outrunning our physical capacities, in turn giving rise to such developments as the new technologies of cyberspace.[74] Enhancing our innate capacities is necessary if failure to cope with rapid change leads to stress and breakdowns in communication.[75]

On the other hand, one might view increased sensitivity to the risks of change, as distinct from the capacity to apprehend and cope with change, as part of an historical process in which earlier agrarian and industrial revolutions are now followed by an ecological revolution, leading to what Dennis Pirages calls 'global ecopolitics'.[76] This does not limit discussion to the obviously global dimensions of climate change and global warming or to the global commons (atmosphere, oceans and Antarctica), since local conditions may be considered either constitutive or contributory elements of the global condition – this is true of both the non-human environment and human value systems. Juxtaposing 'environment' and 'values' right away introduces problems of distinguishing between the two, in as much as modern anthropocentric constructions of 'nature' tend to hide intimate relationships between the human and the non-human (or 'natural'). At the same time, the changing priorities within the dominant culture of western secular industrial societies, which is in many respects synonymous with 'global culture' as a consequence of its influence, are noted by Pirages: 'In the 'postindustrial' world of limited opportunities that is now emerging many of the expansionist industrial norms, values, and modes of international behaviour are increasingly being called into question because they no longer seem appropriate in a more complex world of perceived scarcity'.[77] Pirages suggests that there is a revolutionary change in process, by which the dominant social paradigm will shift as it confronts anomalies and dilemmas, inevitably giving way to a new ecopolitical paradigm.[78] It may be said that such a paradigm shift is a consequence of environmental change, and the inability of the prevailing values of industrial expansionism to cope with such changes. Indeed, evidence of a value shift toward post-materialism in relatively secure post-war advanced industrial societies has been offered by Ronald Inglehart and others, with environmentalism being a key illustration.[79]

In the developing world, the dominant social paradigm of western industrial capitalism and its development model has always been a mixed blessing. Notwithstanding aspirations for industrial development and economic self-sufficiency this paradigm has been consistently challenged in the postcolonial era, and indeed the recent rapid expansion of environmentalism in the developing world has been cited as a manifestation of resistance. Steven Brechin and Willett Kempton, for example, argue that environmentalism in developing countries is not necessarily connected to observed post-materialist values in advanced industrial societies, but is rather a pragmatic (and materialist) response to environmental change under conditions of economic underdevelopment.[80] While the post-materialist thesis does not explain environmental concern in developing countries (other indigenous grievances, and the direct perception of environmental degradation are more important), these authors conclude that concern for the environment has nevertheless become a global value, disseminated through mass media and elite communication centering on the environment and development debate.

These perspectives on environmental concern call attention to underlying theoretical and practical value structures, which may be understood in terms of normatively defined webs of meaning. George Cvetkovitch and Timothy Earle note the importance of recognising the fundamental characteristics of GEC – uncertainty dominates its assessment; environmental changes are simultaneously local and global; and change takes place over a long period of time – and they conclude that values act to attune people to particular GEC themes and influence their perceptions of risk.[81] Incorporating these considerations into the study of international relations may be an awkward task, but 'we still badly need an understanding of how sociocultural systems and ecosystems interact'.[82]

Not surprisingly, an examination of the normative dimensions of environmental change brings us back to concerns addressed above in relation to deterrence and foreign policy; in relation to the former because 'environmental security' is a newly coined term which presents a fundamental challenge to conceptions of security in general (which I discuss at length elsewhere),[83] and in relation to the latter because of the obvious need for at the least policy coordination if not global policy-making through appropriate international institutions. A brief illustration of what is at stake in invoking the concept of 'environmental security' is provided here to further illuminate the normative dimension of policy discourse.

Environment and Security

It has been argued that organised violence, the traditional threat and source of insecurity, is not analytically comparable to environmental threats.[84] Thus a principal difficulty in discussing environment and security is the recalcitrance of traditional politico-military definitions of security. It is a traditional prerogative of nation-states to exercise a monopoly on the use of violence, both as a means of maintaining domestic order, and as a tool of foreign policy. In contrast, the developing logic of international environmental relations increasingly points to relations among regional and local actors in a global context rather than traditional interstate relations. Such 'glocal' (global–local) relations can be seen as succeeding what was begun by the phenomenon of transnational relations by further conditioning, though not eliminating, the role of nation-states. The traditional notion of national security 'becomes profoundly confused' when there is internal instability or insecurity in states, and the 'the image of the state as a referent object for security fades...'.[85] This is compounded where environmental change does not reflect political or territorial boundaries.

Continuing dependence on the troubled concepts of sovereignty, national interest, (state) foreign policy, which have historically provided the framework and rationale for military threats and actions, suggests that the notion of 'security' does not lend itself well to the project of conceptualising a response to emerging global changes – not least global environmental change. Military power is the traditional manifestation of state power, and the locus of value investment for notions of security attaching to the state and (in these terms, by definition) to populations under its jurisdiction. These values are seldom in step with the human environment, but vast resources have been exhausted in their name. Thus the traditional security discourse is not well equipped to address the pressing global issues that a contemporary definition of security must cope with. Consequently, there is an opportunity for reexamining 'the meaning of security',[86] and indeed, the question of redefining security is the topic (and title) of a broad recent literature, much of which addresses environmental security.[87]

Richard Ullman notes that 'the tendency of American political leaders to define security problems and their solutions in military terms is deeply ingrained' and suggests that we 'should not overestimate the achievements of ... nongovernmental organizations' in putting forward alternative conceptions of national security, such as limiting population growth and enhancing environmental quality.[88] This is not perhaps true to the same extent for all countries, but it is to be expected that any sea-change in the world political order will require the acquiescence of the United States, whose security agenda influences others. One might hope the concept of environmental security would find a natural home at the level of international security, but the traditional agenda is merely an extension of national state preoccupations such that collective security, far from escaping the parochialism of state-centric security, is a fundamentally conservative notion, viewed by Herz as 'an attempt to maintain, and render more secure, the "territoriality" or "impermeability" of states upon which their "sovereignty" and "independence" had rested since the beginning of the modern era'.[89]

As a potential improvement on national defence, the idea of international security has a long history which includes various proposals for world government, but perhaps most significantly the initiatives leading to the League of Nations and the United Nations, whose founding documents include collective security provisions. Herz, writing in 1959, is concerned with the new conditions of the 'Atomic Age' (which he characterises in a final chapter entitled 'Universalism as an Alternative to the Power Dilemma'), but his observations remain apposite: 'Any discussion of the details of a more integrated world structure... must of necessity remain rather theoretical and detached from present realities. ...Our task is more basic; it concerns the conclusions to be drawn from the unprecedented condition that has befallen mankind. And the first thing to realize is that the situation confronts for the first time the whole human race as one group...'.[90] Instructively, the conditions are true of global environmental change, yet it is the famous 'security dilemma' which continues to dominate conceptions of security for the 'units' in international relations: '...a feeling of insecurity, deriving from mutual suspicion and mutual fear, compels these units to compete for ever more power in order to find more security, an effort which proves self-defeating because complete security remains ultimately unobtainable'.[91] It is obviously true that the security threats of global environmental change cannot be met simply by the accumulation of state power at the unit level.

Whether or not concepts of environmental security will allow an escape from the essential structure of international relations remains an open question, but to the extent that the present structure remains inadeqate, this must surely be an aspiration. Peter F. Drucker notes in 'The New Realities' that crucial environmental needs such as the protection of the atmosphere and of forests 'cannot be addressed as adversarial issues',[92] and Ken Conca has suggested that it is not clear whether the existing global structures (and their inequalities) will be changed or reinforced by the pursuit of environmental security,[93] and it is even conceivable that environmental security itself could become militarised, and the opportunity for fundamental change lost through the co-option of the environmental agenda by a traditional security agenda.

The complexity and ambiguity of the concept of environmental security, with its definition being tied to 'insecurity' as a social phenomenon with localised variations in perception and valuation as well as a global dimension, leads to a number of different approaches and perspectives in the literature, and a discourse about environmental security which is consequently unclear, exhibiting sometimes contradictory mixed metaphors.[94] Proposals range from attempts at reform of traditional security conceptions to the radical overhaul of world politics, with some advocating the addition of selected parts of the environmental agenda to the list of things to be secured militarily (obviously a very conventional approach), and others calling for a restructuring of the entire political order so as to respond effectively to a perceived environmental crisis of immense proportions.

It is certainly appropriate to acknowledge change, since it is this feature of international relations which has brought existing concepts into disarray, if not disrepute, and any conception of environmental security must surely take into account the challenges that arise from both changes in the global environment and changes in the international political system following the end of the Cold War. This much has been recognised by organisations at the heart of the international system, such as the United Nations and the North Atlantic Treaty Organisation.[95] The question is not, then, about changes in themselves, but rather what these changes mean for our conception of security, and for the study of international relations. International relations theory (and practice) has perhaps already moved in appropriate directions, including its reincorporation into the inclusive compass of political theory,[96] but more specifically it is necessary to consider how the issues of values relating to environmental change can be reflected in the study of international relations, and normative theoretical approaches are well-suited to the task.

CONCLUSIONS

Thus is illustrated by the salience of normative investigations of nuclear deterrence, foreign policy-making, and global environmental change; that is, in both traditional and novel areas of concern to the discipline of international relations. Christopher Hill, writing on future research tasks relating to EPC, points to a 'more directly normative' question which brings the present discussion back to the general theme of normative structures in international society, which must then be held to be among the determinants of foreign policy as much as they are the product of national foreign policy (whether such policy is intentionally or unintentionally supportive of international norms):

> It is the appropriate balance between self-regarding and systemic objectives. This is almost what Arnold Wolfers designated as the divide between possessional and milieu goals, and is a central dilemma for any foreign policy, national or collective. Essentially it refers to the fact that any actor in international relations has to decide, in general and on a case-by-case basis, what balance it is going to strike between pursuing national concerns and looking after the fabric of international society as a whole – which many would characterise as being in its own long-term interest.[97]

Of course, the differences among particular societies in respect to establishing and preserving absolute value references (the substance of nationalism, for example) dictates that their relationship with an international society will be distinctive – there is no prospect of a perfectly shared understanding of world affairs given that each actor views the world from within a different referential context. However, this does not mean that normative theory cannot be employed in understanding the manner in which foreign policies are generated in individual societies, or indeed how they are likely to be percieved by other international actors, regardless of common reference points in an international society. See Peter J. Katzenstein (ed.), *The Culture of National Security: Norms and Identity in World Politics* (New York: Columbia University Press, 1996). As Kratochwil says of the tendency to focus on national decision-making processes:

> By reviving a more philosophically oriented discussion which attempts to assess the role of norms in decision-making, if all goes well we not only counteract such an unwarranted narrowing of focus in regard to international relations, but also gain a better picture of why actors in the international as well as in the domestic arena *have to resort to norms.*[98]

Furthermore, what has been established in the way of an international society can itself generate particular values and apprehensions, and being a part of this 'society' too, individual actors may find sufficient common ground for the conduct of their mutual affairs. What is especially significant is that there now exists a body of vital central issues (security, development, the environment, etc.) which simply cannot be addressed from contingent perspectives, and which admit of no culture-bound solution (notwithstanding that these issues may be produced or conditioned by a dominant or hegemonic global culture: a normative process). These issues, consequently, exemplify objects of study which are uniquely and distinctively the concern of 'international relations'.

A normative understanding of political life, which is conscious of the contingent solutions to the problem of 'the absolute' which individual societies rely on, may provide a means of addressing the difficulties of transferring even a part of this reliance to a system of international values.

What prospects there are for such an international value structure arise principally from the uniqueness (and perhaps also the intransigence) of the issues involved, all of which are the products of modern international relations and consequently have some meaning and reference beyond individual societies. Naturally, this meaning impinges on the practical possibilities of individual actors, as is best appreciated from a theoretical approach which views '*normative* expectations as a filter... on what decision-makers consider worth trying'.[99] Largely because norms 'enable and constrain the playing of roles',[100] the relatively subjective estimation of what is feasible contributes to the shared meaning ascribed to the international milieu, and a shared understanding of the values operating there.

That societies remain individual and distinct nonetheless is a source of difficulty and the challenge for any foreign policy that seeks to address global issues. John Dunn, writing about the broader challenge of formulating state policy in the absence of a coherent conception of the Political Good and under conditions of an abiding nuclear threat, concludes thus:

> On balance it still seems likely – despite the appalling record of organized violence in the twentieth century – that states today do *somewhat* more good than harm. But what is unnerving about the world we live in now is the sense of a challenge... It is hard to see how we can hope to address this challenge except, in the end, through the responses of state powers. But whether states themselves could in principle display the causal capacity to face this challenge successfully for us is at best as yet quite unclear.[101]

It is argued here that global issues, by definition, arise and must be resolved in the context of a global or international political realm with its own history and its own contingent solutions to the problem of political meaning. Thus it is essential to arrive at an adequate understanding of the normative pattern of this broader society, and its relation to the similar if more restricted normative environments of distinct political groups which both act in and constitute international or global society.

NOTES

1. John Dunn, 'Responsibility without Power: States and the Incoherence of the Modern Conception of the Political Good' in his *Interpreting Political Responsibility: Essays 1981–1989* (Cambridge: Polity Press, 1990), p. 130.
2. See, for example, the argument in Robin Brown 'Limited War' in Colin McInnes and G. D. Sheffield (eds), *Warfare in the Twentieth Century: Theory and Practice* (London: Unwin Hyman, 1988).
3. Note the effect of strategic categories spilling over into areas where they are not appropriate: Philip Windsor discusses the case of arms control, where the extended deterrence idea of strategic balance imposed itself in such a way that arms control negotiations proceeded 'in a manner contrary to that which would be the expected norm'. Philip Windsor, 'Towards a Hierarchy for Arms Control', *Millennium* (Vol. 15, No. 2, Summer 1986), p. 173.
4. Philip Bobbitt, *Democracy and Deterrence: The History and Future of Nuclear Strategy* (London: Macmillan, 1988), p. 271.
5. Hugh Macdonald, 'Strategic Studies', *Millennium: Journal of International Studies* (Vol. 16, No. 2, Summer 1987), pp. 335–6.

6. Bobbitt, *op. cit.*, p. 286.
7. Russell Hardin, John J. Mearsheimer, Gerald Dworkin and Robert E. Goodin (eds), *Nuclear Deterrence: Ethics and Strategy* (Chicago, IL and London: University of Chicago Press, 1985). See my review of this volume in *Millennium* (Vol. 16, No. 1, Spring 1987), pp. 141ff.
8. On the relationship between arms control and strategy, see again Windsor, *op. cit.*
9. Jeff McMahan, 'Deterrence and Deontology' in Hardin et al., *op. cit.*, p. 160.
10. Marc Trachtenberg, 'Strategists, Philosophers, and the Nuclear Question' in Hardin et al., *op. cit.*, p. 364.
11. See the discussion in this chapter, under 'Normative Aspects of Foreign Policy'.
12. John Dunn, *Interpreting Political Responsibility: Essays 1981–1989*, *op. cit.*, p. 129.
13. I confess I am unable to identify the original author of the delightfully euphemistic phrase 'technological recalcitrance', but she/he should be congratulated for compressing the wealth of implications attending the simple existence of nuclear weapons (and the impossibility of 'uninventing' them) into such a nutshell. The phrase 'How I learned to stop worrying and love the bomb' is the alternative title of the film Dr. Strangelove, made in the sixties and still well-known as a satire on Cold War paranoia.
14. See again Theodor Adorno, *The Dialectic of Enlightenment*, *op. cit.*
15. See Carl von Clausewitz, *Vom Kriege* (*On War*), especially: Book 1, Chapters I and II; Book 7, Chapter XXII; and all nine chapters of Book 8. He argued that the only rational thing possible is the '...subordination of the military point of view to the political...' (p. 598).
16. See Peter Paret, 'Clausewitz', Chapter 7 in Paret (ed), *Makers of Modern Strategy: from Machiavelli to the Nuclear Age* (Princeton, NJ: Princeton University Press, 1986), p. 190. This volume is a sequel to another by the same principal title (Princeton, 1943 and 1971).
17. B. H. Liddell Hart, *Strategy: the indirect approach* (London: Faber and Faber, 1968), p. 334.
18. Lawrence Freedman, 'The First Two Generations of Nuclear Strategists', Chapter 25 in Paret (ed), *Makers of Modern Strategy*, *op. cit.*, p. 735.
19. Bobbit, *op. cit.*, p. 14.
20. H. J. Laski, *Introduction to Politics*, revised edition prepared by Martin Wight (London: George Allen and Unwin, 1951), pp. 104–5.
21. Bobbitt, *op. cit.*, p. 7.
22. *The Independent*, 8 October 1990.
23. See O. Weaver, P. Lemaitre and E. Tromer (eds), *European Polyphony: Perspectives Beyond the East–West Confrontation* (Basingstoke: Macmillan, 1989), reviewed by Catherine Murray in *Millennium: Journal of International Studies* (Vol. 19, No. 2, Summer 1990).
24. See P. C. Stern, R. Axelrod, R. Jervis and R. Radner (eds), *Perspectives on Deterrence* (Oxford: Oxford University Press, 1989), reviewed by Edward Rhodes in *Millennium: Journal of International Studies* (Vol. 19, No. 2, Summer 1990).
25. Graham Evans, from his review in *Millennium: Journal of International Studies* (Vol. 19, No. 2, Summer 1990).

26. G. M. Dillon (ed.), *Defence Policy Making: A Comparative Analysis* (Leicester: Leicester University Press, 1988), p. 7.
27. *Ibid.*
28. Harold H. Saunders, 'The Arab–Israeli Conflict in a Global Perspective', in John Steinbruner (ed.), *Restructuring American Foreign Policy* (Washington: Brookings, 1989), p. 226.
29. *Ibid.*, p. 227.
30. Neil R. Richardson, 'Dyadic Case Studies in the Comparative Study of Foreign Policy Behaviour' in Charles F. Herman, Charles W. Kegley, Jr., and James N. Rosenau (eds.), *New Directions in the Study of Foreign Policy* (Boston, MA: Allen and Unwin, 1987), p. 161.
31. Charles W. Kegley, Jr., 'Decision Regimes and the Comparative Study of Foreign Policy', in *ibid.*, p. 249.
32. Steve Smith, 'Foreign Policy Analysis and International Relations', *Millennium: Journal of International Studies* (Vol. 16, No. 2, Summer 1987), p. 346.
33. *Ibid.*
34. *Ibid.*
35. *Ibid.*, p. 347.
36. *Ibid.*
37. *Ibid.*, p. 348.
38. Kratochwil, *Rules, Norms, and Decisions, op. cit.*, p. 5.
39. It is worth noting here the significance of Kenneth Arrow's impossibility theorem, from the field of public choice theory, which suggests that the outcome of any collective choice function is necessarily irrational, and that perfect representation of individual preferences in a public choice decision is impossible if even a few basic conditions of democratic politics are to be met.
40. Paul Taylor, *The Limits of European Integration* (London: Croom Helm, 1983), pp. 11–14.
41. *Ibid.*, p. 15, 19.
42. Vernon Van Dyke, 'Values and Interests', *American Political Science Review* (Vol. 56, September 1962), p. 573. The reference is to Morgenthau, *Politics Among Nations*, 3rd. ed. (1960), pp. 4–5.
43. *Ibid.*, p. 572.
44. Note, however, the difficulties associated with 'the domestic analogy'. See Hidemi Suganami, *The Domestic Analogy and World Order Proposals* (Cambridge: Cambridge University Press, 1989).
45. Alfred Pijpers, Elfriede Regelsberger and Wolfgang Wessels (eds), *European Political Cooperation in the 1980s: A Common Foreign Policy for Western Europe?* (Dordrecht, The Netherlands: Martinus Nijhoff, 1988), p. 269.
46. *Ibid.*, p. 232.
47. *Ibid.*, p. 234.
48. Parts of this discussion draw on my 'EcoCultures: Global Culture in the Age of Ecology', *Millennium: Journal of International Studies* (Vol. 22, No. 3, Winter 1993), pp. 483–504 and my 'Environmental Security as a Universal Value: Implications for International Theory' in John Vogler and Mark F. Imber, eds., *The Environment and International Relations* (London and New York: Routledge, 1996).

49. For discussions of values in social science see, for example, David Thomas, *Naturalism and Social Science: A Post-Empiricist Philosophy of Social Science* (Cambridge: Cambridge University Press, 1979) and Christopher G. A. Bryant, *Positivism in Social Theory and Research* (London: Macmillan, 1985), as well as the various themes touched on in Hugh C. Dyer and Leon Mangasarian (eds), *The Study of International Relations: The State of the Art* (London: Macmillan, 1989).

50. Note, for example, the World Climate Research Programme and the International Geosphere-Biosphere Programme.

51. Any number of books touch on policy themes, but see, for example, John E. Carroll (ed), *International Environmental Diplomacy* (Cambridge: Cambridge University Press, 1988); Rudiger Dornbusch and James M. Poterba (eds), *Global Warming: Economic Policy Responses* (Cambridge, MA: MIT Press, 1991); Francis Sandbach, *Environment, Ideology and Policy* (Oxford: Basil Blackwell, 1980); and Caroline Thomas, *The Environment in International Relations* (London: Royal institute of International Affairs, 1992).

52. See, for example, Michael Jacobs, *The Green Economy: Environment, Sustainable Development and the Politics of the Future* (London: Pluto, 1991) and David Pearce (ed), *Blueprint 2: Greening the World Economy* (London: Earthscan, 1991). Pearce is a somewhat controversial advocate of market-led strategies, and contributed 'Economics and the Global Environmental Challenge' to the *Millennium* Special Issue on GEC and IR (Vol. 19, No. 3, 1990).

53. See Kym Anderson and Richard Blackhurst (eds), *The Greening of World Trade Issues* (Hemel Hempstead: Harvester-Wheatsheaf, 1992).

54. See Jiri Pehe, 'The Green Movements in Eastern Europe', *RFE/RL Report on Eastern Europe* (Vol. 1, No. 11, 16 March 1990), pp. 35–7, and also his 'An Annotated Survey of Independent Associations in Eastern Europe', *RFE/RL Radio Free Europe Research*, Background Report (Vol. 14, No. 24, 16 June 1989). See also Barbara Jancar, 'The Environmental Attractor in the Former USSR: Ecology and Regional Change' in Ronnie Lipschutz and Ken Conca (eds), *The State and Social Power in Global Environmental Politics*, *op. cit.*

55. See Stephan Schmidheiny (with the Business Council for Sustainable Development), *Changing Course: A Global Business Perspective on Development and the Environment* (Cambridge, MA: MIT Press, 1992).

56. Paul Craig, Harold Glasser and Willett Kempton, 'Ethics and Values in Environmental Policy: The Said and the UNCED', *Environmental Values* (Vol. 2, No. 2, Summer 1993).

57. See, for example, Vandana Shiva, *Monocultures of the Mind: Perspectives on Biodiversity and Biotechnology* (Penang: Third World Network/London: Zed, 1993) and Marcus Colchester and Larry Lohmann (eds), *The Struggle for Land and the Fate of the Forests* (Penang: World Rainforest Movement/London: Zed, 1993).

58. For a relevant discussion see William E. Connolly, 'Identity and Difference in Global Politics' in James Der Derian and Michael J. Shapiro, *International/Intertextual Relations: Postmodern Readings of World Politics* (Lexington, MA: Lexington Books, 1989), pp. 323–342.

59. Ulf Hannerz, 'Cosmopolitans and Locals in World Culture' in Mike
     Featherstone, *Global Culture, op. cit.*, pp. 249–50.
60. *Ibid.*, p 237.
61. Jeffrey A. McNeely and David Pitt (eds), *Culture and Conservation: The
     Human Dimension in Environmental Planning* (London: Croom Helm,
     1985).
62. See Steve Breyman, 'Knowledge as Power: Ecology Movements and Global
     Environmental Problems' in Lipschutz and Conca (eds), *The State and
     Social Power in Global Environmental Politics, op. cit.*
63. Louis Bruyere, President of the Native Council of Canada, to the World
     Commission on Environmental and Development (WCED) public hearing,
     Ottawa, 26–27 May 1986. Quoted in WCED, *Our Common Future* (Oxford:
     Oxford University Press, 1987), p. 61.
64. See C. K. Omari, 'Traditional African Land Ethics', in J. Ronald Engel and
     Joan Gibb Engel (eds), *Ethics of Environment and Development: Global
     Challenge and International Response* (Tucson, AZ: University of Arizona
     Press, 1990), pp. 167–182.
65. See also Robert Goodland, 'Tribal Peoples and Economic Development:
     The Human Ecological Dimension', in McNeely and Pitt (eds), *Culture and
     Conservation, op. cit.*, p. 15ff.
66. See Chris Tobayiwa and Peter Jackson, 'Shona People, Totems and
     Wildlife', pp. 229–236, and Nicholas V. C. Polunin, 'Traditional Marine
     Practices in Indonesia and Their Bearing on Conservation', pp. 156–159, in
     McNeely and Pitt (eds), *Culture and Conservation, op. cit.*
67. The Independent Commission on International Development Issues chaired
     by Willi Brandt, and the World Commission on Environment and
     Development chaired by Gro Harlem Brundtland.
68. See Paul P. Craig, Harold Glasser and Willett Kempton, 'Ethics and Values
     in Environmental Policy: The Said and the UNCED', *Environmental Values*
     (Vol. 2, No. 2, Summer 1993). See also the survey by Louis Harris and
     Associates, *Public and Leadership Attitudes to the Environment: A Report
     of a Survey in 16 Countries*, conducted for the United Nations Environment
     Programme (New York: Harris and Associates, 1989), and the 1992 survey
     by Riley E. Dunlap, George H. Gallup and Alec M. Gallup, *The Health of
     the Planet Survey: A Preliminary Report on Attitudes on the Environment
     and Economic Growth measured by Surveys of Citizens in 22 Nations to
     Date* (Princeton, NJ: The George Gallup International Institute, 1993). The
     ISSC Human Dimensions of Global Environmental Change Programme
     (HDP) is currently developing a research programme entitled Global
     Omnibus Environmental Survey (GOES) to produce systematic survey data
     on environmental behaviour, knowledge, risk perceptions, attitudes, values,
     and contextual information.
69. Fritjof Capra, *The Turning Point: Science, Society and the Rising Culture*
     (London: Flamingo/HarperCollins, 1983).
70. For useful discussions of the value content of 'nature' see Neil Evernden,
     The Social Construction of Nature (Baltimore, MD: The Johns Hopkins
     University Press, 1992), esp. Chapter 2, 'Nature and Norm', p. 18ff, and the
     useful introduction to the related theories of *human* nature by Leslie
     Stevenson, *Seven Theories of Human Nature* (Oxford: Oxford University

Press, 1974). For broad philosophical discussions of the idea of nature see Clarence Glacken, *Traces on the Rhodian Shore: Nature and Culture in Western Thought from Ancient Times to the End of the Eighteenth Century* (Berkeley: University of California Press, 1967) and the more recent and very readable Max Oelschlaeger, *The Idea of Wilderness: From Prehistory to the Age of Ecology* (New Haven, CT: Yale University Press, 1991).

71. The principal thrust of this distinction is to illuminate the modernist conception of the non-human environment as 'nature', which underwrites resource exploitation in the interest of *human* progress. See Oelschlaeger, *The Idea of Wilderness, ibid.*, Chapter 3, 'The Alchemy of Modernism: The Transmutation of Wilderness into Nature', pp. 68ff.
72. Ulrich Beck, *Risk Society: Towards a New Modernity* (London: Sage, 1992). See also his *Ecological Politics in an Age of Risk* (Cambridge: Polity Press, 1995).
73. Mary Douglas and Aaron Wildavsky, *Risk and Culture: An Essay on the Selection of Technical and Environmental Dangers* (Berkeley, CA: University of California Press, 1982), pp. 1, 5 and 8.
74. See, among his many works, Paul Virilio, *Speed and Politics: An Essay on Dromology*, trans. M. Polizzotti (New York: Semiotext(e), 1986), and an application of 'speed' to international relations in James Der Derian, *Antidiplomacy: Spies, Terror, Speed, and War* (Oxford: Blackwell, 1992). On the last point see Allucquere Rosanne Stone, 'Will the Real Body Please stand Up? Boundary Stories about Virtual Cultures' in Michael Benedikt, *Cyberspace: First Steps* (Cambridge, MA: MIT Press, 1991), p. 110.
75. See Donna Haraway, *Primate Visions: Gender, Race and Nature in the World of Modern Science* (New York: Routledge, 1990), pp. 186–230.
76. Dennis Pirages, *The New Context for International Relations: Global Ecopolitics* (North Scituate, MA: Duxbury Press, 1978).
77. Pirages, *op. cit.*, from the Preface, p. ix.
78. *Ibid.*, p. 7ff.
79. See Ronald Inglehart, *The Silent Revolution: Changing Values and Political Styles Among Western Publics* (Princeton, NJ: Princeton University Press, 1977) and *Cultural Shift in Advanced Industrial Society* (Princeton, NJ: Princeton University Press, 1990), and Nicholas Watts and Geoffrey Wandesforde-Smith, 'Postmaterial Values and Environmental Policy Change' in Dean E. Mann (ed), *Environmental Policy Formation: The Impact of Values, Ideology and Standards* (Lexington, MA: Lexington Books, 1981).
80. Steven R. Brechin and Willett Kempton, 'Global Environmentalism: A Challenge to the Postmaterialism Thesis?', *Social Science Quarterly* (Vol. 75, 1994). This article provides a useful analysis of information gathered in the Harris and Gallup polls, *op. cit.*
81. George Cvetkovich and Timothy C. Earle, 'Values and Responses to News Media Signals About Global Environmental Changes: A Preliminary Study with American University Students', Western Institute for Social and Organizational Research Report No. 1991-03 (Bellingham, WN: WISOR/Western Washington University, 1991).
82. Karl Dake, 'Myths of Nature: Culture and the Social Construction of Risk', *Journal of Social Issues* (Vol. 48, No. 4, 1992), pp. 33–4.

83. For a more extensive treatment of environmental security situated in the context of normative theory see my 'Environmental Security as a Universal Value: Implications for International Theory' in John Vogler and Mark F. Imber, eds., *The Environment and International Relations* (London and New York: Routledge, 1996).

84. Daniel Deudney, 'The Case Against Linking Environmental Degradation and National Security', *Millennium* (Vol. 19, No. 3, Winter 1990), pp. 461ff. See also his 'Environmental Security: Muddled Thinking', *Bulletin of The Atomic Scientists* (April 1991), pp. 22–28.

85. Barry Buzan, *People, States and Fear*, 2nd ed. (Hemel Hempstead, Herts: Harvester Wheatsheaf, 1991), p. 103.

86. Dennis Pirage, 'Environmental Security and Social Evolution', *International Studies Notes* (Vol. 16, No. 1, Winter 1991), p. 8.

87. Lester R. Brown, *Redefining National Security* Worldwatch Institute Paper No. 14 (Washington, DC: Worldwatch Institute, 1977) and Lester R. Brown, 'Redefining National Security' in Lester R. Brown, et al., *State of the World 1986* A Worldwatch Institute Report on Progress Toward a Sustainable Society (New York: Norton 1986); Neville Brown, 'Climate Ecology and International Security', *Survival* (Vol. 31 No. 6, 1989), pp. 519–32; Simon Dalby, 'Modernity, Ecology and the Dilemmas of Security' (paper presented at the 33rd Annual Convention of the International Studies Association, Atlanta, 4 April 1992). See also his 'Security, Modernity, Ecology: The Dilemmas of Post-Cold War Security Discourse', *Alternatives* (Vol. 17, No. 1, 1992); Thomas F. Homer-Dixon, 'On the Threshold: Environmental Changes as Causes of Acute Conflict', *International Security* (Vol. 16, No. 2, Fall 1991), pp. 76–116; Jessica T. Mathews, 'Redefining Security', *Foreign Affairs* (Vol. 68, No. 2 (1989), pp. 162–77; Norman Myers, 'Environment and Security', *Foreign Policy* (No. 74, 1989), pp. 23–41; Dennis Pirages, 'Environmental Security and Social Evolution', *International Studies Notes* (Vol. 16, No. 1, Winter 1991), pp. 8–13; Michael Renner, *National Security: The Economic and Environmental Dimensions* (Washington, DC: Worldwatch Institute Paper No. 89, 1989); Michael Renner, 'Enhancing Global Security' in Lester R. Brown, et al., *State of the World 1989*, A Worldwatch Institute Report on Progress Toward a Sustainable Society (New York: Norton 1989); Ian H. Rowlands, 'The Security Challenges of Global Environmental Change', *Washington Quarterly* (Vol. 14, No. 1, Winter 1991), pp. 99–114; Theodore C. Sorenson, 'Rethinking National Security', *Foreign Affairs* (Vol. 69, No. 3 (1990), pp. 1–18; Ann Tickner, 'Redefining Security: A Feminist Perspective' (unpublished, 1989); Richard H. Ullman, 'Redefining Security', *International Security* (Vol. 8, No. 1, Summer 1983), pp. 129–53; see also the *Environmental Security Network Newsletter*. (Vol. 1, No. 1, Fall 1991).

88. Ullman, *op. cit.*, pp. 152–3.

89. John H. Herz, *International Politics in the Atomic Age*, pbk. ed. (New York and London: Columbia University Press, 1959), p. 76.

90. *Ibid.*, p. 303

91. *Ibid.*, p. 231. For alternative discussions of the essentially tragic 'security dilemma', see Herbert Butterfield, *History and Human Relations* (London:

Collins, 1951), pp. 19–20; Arnold Wolfers, *Discord and Collaboration* (Baltimore, MD: Johns Hopkins Press, 1962), pp. 3–24, and Robert Jervis, *Perception and Misperception in International Politics* (Princeton, NJ: Princeton University Press, 1976), p. 66.

92. Peter F. Drucker, *The New Realities* (London: Mandarin, 1990), pp. 110–111.

93. Ken Conca, 'Peace Studies and the Multiple Meanings of the Global Environment' (paper presented at the 33rd Annual Convention of the International Studies Association, Atlanta, 4 April 1992), and his 'Environmental Change and the Deep Structure of World Politics', in R. D. Lipschutz and K. Conca (eds.), *The State and Social Power in Global Environmental Politics* (New York: Columbia University Press, 1993).

94. *Ibid.*

95. The NATO Committee on the Challenges of Modern Society (CCMS) met for the first time in sixteen years in Washington, DC on 13 November 1995, to consider, among other things, a proposal for a pilot study on environmental security. NATO Press Release (95) 116, 24 November 1995 (see Internet/World Wide Web gopher site at <gopher://marvin.stc.nato.int:70/00/natodata/press...>).

96. See R. B. J. Walker, *Inside/Outside: International Relations as Political Theory* (Cambridge: Cambridge University Press, 1993) and Howard Williams, *International Relations in Political Theory* (Milton Keynes: Open University Press, 1992). Note also the revisiting of an old debate in the context of late twentieth century developments, touching on the issues of anarchy, interdependence and international cooperation, in David A. Baldwin (ed.), *Neorealism and Neoliberalism: The Contemporary Debate* (New York: Columbia University Press, 1993).

97. Alfred Pijpers *et al*, *op. cit.*, p. 222.

98. Friedrich V. Kratochwil, *Rules, Norms, and Decisions*, *op. cit.*, p.5.

99. Martin Hollis and Steve Smith (eds), *Explaining and Understanding International Relations* (Oxford: Clarendon Press, 1990), pp. 191–193.

100. *Ibid.*, p. 193.

101. John Dunn, *Interpreting Political Responsibility: Essays 1981–1989*, *op. cit.*, p. 141.

Conclusion

Thus do philosophy and reality, theory and action, work in the same circle indefinitely.

William James[1]

It has been shown that normative theory plays a central role in the study of international relations, in accordance with the initial premise. The questions posed at the outset concerning the role of normative theory – how, why, what – have been addressed by reference to methodological distinctions, to traditions reflected in the literature, and to the depth and breadth of the normative dimensions of international relations.

How normative theory plays a role was shown by examination of methodological problems raised in the first chapter, problems which resurfaced throughout, although their importance is not simply in indicating how normative theory accounts for choice of methods (and not just methods which locate values), since the questions about method right away implicate epistemological justifications of methodology. The role of normative theory was shown to be the establishment of the relationship between values and facts arising from the interpretive function of theory.

Why normative theory plays a role is consequent upon theoretical traditions which govern the disciplinary study of international relations, and a reading of the literature shows that these traditions have both implicitly included and explicitly marginalised normative theory. Here the role of normative theory was shown to be the re-introduction of values into a body of theory otherwise preoccupied with interests.

What the role of normative theory amounts to has been shown in chapters addressing the philosophical foundations of a normative approach dicovered in the realm of ideas and ideology (indicating limitations), in the communicative dynamic of norms in ethics, epistemology and political practice, in the influence of values in the formation of world views supporting political action, and in the applied cases of deterrence and foreign policy which indicate the explanatory capacity of normative theory in key areas of study. The twin strands of epistemological and political significance have been shown to give normative theory a broad ambit in the study of international relations.

THE LINE OF ARGUMENT

The argument presented here has developed along two intertwining strands or themes: the first is epistemological; the second political, in respect to theory. Which of these strands dominates depends to some extent upon the nature of the relation between theory and practice, but also on the perspective of the interlocutor.

On one hand the empirical contingencies of life on earth create the demand for knowledge and understanding of empirical facts which impinge upon our lives without regard to our values or designs, while at the same time many of the salient features of our world are social, economic and cultural and subject to political processes in which historical consciousness of value choices and collective aspirations is a vital component – these latter are social or institutional facts.

On the other hand, political practices and policy choices depend on some relatively stable conception of the world in which they are made, on grounds of effectiveness, while at the same time unfolding events or trends in or around a political system may escape detection and response if they are not accounted for in the operative political understanding.

Thus, the two strands of epistemology (or ontology, in the context of culture) and politics are tied up with one another such that knowledge is always conditioned by political processes (including the politics of knowledge itself) and politics is always conditioned by the state of knowledge as it bears on political choice and action.[2]

The point of arguing for the epistemological priority of values is not simply to deny factual aspects of international life, but to say that whatever facts are apprehended are apprehended as a consequence of normative influences. The intimate relationship of facts and values has been acknowledged here from the start. The issue is the nature of this relationship, which has been examined here to show that in every respect values are prior; prior in knowledge and prior in politics. Therefore, we should not be inclined to make out the facts of international relations in order to choose appropriate values, but rather to consider what can be made of these facts in light of our value choices. Unger puts it well:

Until the present time, few ideas were so widely shared among thinkers of the most diverse persuasions as the belief that the decisive question for political thought is, What can we know? This belief was accompanied by the doctrine that the manner in which we solve the problems of the theory of knowledge in turn depends on the way we answer questions in political thought. The theory of knowledge, according to this conception, is part of an inquiry into the psychological question, Why do we, as individuals, act as we do? Political theory is defined as the study of how men [and women] organize their societies and of how society should be organized.[3]

In the end, the discussion must come full circle and consider once again the character of the is–ought distinction and the separation of ethics and politics which has generated a marginalised and limited form of normative theorising in international relations. The determination of 'what ought to be' in international relations is not the only or even the chief role of normative theory in the study of international relations. Prior to and more important than any prescriptive statements that a normative theory of international relations can produce is the possibility it affords of revealing value-laden epistemologies and engaging in descriptive analysis of the moral order of the age.

The preceding examination of normative international relations theory has focussed on these latter aspects of its role, partly by making the necessary distinctions to indicate its potential for descriptive application in international relations, and partly by showing how realist international relations theory has hidden the normative dimension of descriptions and explanations. Political theory is only possible when the conception of politics is possible, and theory is consequently tied to human experience of political practice – in its several guises. This apparently self-evident condition is perhaps neglected in any study which takes a given theory or interpretation of reality for granted.

A theory of politics must be a theory of collective life, based on shared experience, regardless of what transcendent grounds there may be for human choice – these latter do not relieve us of the responsibility (jointly or severally) for choosing the form of our collective life. Realism, like religion, allows the world to come to terms with its failings. Yet it is insubstantial; political substance resides in values, and these are not subject to a final settlement.

In international relations, the natural history of social interactions ('the history through which they were established and naturalized'[4]) which generate normative structures is characterised, and challenged, by differences. Differences abound, typically as a result of identities grounded in nationhood and citizenship, but also in the miriad of cross-cutting experiences and loyalties that grow out of culture, class, race, religion and gender. Unlimited by the parameters of the nation-state, these islands of difference and identity rise out of a sea of human values. The choice of values gives rise to political issues or struggles, whose resolution is necessarily normative; normative not simply in the sense that resolutions determine which values ought to prevail, but because resolutions represent acknowledgement and acceptance as the product of a political engagement.

If it is granted that theory and practice are in a dialectical relationship, it is unlikely that practice will ever conform closely to the latest theoretical developments or that theories will necessarily address the pressing demands of everyday life. Nevertheless, the two inform one another, and knowledge and politics share characteristics which make them in some sense compatible. It is argued here that these characteristics are normative, and implicate values. Values exist both in static empirical facts, and in processes. Thus the argument of the combined strands, epistemological and political, is that the study of international relations stands in relation to the values permeating both its epistemologies and its subject matter. Consequently the role of normative theory, capable of addressing these values, is central to the project of international relations in both theory and practice.

It is particularly important to the present discussion that this relationship between theory and practice – or experience of practice – reflects a limitation of normative explanations. It has already been said that normative theory cannot account for transcendent belief systems except by reducing them to social norms, and that normative theory must remain agnostic about the transcendental categories of some philosophies. At the same time, it is clear that experience itself is not limited to an objective reality, and therefore that transcendental features of human experience may influence the apprehension of an acknowledged reality or its attributes. Recall Kolakowski's previously cited observation that 'we may not *a priori* exclude the reality of mystical experience that provides some people with this privileged access; but their experience cannot be re-forged into a theory'.[5] Thus it remains the case that normative theory can only account for values that are 'there', in the political world, and not for those to which access is privileged. Normative theory is concerned with the description and prescription of political practice, rather than with an ascription of Truth, notwithstanding that ethics and epistemology can be viewed as political practices. The well-known normative categories of truth, goodness, and beauty must be understood as having an application in the world of human experience, and therefore always presenting opportunities for establishing ultimate – if contingent – ends.

Normative theory must not fall back upon the '...teleology and essentialism that the modern philosophical tradition was born combating'.[6] On the contrary, it should partake of the anti-foundationalist, deconstructionist and constructivist developments of post-modern thought where the debate

is between a 'code of paradox and a code of coherence' – Derrida and
Foucault versus Habermas and Taylor.[7]

BACKGROUND THEORY

In order to conclude how and why normative theory is part of the study of
international relations it is necessary to consider what this larger project
entails. Ordinary accounts of any disciplinary study, or science, include
the attributes of description, explanation and understanding, which are
valued and justified in terms of the desire for prediction. This is not to say
that predictive capacity is the only or even the most important criterion of
good theory, but wherever the applied purposes of choice and action are at
issue some element of prediction is inevitable. It is hardly necessary at
this point to reiterate the disciplinary characteristics of the study of international relations, beyond noting that predictive capacity is at least as
much valued in respect to the weighty issues of international affairs as in
any of the more restricted ambits of social science or in respect to the
moral order of any constituent part of international society.

While it may be true that claims to predictive capacity are weaker in the
social sciences than in the natural sciences and that prediction is largely
tangential to social theory, there is nevertheless a clear and continuous
demand for knowledge about societies, including the global community
(hence international relations), with the end-in-view or ultimate purpose of
choosing options and planning for the future. It would not be an overstate-
ment to claim for normative theory the capacity to uncover, examine and
criticise the foundations of the theory and practice of international
relations, and thereby create opportunities for choosing and planning the
moral order of a new age.

If this characterises the task at hand, what contribution does normative
theory make? The extent of normative structures and influences suggests
endless actual and possible roles for normative theory, but of greatest
interest is the notion of a normative background theory, as a basis for particular investigations or theoretical constructs. Given its particular usefulness in epistemological applications, normative theory can provide a
stabilising *background theory* for epistemological competition within the
study of international relations, since it does not readily allow an over-
simplified or particularistic version of 'truth'. Normative theory, as a form
of engagement in political understanding, also provides a background for
purposive engagement in political life; a means of coping with the rise
and fall of particular practices, and a framework for comprehending the

nature of the political processes by which these practices come to be known, accepted, and ultimately discarded.

The possible applications of theory 'in the background' are as numerous as the practical applications which rely on it, and normative theory is relevant to all aspects of social interaction. This is significant in a world which is changing rapidly, and in which change has an impact on the everyday life of diverse populations. The normative dimension of international relations shares the cultural aspect of more familiar normative activities (influenced by fashion, for example) in as much as many features of everyday life involve conscious reference to international or global cultural trends which have importance in the immediate social context. The meaning of the global normative structure is played out contingently, in a local context – it is a case of the local–global nexus in the realm of ideas.[8]

Furthermore, we all live – physically and morally – on one planet and in one world, whatever 'other worlds' are relevant to us or inform our lives.

> Because of our common humanity and because of the needs which every society has to provide for, there is always available, if not always in evidence, a common basis for intercultural communication and mutual appraisal, moral appraisal not excluded.[9]

A pertinent example is radical social change in the USSR and Eastern Europe in and around 1989 (and its continuing effects), which illustrates socio-political norms dictating social realities in a concrete way, with 'reality' changing as a direct result of changing ethical, epistemological, theoretical and ideological principles (the catalyst being *glasnost*) – literally, a change of mind leading to a change of politics. These changes have come about in a global context, even though they are played out in the local (national) life of the region. A normative theoretical background can usefully inform investigation of such events by calling attention to the normative features of change, rather than simply the machinations of power and wealth.

No doubt general recognition of this background role is only a distant possibility, given the tenacity of traditions in international relations theory. It may even be a disservice to normative theorising to link it to the particular activity of international relations scholarship. Chris Brown argues (after Kant) that well intentioned 'international theory' can only offer sorry comfort to the oppressed by attempting to produce normative theory, because 'acceptance of the idea that such theory can be constructed within the limits imposed by a separate discourse of international relations is a crucial handicap to their enterprise'.[10] On this view, the broader tradition of political theory may be a more appropriate standpoint for theorising about international relations. For example, David Held (a political theorist), in characterising the present international order as a hybrid system of persistent sovereign states and developing plural authority structures, says that the dangers this hybrid signals 'may in principle be surmounted if a multiple system of authority is bound by fundamental ordering principles and rules'.[11] Elsewhere, David Beetham (another political theorist), in his investigation of legitimacy, notes that: 'To be sure, the interdependence of all our interests in securing the conditions for human survival is becoming everyday more evident. Yet it may take the institutional embodiment of this interdependence to develop at the global level before liberal democracy can be realised as a universal, and not merely a localised, political form'.[12] Held's 'bounded multiple system' and Beethams 'institutional embodiment' go beyond an exclusive concern with the policies of nation-states, and reflect a renewed concern in the late twentieth century with the prospects for global governance which is better addressed by innovative perspectives on international relations that challenge tradition. The present argument maintains that there are sufficient specific characteristics of international relations to warrant a specialised body of theory about the subject, but agrees that such theory can draw on a broad base of philosophy and social science and should not be restricted by essentialist or absolutist conceptions of its subject matter.

It does not follow from the foregoing arguments that normative theory is the only kind of theorising worth doing, and clearly it has limitations. Yet the normative perspective is sufficiently vital to the study of international relations that the case for it should be made strongly. If the case is made strongly enough, and normative consciousness is incorporated or reincorporated into the whole range of approaches to the subject, normative theory can quickly recede into the background – where it belongs.[13]

Finally, it must be said that the incentive for a study such as this is concern with the distance between political practices and the human values that they are intended to further. This is not the place to describe the suffering brought by the four horsemen of the apocalypse, and in equal measure by political folly, but it should be clear enough that the general purpose of political systems is to improve the human condition. This critical assessment of the role of normative theory in the study of international relations is therefore also a call for change in theoretical practices, since both theoretical and practical goals are furthered by reintegrating human values into the study of international relations. A consequence of such reintegration would be a better understanding of the moral order that underpins world order.

NOTES

1. William James, *A Pluralistic Universe* (Cambridge, MA and London: Harvard University Press, 1977), p. 149.
2. The phrase 'as it bears' distinguishes between the state of knowledge as among academic theoreticians, who may overestimate their influence, and the state of knowledge that informs political processes of everyday life.
3. Roberto Mangabeira Unger, *Knowledge and Politics* (New York: The Free Press, 1975), p. 3.
4. William E. Connolly, 'Identity and Difference in Global Politics' in James Der Derian and Michael J. Shapiro (eds), *International/Intertextual Relations: Postmodern Readings of World Politics* (Lexington, MA: Lexington Books, 1989), p. 341.
5. Laszek Kolakowski, *Metaphysical Horror* (Oxford: Basil Blackwell, 1988), p. 98.
6. Roberto Mangabeira Unger, *Knowledge and Politics* (New York: The Free Press, 1975), p. 341.
7. William E. Connolly, 'Identity and Difference in Global Politics', *op. cit.*, p. 340. See also K. Baynes, J. Bohman and T. McCarthy (eds), *After Philosophy* (Cambridge, MA: MIT Press, 1987).
8. See 'The Local–Global Nexus', *International Social Science Journal*, (Vol. 40, No. 117, 1988).
9. Robin Attfield, *A Theory of Value and Obligation* (London: Croom Helm, 1987), p. 220.
10. Chris Brown, 'Sorry Comfort? The Case Against "International Theory" ', unpublished conference paper presented to the Inaugural Pan-European Conference on International Studies of the European Consortium for Political Research, Standing Group on International Relations (panel on 'Power and Morality in International Relations'), Heidelberg, 16–20 September 1992, p. 4.
11. David Held, 'Democracy, the Nation-State and the Global System' in David Held (ed), *Political Theory Today* (Cambridge: Polity Press, 1991), p. 226.
12. David Beetham, *The Legitimation of Political Power* (London: Macmillan, 1991), p. 250.
13. Note again Beitz's remark that normative ideas are most powerful when operating 'in the background'. Charles R. Beitz, 'Recent International Thought', *International Journal* (Vol. 43, No. 2, Spring 1988), p. 203. Note also Mervyn Frost's discussion of 'background theory' in his *Ethics in International Relations: A Constitutive Theory* (Cambridge: Cambridge University Press, 1996), pp. 124–5, and p. 167, as well as Chapter 5 on his 'constitutive theory of individuality'.

Bibliography

Akehurst, Michael, 'Humanitarian Intervention' in Hedley Bull (ed.), *Intervention in World Politics* (Oxford: Clarendon Press, 1984).

Anderson, Kym and Richard Blackhurst (eds), *The Greening of World Trade Issues* (Hemel Hempstead: Harvester Wheatsheaf, 1992).

Archibugi, Daniele, 'Models of International Organization in Perpetual Peace Projects', *Review of International Studies* (Vol. 18, No. 4, October 1992).

Ashley, Richard K., 'Political Realism and Human Interests', *International Studies Quarterly* (Vol. 25, No. 2, 1981).

Ashley, Richard K., 'The Poverty of Neorealism', *International Organisation* (Vol. 38, No. 2, 1984).

Attfield, Robin, *A Theory of Value and Obligation* (London: Croom Helm, 1987).

Baldwin, David A. (ed.), *Neorealism and Neoliberalism: The Contemporary Debate* (New York: Columbia University Press, 1993).

Baldwin, J. M. (ed.), *Dictionary of Philosophy and Psychology* (New York: Peter Smith, 1940).

Banks, Michael, 'The Inter-Paradigm Debate' in Light and Groom (eds), *International Relations: A Handbook of Current Theory* (London: Francis Pinter, 1985).

Bartelson, Jens, *A Geneology of Sovereignty* (Cambridge: Cambridge University Press, 1995).

Baynes, K., J. Bohman and T. McCarthy (eds), *After Philosophy* (Cambridge, MA: MIT Press, 1987).

Beck, Ulrich, *Ecological Politics in an Age of Risk* (Cambridge: Polity Press, 1995).

Beck, Ulrich, *Risk Society: Towards a New Modernity* (London: Sage, 1992).

Beetham, David, *The Legitimation of Political Power* (London: Macmillan, 1991).

Beitz, Charles R., 'Cosmopolitan Ideals and National Sentiment', *Journal of Philosophy* (Vol. 80, No. 10, October 1983).

Beitz, Charles R., 'Recent International Thought', *International Journal* (Vol. 43, No. 2, Spring 1988).

Beitz, Charles R., *Political Equality: An Essay in Democratic Theory* (Princeton: Princeton University Press, 1989).

Beitz, Charles R., *Political Theory and International Relations* (Princeton: Princeton University Press, 1979).

Benhabib, Seyla, *Critique, Norm, and Utopia: A Study of the Foundations of Critical Theory* (New York: Columbia University Press, 1986).

Berger, Peter L. and Thomas Luckman, *The Social Construction of Reality* (New York: Doubleday, 1966).

Berki, R. N., *On Political Realism* (London: J. M. Dent, 1981).

Bernstein, Richard J., *The Restructuring of Social and Political Theory* (Oxford: Basil Blackwell, 1976).

Bobbitt, Philip, *Democracy and Deterrence: The History and Future of Nuclear Strategy* (London: Macmillan, 1988).

208

Boyd, Richard N., 'The Current Status of Scientific Realism' in J. Leplin (ed.), *Scientific Realism* (Berkeley, CA: University of California Press, 1984).

Brandt, Richard, 'Epistemology and Ethics, Parallel Between' in the *Encyclopedia of Philosophy*.

Brechin, Steven R. and Willett Kempton, 'Global Environmentalism: A Challenge to the Postmaterialism Thesis?', *Social Science Quarterly* (Vol. 75, 1994).

Breyman, Steve, 'Knowledge as Power: Ecology Movements and Global Environmental Problems' in Ronnie D. Lipschutz and Ken Conca (eds), *The State and Social Power in Global Environmental Politics* (New York: Columbia University Press, 1993).

Broecker, Wallace S., 'Global Warming on Trial', *Natural History* (April 1992).

Brown, Chris, 'Sorry Comfort? The Case Against "International Theory"', unpublished conference paper presented to the Inaugural Pan-European Conference on International Studies of the European Consortium for Political Research, Standing Group on International Relations (panel on 'Power and Morality in International Relations'), Heidelberg, 16–20 September 1992.

Brown, Chris, 'The Modern Requirement? Reflections on Normative International Theory in a Post-Western World', *Millennium: Journal of International Studies* (Vol. 17, No. 2, Summer 1988).

Brown, Chris, *International Relations Theory: New Normative Approaches* (London: Harvester Wheatsheaf, 1992).

Brown, Lester R., *et al.*, *State of the World 1986* A Worldwatch Institute Report on Progress Toward a Sustainable Society (New York: Norton 1986).

Brown, Lester R., *Redefining National Security* Worldwatch Institute Paper No. 14 (Washington, DC: Worldwatch Institute, 1977).

Brown, Neville, 'Climate Ecology and International Security', *Survival* (Vol. 31 No. 6, 1989).

Brown, Robin, 'Limited War' in Colin McInnes and G. D. Sheffield (eds), *Warfare in the Twentieth Century: Theory and Practice* (London: Unwin Hyman, 1988).

Bryant, Christopher G. A., *Positivism in Social Theory and Research* (London: Macmillan, 1985).

Buchler, J. (ed.), *Philosophical Writings of Pierce* (New York: Dover Publications, 1955).

Bull, Hedley and Adam Watson (eds), *The Expansion of International Society* (Oxford: Clarendon Press, 1984).

Bull, Hedley, 'International Relations as an Academic Pursuit', *Australian Outlook* (Vol. 26, No. 3, December 1972).

Bull, Hedley, 'International Theory: The Case for a Classical Approach', *World Politics* (Vol. 18, No. 3, 1966).

Bull, Hedley, *The Anarchical Society* (London: Macmillan, 1977).

Butterfield, Herbert and Martin Wight (eds), *Diplomatic Investigations: Essays in the Theory of International Politics* (London: George Allen and Unwin Ltd., 1966).

Butterfield, Herbert, *History and Human Relations* (London: Collins, 1951).

Buzan, Barry, *People, States and Fear*, 2nd ed. (Hemel Hempstead: Harvester Wheatsheaf, 1991).

Capra, Fritjof, *The Turning Point: Science, Society and the Rising Culture* (London: Flamingo/HarperCollins, 1983).

Carr, E. H., *The Twenty Years' Crisis* (London: Macmillan, 1939).

Carroll, John E. (ed.), *International Environmental Diplomacy* (Cambridge: Cambridge University Press, 1988).

Castañeda, Hector-Neri, 'Ought, Reasons, Motivation, and the Unity of the Social Sciences: The Meta-theory of the Ought–Is Problem', in Giuliano di Bernardo (ed.), *Normative Structures of the Social World* (Amsterdam: Editions Rodopi, 1988).

Channel 4, 'Voices: The Trouble with Truth' (London: Channel 4 Television, April 1988).

Chomsky, Noam, *Problems of Knowledge and Freedom* (London: Fontana/Collins, 1972).

Cleveland, Harlan, *The Global Commons: Policy for the Planet* (London: University Press of America / Aspen Institute, 1990).

Colchester, Marcus and Larry Lohmann (eds), *The Struggle for Land and the Fate of the Forests* (Penang: World Rainforest Movement / London: Zed, 1993).

Conca, Ken, 'Environmental Change and the Deep Structure of World Politics', in Ronnie D. Lipschutz and Ken Conca (eds), *The State and Social Power in Global Environmental Politics* (New York: Columbia University Press, 1993).

Conca, Ken, 'Peace Studies and the Multiple Meanings of the Global Environment' (paper presented at the 33rd Annual Convention of the International Studies Association, Atlanta, 4 April 1992).

Connolly, William E., 'Identity and Difference in Global Politics' in James Der Derian and Michael J. Shapiro, *International/Intertextual Relations: Postmodern Readings of World Politics* (Lexington, MA: Lexington Books, 1989).

Cox, Robert W., 'Social Forces, States and World Orders: Beyond International Relations Theory', *Millennium: Journal of International Studies* (Vol. 10, No. 2, Summer 1881).

Craig, Paul P., Harold Glasser and Willett Kempton, 'Ethics and Values in Environmental Policy: The Said and the UNCED', *Environmental Values* (Vol. 2, No. 2, Summer 1993).

Cvetkovich, George and Timothy C. Earle, 'Values and Responses to News Media Signals About Global Environmental Changes: A Preliminary Study with American University Students', Western Institute for Social and Organizational Research Report No. 1991-03 (Bellingham, WN: WISOR/Western Washington University, 1991).

Dake, Karl, 'Myths of Nature: Culture and the Social Construction of Risk', *Journal of Social Issues* (Vol. 48, No. 4, 1992).

Dalby, Simon, 'Security, Modernity, Ecology: The Dilemmas of Post-Cold War Security Discourse', *Alternatives* (Vol. 17, No. 1, 1992).

Der Derian, James and Michael J. Shapiro (eds), *International/Intertextual Relations: Post-modern Readings in World Politics* (Lexington, MA: Lexington Books, 1989).

Der Derian, James, *Antidiplomacy: Spies, Terror, Speed, and War* (Oxford: Blackwell, 1992).

Der Derian, James, *On Diplomacy: A Geneology of Western Estrangement* (Oxford: Blackwell, 1987).

Derrida, Jacques, *On Grammatology* (Baltimore: Johns Hopkins University Press, 1976).

Derrida, Jacques, *Speech and Phenomena* (Evanston, IL: Northwestern University Press, 1973).

Deudney, Daniel, 'Environmental Security: Muddled Thinking', *Bulletin of The Atomic Scientists* (April 1991).

Deudney, Daniel, 'The Case Against Linking Environmental Degradation and National Security', *Millennium: Journal of International Studies* (Vol. 19, No. 3, Winter 1990).

Deutsch, Karl, *The Analysis of International Relations* (Englewood Cliffs, NJ: Prentice-Hall, 1978).

Dewey, John, 'Challenge to Liberal Thought' in *Fortune* (Vol. 30, 1944).

Dewey, John, 'Theory of Valuation', *International Encyclopedia of Unified Science*, Volume II, Number 4 (Chicago: University of Chicago Press, 1939).

di Bernardo, Giuliano (ed.), *Normative Structures of the Social World* (Amsterdam: Editions Rodopi, 1988).

Dillon, G. M. (ed.), *Defence Policy Making: A Comparative Analysis* (Leicester: Leicester University Press, 1988).

Donelan, Michael, *Elements of International Political Theory* (Oxford: Clarendon Press, 1990).

Dornbusch, Rudiger and James M. Poterba (eds), *Global Warming: Economic Policy Responses* (Cambridge, MA: MIT Press, 1991).

Dougherty, James E. and Robert L Pfaltzgraff, Jr., *Contending Theories of International Relations* (New York: Lippincott, 1971).

Douglas, Mary and Aaron Wildavsky, *Risk and Culture: An Essay on the Selection of Technical and Environmental Dangers* (Berkeley, CA: University of California Press, 1982).

Drucker, Peter F., *The New Realities* (London: Mandarin, 1990).

Dunlap, Riley E., George H. Gallup and Alec M. Gallup, *The Health of the Planet Survey: A Preliminary Report on Attitudes on the Environment and Economic Growth measured by Surveys of Citizens in 22 Nations to Date* (Princeton, NJ: The George Gallup International Institute, 1993).

Dunn, John, 'Responsibility without Power: States and the Incoherence of the Modern Conception of the Political Good' in John Dunn, *Interpreting Political Responsibility: Essays 1981–1989* (Cambridge: Polity Press, 1990).

Dyer, Hugh C. and Leon Mangasarian (eds), *The Study of International Relations: The State of the Art* (London: Macmillan, 1989).

Dyer, Hugh C., 'EcoCultures: Global Culture in the Age of Ecology', *Millennium: Journal of International Studies* (Vol. 22, No. 3, Winter 1993).

Dyer, Hugh C., 'Environmental Security as a Universal Value: Implications for International Theory' in John Vogler and Mark F. Imber, eds., *The Environment and International Relations* (London and New York: Routledge, 1996).

Dyer, Hugh C., *Justice in World Order: A Conceptual Analysis* (unpublished M.A. thesis, Dalhousie University, 1984).

Easton, David, *A Systems Analysis of Political Life* (New York: John Wiley, 1965).

Eccleshall, Robert, Vincent Geoghagen, Richard Jay and Rick Wilford, *Political Ideologies: An Introduction* (London: Hutchinson, 1984).

Eco, Umberto, *Travels in Hyperreality: Essays* (London: Picador, 1987).

Edel, Abraham, *Analyzing Concepts in Social Science: Science, Ideology, and Value*, Vol. 1 (New Brunswick, NJ: Transaction Books, 1979).

Elshtain, Jean Bethke , *Women and War* (New York: Basic Books, 1987).

Engel, J. Ronald and Joan Gibb Engel (eds), *Ethics of Environment and Development: Global Challenge and International Response* (Tucson, AZ: University of Arizona Press, 1990).

Enloe, Cynthia, *Bananas, Beaches, and Bases: Making Feminist Sense of International Politics* (London: Pandora, 1989).

Evernden, Neil, *The Social Construction of Nature* (Baltimore, MD: The Johns Hopkins University Press, 1992).

Fay, Brian, *Social Theory and Political Practice* (London: Allen and Unwin, 1975).

Featherstone, Michael (ed.), *Global Culture: Nationalism, Globalization and Modernity* (London: Sage, 1990).

Ferguson, Yale H. and Richard W. Mansbach, 'Beyond the Elusive Quest: A Search for Authority Patterns in History' (a paper given at the joint BISA/ISA convention, London, 31 March 1989.

Ferguson, Yale H. and Richard W. Mansbach, *The Elusive Quest: Theory and International Politics* (Columbia, SC: University of South Carolina Press, 1988).

Ferguson, Yale H. and Richard W. Mansbach, *The State, Conceptual Chaos, and the Future of International Relations Theory* (Boulder, CO: Lynne Rienner, 1989).

Fishkin, James S., *Beyond Subjective Morality: Ethical Reasoning and Political Philosophy* (London and New Haven, CT: Yale University Press, 1984).

Foucault, Michel, *Power/Knowledge: Selected Interviews and Other Writings* (New York: Pantheon, 1980).

Foucault, Michel, *The Archeology of Knowledge* (New York: Pantheon, 1972).

Freedman, Lawrence, 'The First Two Generations of Nuclear Strategists', Chapter 25 in Peter Paret (ed.), *Makers of Modern Strategy* (Princeton, NJ: Princeton University Press, 1986).

Frost, Mervyn, 'Normative Theory and International Relations: Overcoming the Positivist Bias', *Politikon: South African Journal of Political Science* (Vol. 12, No. 1, June 1985).

Frost, Mervyn, *Ethics in International Relations: A Constitutive Theory* (Cambridge: Cambridge University Press, 1996).

Frost, Mervyn, *Towards a Normative Theory of International Relations* (Cambridge: Cambridge University Press, 1986).

Gallie, W. B., 'Essentially Contested Concepts', *Proceedings of the Aristotelian Society* (Vol. 56, 1955–6).

Geertz, Clifford, *The World as a Stage. Negara: The Theatre State in Nineteenth-Century Bali* (Princeton, NJ: Princeton University Press, 1981).

Gellman, Barton, *Contending with Kennan: Toward a Philosophy of American Power* (New York: Praeger, 1984).

Gilpin, Robert, 'The Richness of the Tradition of Political Realism', *International Organization* (Vol. 38, No. 2, Spring 1984), reprinted in Robert O. Keohane (ed.), *Neorealism and its Critics* (New York: Columbia University Press, 1986).

Glacken, Clarence, *Traces on the Rhodian Shore: Nature and Culture in Western Thought from Ancient Times to the End of the Eighteenth Century* (Berkeley: University of California Press, 1967).

Goodland, Robert, 'Tribal Peoples and Economic Development: The Human Ecological Dimension', in Jeffrey A. McNeely and David Pitt (eds), *Culture and Conservation: The Human Dimension in Environmental Planning* (London: Croom Helm, 1985).

Goodman, Nelson, *Ways of Worldmaking* (Indianapolis: Hackett Publishing, 1978).

Greimas, Algirdas Julien, *On Meaning: Selected Writings in Semiology* (London: Francis Pinter, 1987).

Griffiths, Martin, *Realism, Idealism and International Politics: A Reinterpretation* (London Routledge, 1992).

Guastini, Ricardo, 'Constitutive Rules and the Is–Ought Dichotomy' in Giuliano di Bernardo (ed.), *Normative Structures of the Social World* (Amsterdam: Editions Rodopi, 1988).

Halliday, Fred, 'State and Society in International Relations: A Second Agenda', *Millennium: Journal of International Studies* (Vol. 16, No. 2, Summer 1987), reprinted in Hugh C. Dyer and Leon Mangasarian (eds), *The Study of International Relations: The State of the Art* (London: Macmillan, 1989).

Hannerz, Ulf, 'Cosmopolitans and Locals in World Culture' in Michael Featherstone (ed.), *Global Culture: Nationalism, Globalization and Modernity* (London: Sage, 1990).

Haraway, Donna, *Primate Visions: Gender, Race and Nature in the World of Modern Science* (New York: Routledge, 1990).

Hardin, Russell, John J. Mearsheimer, Gerald Dworkin and Robert E. Goodin (eds), *Nuclear Deterrence: Ethics and Strategy* (Chicago, IL and London: University of Chicago Press, 1985).

Hare, R. M., 'Why Moral Language?' in Philip Pettit, Richard Sylvan and Jean Norman (eds), *Metaphysics and Morality* (Oxford: Basil Blackwell, 1987).

Harris, Louis and Associates, *Public and Leadership Attitudes to the Environment: A Report of a Survey in 16 Countries* (New York: Harris and Associates, 1989)

Harrison, Horace V. (ed.), *The Role of Theory in International Relations* (Litton Educational Publishing, 1964).

Hegel, G. W. F., *The Philosophy of Right* (Oxford: Oxford University Press, 1980 [1821]).

Held, David (ed.), *Political Theory Today* (Cambridge: Polity Press, 1991).

Held, David, 'Democracy, the Nation-State and the Global System' in David Held (ed.), *Political Theory Today* (Cambridge: Polity Press, 1991).

Heller, Agnes and Ferenc Fehér, *The Postmodern Political Condition* (Cambridge: Polity Press, 1988).

Herman, Charles F., Charles W. Kegley, Jr., and James N. Rosenau (eds), *New Directions in the Study of Foreign Policy* (Boston, MA: Allen and Unwin, 1987).

Herz, John H., *International Politics in the Atomic Age* (New York and London: Columbia University Press, 1959).

Hobhouse, L. T., *Elements of Social Justice* (London: George Allen and Unwin, 1922, reprinted 1958).

Hoffman, Mark J., 'Normative Approaches' in Margot Light and A. J. R. Groom (eds), *International Relations: A Handbook of Current Theory* (London: Francis Pinter, 1985).

Hoffman, Mark, 'Critical Theory and the Inter-Paradigm Debate' in Hugh C. Dyer and Leon Mangasarian (eds), *The Study of International Relations: The State of the Art* (London: Macmillan, 1989).

Hoffmann, Stanley, 'An American Social Science: International Relations', *Daedalus*, (Vol. 106, No. 3, 1977).

Hoffmann, Stanley, 'International Society' in J. D. B. Miller and R. J. Vincent (eds), *Order and Violence: Hedley Bull and International Relations* (Oxford: Clarendon Press, 1990).

Holiday, Anthony, *Moral Powers: Normative Necessity in Language and History* (London: Routledge, 1988).

Hollis, Martin and Steve Smith (eds), *Explaining and Understanding International Relations* (Oxford: Clarendon Press, 1990).

Homer-Dixon, Thomas F., 'On the Threshold: Environmental Changes as Causes of Acute Conflict', *International Security* (Vol. 16, No. 2, Fall 1991).

Hume, David, *A Treatise of Human Nature*, in Henry D. Aiken (ed.), *Hume's Moral and Political Philosophy* (London: Collier Macmillan, 1948).

Inglehart, Ronald, *Cultural Shift in Advanced Industrial Society* (Princeton, NJ: Princeton University Press, 1990).

Inglehart, Ronald, *The Silent Revolution: Changing Values and Political Styles Among Western Publics* (Princeton, NJ: Princeton University Press, 1977).

International Social Science Journal, 'The Local-Global Nexus' (Vol. 40, No. 117, August 1988).

Jackson, Robert, 'Martin Wight, International Theory and the Good Life', *Millennium: Journal of International Studies* (Vol. 19, No. 2, Summer 1990).

Jacobs, Michael, *The Green Economy: Environment, Sustainable Develoment and the Politics of the Future* (London: Pluto, 1991).

James, William, *A Pluralistic Universe* (Cambridge, MA and London: Harvard University Press, 1977).

Jancar, Barbara, 'The Environmental Attractor in the Former USSR: Ecology and Regional Change' in Ronnie D. Lipschutz and Ken Conca (eds), *The State and Social Power in Global Environmental Politics* (New York: Columbia University Press, 1993).

Jervis, Robert, *Perception and Misperception in International Politics* (Princeton, NJ: Princeton University Press, 1976).

Johansen, Robert C., *The National Interest and the Human Interest: An Analysis of U.S. Foreign Policy* (Princeton: Princeton University Press, 1980).

Jones, Dorothy V., *Code of Peace: Ethics and Security in the World of Warlord States* (Chicago: University of Chicago Press, 1991).

Jones, Roy, 'The English School of International Relations: A Case for Closure', *Review of International Studies* (Vol. 7, No. 1, 1981).

Kaplan, Morton, 'The New Great Debate: Traditionalism vs Science in International Relations' in K. Knorr and J. Rosenau (eds), *Contending Approaches to International Politics* (Princeton, NJ: Princeton University Press, 1969).

Kariel, Henry S., *The Desperate Politics of Postmodernism* (Amherst, MA: University of Massachusetts Press, 1989).

Katzenstein, Peter J. (ed.), *The Culture of National Security: Norms and Identity in World Politics* (New York: Columbia University Press, 1996).

Kegley, Charles W., Jr. and Gregory A. Raymond, *When Trust Breaks Down: Alliance Norms and World Politics* (Columbia, SC: University of South Carolina Press, 1990).

Kegley, Charles W., Jr., 'Decision Regimes and the Comparative Study of Foreign Policy', in Charles F. Herman, Charles W. Kegley, Jr., and James N. Rosenau (eds), *New Directions in the Study of Foreign Policy* (Boston, MA: Allen and Unwin, 1987).

Kegley, Charles W., Jr., *Controversies in International Relations Theory: Realism and the Neoliberal Challenge* (New York: St. Martin's Press, 1995).

Kellner, Douglas, *Critical Theory, Marxism and Modernity* (Oxford: Polity Press, 1989).

Kennan, George F., 'Morality and Foreign Policy', *Foreign Affairs* (Vol. 64, No. 2, Winter 1985–86).

Kennan, George F., *Realities of American Foreign Policy* (New York: W. W. Norton, 1966; first published by Princeton University Press, 1954).

Kennan, George Frost, *Memoirs, 1925–1950 [Volume One]* (Boston: Little, Brown, 1967).

Keohane, Robert O. (ed.), *Neorealism and Its Critics* (New York: Columbia University Press, 1986).

Keohane, Robert O., 'International Institutions: Two Approaches', *International Studies Quarterly* (Vol. 32, No. 4, December 1988).

King, Anthony D., *Culture, Globalization and the World System* (London: Macmillan, 1991).

King, Preston and B. C. Parekh (ed.), *Politics and Experience* (Cambridge: Cambridge University Press, 1968).

Knorr, K. and J. Rosenau (eds), *Contending Approaches to International Politics* (Princeton, NJ: Princeton University Press, 1969).

Knutsen, Torbjörn L., *A History of International Relations Theory* (Manchester: Manchester University Press, 1992)

Kolakowski, Laszek, *Metaphysical Horror* (Oxford: Basil Blackwell, 1988).

Kratochwil, Friedrich V., 'Norms and Values: Rethinking the Domestic Analogy', *Ethics and International Affairs* (Vol. 1, 1987), p. 136.

Kratochwil, Friedrich V., *Rules, Norms, and Decisions: On the conditions of practical and legal reasoning in international relations and domestic affairs* (Cambridge: Cambridge University Press, 1989).

Krippendorff, Ekkehart, *International Relations as a Social Science* (Brighton: Wheatsheaf, 1982).

Kuhn, Thomas S., *The Structure of Scientific Revolutions*, 2nd ed. (Chicago: University of Chicago Press, 1970).

Kukathas, Chandran and Philip Pettit, *Rawls: A Theory of Justice and its Critics* (Cambridge: Polity Press, 1990).

Laski, H. J., *Introduction to Politics*, revised edition prepared by Martin Wight (London: George Allen and Unwin, 1951).

Lauener, Henri, 'Philosophie als normative Tätigkeit (offener Transzendentalismus versus Naturalismus)', (*Dialectica*, Vol. 41, 1987).

Liddell Hart, B. H., *Strategy: the indirect approach* (London: Faber and Faber, 1968).

Light, Margot and A. J. R. Groom (eds), *International Relations: A Handbook of Current Theory* (London: Francis Pinter, 1985).

Linklater, Andrew, 'Realism, Marxism and Critical International Theory', *Review of International Studies* (Vol. 12, No. 2, 1986).

Linklater, Andrew, *Beyond Realism and Marxism: Critical Theory and International Relations* (London: Macmillan, 1990).

Linklater, Andrew, *Men and Citizens in the Theory of International Relations* (London: Macmillan, 1982).

Lorenz, Kuno, 'Is and Ought Revisited', *Dialectica* (Vol. 41, 1987).

Lukes, Steven, *Power: A Radical View* (London: Macmillan, 1974).

Lyotard, Jean-Francois, *The Postmodern Condition: A Report on Knowledge* (Minneapolis: University of Minnesota Press, 1984).

Macdonald, Hugh, 'Strategic Studies', *Millennium: Journal of International Studies* (Vol. 16, No. 2, Summer 1987), and reprinted in Hugh C. Dyer and Leon Mangasarian (eds), *The Study of Intrnational Relations: The State of the Art* (London: Macmillan, 1989).

Machiavelli, N., *Discourses*, ed. Bernard Crick, trans. L. J. Walker (Harmondsworth: Penguin 1970).

MacIntyre, Alasdair, *Whose Justice? Which Rationality?* (London: Duckworth, 1989).

Manning, D. J. (ed.), *The Form of Ideology* (London: George Allen and Unwin, 1980).

Marcuse, Herbert, *One Dimensional Man* (Boston: Beacon Press, 1964).

Marti-Huang, Duen, 'The "Is" and "Ought" Convention', *Dialectica* (Vol. 41, 1987).

Marx, Karl and Freidrich Engels, *The German Ideology* (London: Lawrence and Wishart, 1965).

Mathews, Jessica T., 'Redefining Security', *Foreign Affairs* (Vol. 68, No. 2, 1989).

McGrew, Andrew G. and Paul G. Lewis, *et al.*, *Global Politics: Globalization and the Nation-State* (Cambridge: Polity Press, 1992).

McMahan, Jeff, 'Deterrence and Deontology' in Russell Hardin, *et al.*, (eds), *Nuclear Deterrence: Ethics and Strategy* (Chicago, IL and London: University of Chicago Press, 1985).

McNeely, Jeffrey A. and David Pitt (eds), *Culture and Conservation: The Human Dimension in Environmental Planning* (London: Croom Helm, 1985).

Meinecke, F., *Machiavellism: The Doctrine of Raison d'État and its Place in Modern History* trans. D. Scott (London: Routledge and Kegan Paul, 1957, 1962; first published as *Die Idee der Staatsräson in der Neueren Geschichte*, Munich: R. Ouldenbourg Verlag, 1924).

Meja, V. and N. Stehr, *Knowledge and Politics: The Sociology of Knowledge Dispute* (London: Routledge, 1990).

Merle, Marcel, *The Sociology of International Relations*, trans. Dorothy Parkin (Leamington Spa: Berg Publishers, 1987).

Miller, J. D. B. and R. J. Vincent (eds), *Order and Violence: Hedley Bull and International Relations* (Oxford: Clarendon Press, 1990).

Minogue, K. R., 'Epiphenomenalism in Politics: The Quest for Political Reality', *Political Studies* (Vol. XX, No. 4, December 1972).

Minsky, Marvin, *The Society of Mind* (London: Picador, 1988).

Morgan, Patrick, *Theories and Approaches to International Politics: What Are We to Think?* (New Brunswick, NJ: Transaction Books, 1987).

Morgenthau, Hans J., *Politics Among Nations*, 5th. ed., revised (New York: Alfred A. Knopf, 1978).

Morgenthau, Hans J., 'The Intellectual and Political Functions of Theory' in Morgenthau, *Truth and Power: Essays of a Decade, 1960–70* (London: Pall Mall Press, 1970).

Morgenthau, Hans J., *Scientific Man vs. Power Politics* (Chicago: University of Chicago Press, 1946).

Morgenthau, Hans, J., *Truth and Power: Essays of a Decade, 1960–70* (London: Pall Mall Press, 1970).

Morgenthau,, Hans J. 'International Relations: Common Sense and Theories', *Journal of International Affairs* (Vol. 21, No. 2, 1967).

Myers, 'Environment and Security', *Foreign Policy* (No. 74, 1989).

Nardin, Terry, 'The Problem of Relativism in International Ethics', *Millennium: Journal of International Studies* (Vol. 18, No. 2, Summer 1989).

Nardin, Terry, *Law, Morality and the Relations of States* (Princeton, NJ: Princeton University Press, 1983).

NATO Press Release (95) 116, 24 November 1995 (Internet/World Wide Web gopher site at <gopher://marvin.stc.nato.int:70/00/natodata/press...>).

Navari, Cornelia (ed.), *The Condition of States* (Milton Keynes: Open University Press, 1992).

Navari, Cornelia, 'Introduction: The State as a Contested Concept in International Relations' in Cornelia Navari (ed.), *The Condition of States* (Milton Keynes: Open University Press, 1992).

New York Review of Books, March 26, 1970.

Niebuhr, Reinhold , 'Ideology and the Scientific Method' in Niebuhr, *Christian Realism and Political Problems* (New York: Scribner's, 1953).

Niebuhr, Reinhold, *Christian Realism and Political Problems* (New York: Scribner's, 1953).

Niebuhr, Reinhold, *Christianity and Power Politics* (New York: Scribner's, 1940).

Oakeshott, Michael, *On History and Other Essays* (Oxford: Basil Blackwell, 1983).

Oakeshott, Michael, *On Human Conduct* (Oxford: Clarendon Press, 1975).

Oelschlaeger, Max, *The Idea of Wilderness: From Prehistory to the Age of Ecology* (New Haven, CT: Yale University Press, 1991).

Olson, William C. and A. J. R. Groom, *International Relations Then and Now: Origins and Trends in Interpretation* (London: Harper Collins, 1991).

Omari, C. K., 'Traditional African Land Ethics', in J. Ronald Engel and Joan Gibb Engel (eds), *Ethics of Environment and Development: Global Challenge and International Response* (Tucson, AZ: University of Arizona Press, 1990).

Onuf, Nicholas G., *World of Our Making: Rules and Rule in Social Theory and International Relations* (Columbia, SC: University of South Carolina Press, 1989).

Paret, Peter (ed.), *Makers of Modern Strategy: from Machiavelli to the Nuclear Age* (Princeton, NJ: Princeton University Press, 1986).

Paret, Peter, 'Clausewitz', Chapter 7 in Paret (ed.), *Makers of Modern Strategy* (Princeton, NJ: Princeton University Press, 1986).

Parkinson, F., *The Philosophy of International Relations: A Study in the History of Thought* (London: Sage, 1977).

Parsons, Talcott, 'An Approach to the Sociology of Knowedge', *Transaction of the Fourth World Congress of Sociology* (Vol. 4, September 1959), reprinted as Chapter 5 in Talcott Parsons, *Sociological Theory and Modern Society* (New York: The Free Press and London: Collier-Macmillan, 1967).

Parsons, Talcott, *Sociological Theory and Modern Society* (New York: The Free Press and London: Collier-Macmillan, 1967).

Pearce, David (ed.), *Blueprint 2: Greening the World Economy* (London: Earthscan, 1991).

Pearce, David, 'Economics and the Global Environmental Challenge', *Millennium: Journal of International Studies* (Vol. 19, No. 3, 1990).

218 *Bibliography*

Pehe, Jiri, 'An Annotated Survey of Independent Associations in Eastern Europe', *RFE/RL Radio Free Europe Research*, Background Report (Vol. 14, no. 24, 16 June 1989).

Pehe, Jiri, 'The Green Movements in Eastern Europe', *RFE/RL Report on Eastern Europe* (Vol. 1, No. 11, 16 March 1990).

Perry, Ralph Barton, *Realms of Value: A Critique of Human Civilization* (Cambridge, MA: Harvard University Press, 1954).

Pettit, Philip, Richard Sylvan and Jean Norman (eds), *Metaphysics and Morality* (Oxford: Basil Blackwell, 1987).

Pijpers, Alfred, Elfriede Regelsberger and Wolfgang Wessels (eds), *European Political Cooperation in the 1980s: A Common Foreign Policy for Western Europe?* (Dordrecht, The Netherlands: Martinus Nijhoff, 1988).

Pirage, Dennis, 'Environmental Security and Social Evolution', *International Studies Notes* (Vol. 16, No. 1, Winter 1991).

Pirages, Dennis, *The New Context for International Relations: Global Ecopolitics* (North Scituate, MA: Duxbury Press, 1978).

Plamenatz, John, *Ideology* (London: Pall Mall, 1970).

Plato, the *Gorgias*, trans W. C. Helmbold (Indianapolis: Bobbs-Merrill, 1952).

Plato, the *Phaedrus*, trans C. J. Rowe (Warminster: Aris & Phillips 1986).

Polunin, Nicholas V. C., 'Traditional Marine Practices in Indonesia and Their Bearing on Conservation', in Jeffrey A. McNeely and David Pitt (eds), *Culture and Conservation: The Human Dimension in Environmental Planning* (London: Croom Helm, 1985).

Popper, Karl, *The Open Society and Its Enemies* (London: Routledge and Kegan Paul, 1945; 2nd ed., revised, 1952).

Potter, V. G., *Charles S. Pierce On Norms and Ideals* (Worcester, MA: U. Mass Press, 1967).

Renger, N. J., 'Serpents and Doves in International Theory', *Millennium: Journal of International Studies* (Vol. 17, No. 2, Summer 1988)

Renner, Michael, 'Enhancing Global Security' in Lester R. Brown, *et al.*, *State of the World 1989* A Worldwatch Institute Report on Progress Toward a Sustainable Society (New York: Norton 1989).

Renner, Michael, *National Security: The Economic and Environmental Dimensions* (Washington, DC: Worldwatch Institute Paper No. 89, 1989).

Ricci, David M., *The Tragedy of Political Science: Politics, Scholarship, and Democracy* (New Haven, CT: Yale University Press, 1984).

Richardson, Neil R., 'Dyadic Case Studies in the Comparative Study of Foreign Policy Behaviour' in Charles F. Herman, Charles W. Kegley, Jr., and James N. Rosenau (eds), *New Directions in the Study of Foreign Policy* (Boston, MA: Allen and Unwin, 1987).

Robertson, Roland, *Globalization: Social Theory and Global Culture* (London: Sage, 1992).

Robertson, Roland, 'Mapping the Global Condition: Globalization as the Central Concept' in *Theory, Culture and Society* (Vol. 7, Nos. 2 & 3, June 1990 – Special Issue on Global Culture).

Rorty, Richard, *Philosophy and The Mirror of Nature* (Princeton, NJ: Princeton University Press, 1979).

Rorty, Richard, *The Consequences of Pragmatism* (Brighton: Harvester Press, 1982).

Rowlands, Ian H., 'The Security Challenges of Global Environmental Change', *Washington Quarterly* (Vol. 14, No. 1, Winter 1991).

Sabine, George H. (revised by Thomas L. Thorson), *A History of Political Theory*, 4th ed. (Hinsdale, IL: Holt, Rinehart and Winston, The Dryden Press, 1973).

Sandbach, Francis, *Environment, Ideology and Policy* (Oxford: Basil Blackwell, 1980).

Saunders, Harold H., 'The Arab-Israeli Conflict in a Global Perspective', in John Steinbruner (ed.), *Restructuring American Foreign Policy* (Washington: Brookings, 1989).

Schmidheiny, Stephan (with the Business Council for Sustainable Development), *Changing Course: A Global Business Perspective on Development and the Environment* (Cambridge, MA: MIT Press, 1992).

Schwarzenberger, George, *Power Politics: A Study of World Society*, 3rd ed. (London: Stevens & Sons, 1964).

Searle, John R., 'How to Derive "Ought" from "Is"', *Philosophical Review* (Vol. 73, 1964).

Searle, John R., *Expression and Meaning: Studies in the Theory of Speech Acts* (Cambridge: Cambridge University Press, 1979).

Searle, John R., *Speech Acts: An Essay in the Philosophy of Language* (Cambridge: Cambridge University Press, 1969).

Shapiro, Michael J., *Language and Politics* (New York: New York University Press, 1984)

Shapiro, Michael J., *Reading the Post-modern Polity: Political Theory as Textual Practice* (Minneapolis: University of Minnesota Press, 1992).

Shiva, Vandana, *Monocultures of the Mind: Perspectives on Biodiversity and Biotechnology* (Penang: Third World Network / London: Zed, 1993).

Skinner, Quentin, review of Clifford Geertz, *The World as a Stage. Negara: The Theatre State in Nineteenth-Century Bali* (Princeton, NJ: Princeton University Press, 1981), in *The New York Review*, 16 April 1981.

Smith, Anthony D., 'The Nation: Invented, Imagined, Reconstructed?', *Millennium: Journal of International Studies* (Vol. 20, No. 3, Winter 1991).

Smith, Michael Joseph , *Realist Thought from Weber to Kissinger* (Baton Rouge and London: Louisiana State University Press, 1986).

Smith, Steve, 'Foreign Policy Analysis and International Relations', *Millennium: Journal of International Studies* (Vol. 16, No. 2, Summer 1987), reprinted in Hugh C. Dyer and Leon Mangasarian (eds), *The Study of International Relations: The State of the Art* (London: Macmillan, 1989).

Smith, Steve, *International Relations: British and American Perspectives* (Oxford: Basil Blackwell, 1985).

Sofer, Sasson, 'International Relations and the Invisibility of Ideology', *Millennium: Journal of International Studies* (Vol. 16, No. 3, Winter 1987).

Solomon, Robert C., *From Rationalism to Existentialism: The Existentialists and their Nineteenth-Century Backgrounds* (New York: Humanities Press, 1978).

Sorenson, Theodore C., 'Rethinking National Security', *Foreign Affairs* (Vol. 69, No. 3, 1990).

Spivak, Gyatri C., *In Other Worlds: Essays in Cultural Politics* (New York and London: Methuen, 1987).

Steinbruner, John (ed.), *Restructuring American Foreign Policy* (Washington: Brookings, 1989).

220 *Bibliography*

Stern, P. C., R. Axelrod, R. Jervis and R. Radner (eds), *Perspectives on Deterrence* (Oxford: Oxford University Press, 1989).

Stevenson, Leslie, *Seven Theories of Human Nature* (Oxford: Oxford University Press, 1974).

Stone, Allucquere Rosanne, 'Will the Real Body Please Stand Up? Boundary Stories about Virtual Cultures' in Michael Benedikt, *Cyberspace: First Steps* (Cambridge, MA: MIT Press, 1991).

Stopford, John and Susan Strange, *Rival States, Rival Firms: Competition for World Market Shares* (Cambridge: Cambridge University Press, 1991).

Strange, Susan, 'States, Firms and Diplomacy', *International Affairs* (Vol. 68, No. 1, January 1992).

Strange, Susan, *States and Markets* (London: Pinter, 1988).

Stroll, Avrum, 'Norms' *Dialectica* (Vol. 41, 1987; Proceedings of the VIIIth International Colloquium in Vienna/Biel May 1–4, 1986).

Suganami, Hidemi, *The Domestic Analogy and World Order Proposals* (Cambridge: Cambridge University Press, 1989).

Sylvester, Christine, 'Homeless in International Relations? "Women's" Place in Canonical Texts and in Feminist Reimaginings' in Adam Lerner and Marjorie Ringrose (eds) *Reimagining the Nation* (London: Open University Press, 1993).

Sylvester, Christine, *Feminist Theory and International Relations in a Postmodern Era* (Cambridge: Cambridge University Press, forthcoming).

Taylor, Paul, *The Limits of European Integration* (London: Croom Helm, 1983).

Theodor Adorno, *The Dialectic of Enlightenment* (London: Verso, 1979).

Thomas, Caroline, *The Environment in International Relations* (London: Royal Institute of International Affairs, 1992).

Thomas, David, *Naturalism and Social Science: A Post-Empiricist Philosophy of Social Science* (Cambridge: Cambridge University Press, 1979).

Thompson, Kenneth W., *Masters of International Thought: Major Twentieth-Century Theorists and the World Crisis* (Baton Rouge, LA: Louisiana State University Press, 1980).

Thucydides, *History of the Peloponnesian War*, trans. B. Jowett (London: Oxford University Press, 1900).

Tickner, Ann, 'Redefining Security: A Feminist Perspective' (unpublished, 1989).

Tobayiwa, Chris and Peter Jackson, 'Shona People, Totems and Wildlife', in Jeffrey A. McNeely and David Pitt (eds), *Culture and Conservation: The Human Dimension in Environmental Planning* (London: Croom Helm, 1985).

Trachtenberg, Marc, 'Strategists, Philosophers, and the Nuclear Question' in Russell Hardin, *et al.,*.(eds), *Nuclear Deterrence: Ethics and Strategy* (Chicago, IL and London: University of Chicago Press, 1985).

Turner, Stephen P. and Regis A. Factor, *Max Weber and the dispute over reason and value: a study in philosophy, ethics, and politics*, International Library of Sociology (London: Routledge and Kegan Paul, 1984).

Ullman, Richard H., 'Redefining Security', *International Security* (Vol. 8, No. 1, Summer 1983).

Ullmann-Margalit, Edna, *The Emergence of Norms* (Oxford: Oxford University Press, 1977).

Unger, Roberto Mangabeira, *Knowledge and Politics* (New York: The Free Press and London: Collier Macmillan, 1975).

Van Dyke, Vernon, 'Values and Interests', *American Political Science Review* (Vol. 56, September 1962).

van Fraasen, Bas C., *The Scientific Image* (Oxford: Oxford University Press, 1981).

Vasquez, John A., *The Power of Power Politics* (London: Pinter, 1983).

Vincent, R. J., 'Order in International Politics' in Miller, J. D. B. and R. J. Vincent (eds), *Order and Violence: Hedley Bull and International Relations* (Oxford: Clarendon Press, 1990).

Vincent, R. J., *Human Rights and International Relations* (Cambridge: Cambridge University Press, 1986).

Vincent, R. J., *Non-Intervention and International Order* (Princeton, NJ: Princeton University Press, 1974).

Virilio, Paul, *Speed and Politics: An Essay on Dromology*, trans. M. Polizzotti (New York: Semiotext(e), 1986).

Vogler, John and Mark F. Imber, (eds), *The Environment and International Relations* (London and New York: Routledge, 1996).

von Clausewitz, Carl, *Vom Kriege* (*On War*), trans. Michael Howard and Peter Paret (eds) (Princeton: Princeton University Press, 1976).

von Wright, Georg Henrik, *Norm and Action* (London: Routledge & Kegan Paul, 1977).

Walker, R. B. J., 'History and Structure in the Theory of International Relations', *Millennium: Journal of International Studies* (Vol. 18, No. 2, Summer 1989).

Walker, R. B. J., *The Prince* and the "Pauper": Tradition, Modernity, and Practice in the Theory of International Relations' in James Der Derian and Michael J. Shapiro (eds), *International/Intertextual Relations: Post-modern Readings in World Politics* (Lexington, MA: Lexington Books, 1989).

Walker, R. B. J., *Inside/Outside: International Relations as Political Theory* (Cambridge: Cambridge University Press, 1993).

Waltz, Kenneth N., *Man, the State and War* (New York: Columbia University Press, 1959).

Waltz, Kenneth N., *Theory of International Politics* (Reading. MA: Addison-Wesley, 1979).

Warner, Daniel, *An Ethic of Responsibility in International Relations* (London: Lynne Reiner, 1992).

Warnock, G. J., *Morality and Language* (Totowa, NJ: Barnes and Noble, 1983).

Watts, Nicholas and Geoffrey Wandesforde-Smith, 'Postmaterial Values and Environmental policy Change' in Dean E. Mann (ed.), *Environmental Policy Formation: The Impact of Values, Ideology and Standards* (Lexington, MA: Lexington Books, 1981).

Watzlawick, Paul, *How Real is Real? Communication, Disinformation, Confusion* (New York: Random House, 1976).

Weaver, O., P. Lemaitre and E. Tromer (eds), *European Polyphony: Perspectives Beyond the East-West Confrontation* (Basingstoke: Macmillan, 1989).

Wendt, A., 'Anarchy is What States Make of it: The Social Construction of Power Politics', *International Organisation* (Vol. 46, No. 2, 1992).

Weston, D. E., *Realism, Language and Social Theories: Studies in the Relation of the Epistemology of Science and Politics* (PhD thesis, University of Lund, Sweden, 1978).

Wight, M., 'Western Values in International Relations' in H. Butterfield and M. Wight (eds), *Diplomatic Investigations* (London: Allen and Unwin, 1967).

Wight, Martin, 'Why Is There No International Theory?', *International Relations* (Vol. 2, No. 1, April 1960).

Wight, Martin, *Power Politics*, 2nd ed., edited by Hedley Bull and Carsten Holbraad (Leicester: Leicester University Press for the Royal Institute of International Affairs, 1978).

Williams, Howard, 'Machiavelli: *Realpolitik*' in Howard Williams, *International Relations in Political Theory* (Milton Keynes: Open University Press, 1992).

Williams, Howard, *International Relations in Political Theory* (Milton Keynes: Open University Press, 1992).

Williams, Robert M., 'The Concept of Norms', in David L. Sills (ed.) *International Encyclopedia of the Social Sciences* (New York: Macmillan and Free Press, 1968–1979).

Windsor, Philip, 'Superpower Intervention' in Hedley Bull (ed.), *Intervention in World Politics* (Oxford: Clarendon Press, 1984).

Windsor, Philip, 'The State and War' in Cornelia Navari (ed.), *The Condition of States* (Milton Keynes: Open University Press, 1991).

Windsor, Philip, 'Towards a Hierarchy for Arms Control', *Millennium: Journal of International Studies* (Vol. 15, No. 2, Summer 1986).

Wolfers, Arnold, *Discord and Collaboration* (Baltimore, MD: Johns Hopkins Press, 1962).

Wolin, Sheldon, 'Paradigms and Political Theories' in Preston King and B. C. Parekh (eds), *Politics and Experience* (Cambridge: Cambridge University Press, 1968).

Wolin, Sheldon, 'Political Theory as a Vocation', *American Political Science Review* (December, 1966).

Wróblewski, Jerzy, 'Cognition of Norms and Cognition Through Norms', in Giuliano di Bernardo (ed.), *Normative Structures of the Social World* (Amsterdam: Editions Rodopi, 1988).

Index